DRINKING MUDDY WATER

Sudden Change Media
Washington, DC

DRINKING MUDDY WATER

THE STREETS, THE SCANDALS,

THE PARTY OF LINCOLN

RONALD MOTEN

Sudden Change Media
Washington, DC

Drinking Muddy Water
The Streets, the Scandals, the Party of Lincoln

Copyright © 2012 by Ronald Moten

ISBN-10 0615702090
ISBN-13 9780615702094

Additional copies of this book can be purchased online at:

www.drinkingmuddywater.info

Address requests for information to:

Sudden Change Media
455 Massachusetts Avenue, NW
Suite # 150-144
Washington, DC 20001

publisher@suddenchangemedia.com

Dedication

To my grandparents Thaddina and Edward Floyd, my angels from God whose love for me gives me chills whenever I think of them.

To my parents, Arlene Moten and Ronald Starks, who planted and cultivated the seed that would not be here without them and their love.

To my children, who have given me so much love and shared me with the other children of the world.

To my Great-Great-Grandma Toasting, Great-Grandma Winslow, Grandma Minnie Burns, Aunties Dovey Roundtree and Gwendolyn Haywood, and Aunt Geneva.

To the Winslow, Starks, and Moten sides of the family.

To Tyrone F. General for believing in me and always being there for me even after I decided to switch parties.

To two of my mentors, Mr. Brown, whose first name I never knew because my grandparents taught me respect for my elders, and Mr. Bill Butler from No. 2 Boys Club who helped me and my mother and countless youth and families throughout D.C.

To Ballou Senior High School for never always showing appreciation and never turning its back on me even with all the politics.

To everyone at Peaceoholics who sacrificed so much and believed in the work that Jauhar Abraham and I started. We could not have done it without you.

To everybody who had to "drink muddy water" for me to still be standing strong. I know without God's help and your sacrifices I would not have the insights and privilege to write this book, which is intended to honor you by passing the torch to the next generation.

About the Author

Ronald L. Moten is a fifth generation Washingtonian and attended Theodore Roosevelt Senior High School. He is a proud father of three boys and two girls. Two of his sons are adult men and productive citizens in the Nation's Capital.

In his youth, Ron had brushes with the law and later was incarcerated at Danbury FCI (Federal Correction Institution) where he earned his GED (General Equivalency Diploma) from the state of Connecticut. He also attended Park Community College in Allenwood, Pennsylvania where he majored in Liberal Arts and studied History. His college experience opened his mind to the power of community activism to create positive change.

Immediately upon his release from Danbury FCI, Mr. Moten began doing outreach for Cease Fire Don't Smoke the Brothers and had the opportunity to meet Mrs. Mandela in the office of Mayor Marion Barry. She graciously shared words of wisdom and inspiration with him. Through this and other personal experiences, education, divine guidance, and inspiration from great leaders such as Winnie Mandela, the Freedom Riders, and Kwame Ture (Stokeley Carmichael) of SNCC (Student Nonviolent Coordinating Committee), he began to practice the principles of nonviolence and became more aware of the struggles of the African-American community and his responsibilities as a citizen.

Mr. Moten was a Health and Physical Education instructor at the Village Learning Center from 2000 to 2002. This was one of D.C.'s first public charter schools. He was honored with numerous awards for his commitment to the school's youth and the surrounding community.

In 2004, Mr. Moten co-founded the Peaceoholics with Jauhar Abraham and served as the chief operating officer until his departure in

2009. This nationally known nonprofit organization was established to combat violence and promote peace among youth. While with Peaceoholics, he was responsible for managing and training the staff and for program operations. He soon became the public face and lightning rod of the organization. He built relationships with community, city, and state governments and helped them develop effective programs that strategically engaged at-risk youth to better understand the importance of education, peace, and economic empowerment. The goal was always to transform youth and adults into productive citizens.

He helped the District of Columbia government create strategies to reduce homicides and unemployment and to vastly improve education. He and Jauhar Abraham developed a curriculum called Rebuild the Village Model® for schools, institutions, and communities that focuses on positive engagement through youth development. He also assisted the city in developing numerous initiatives to strengthen families and communities and to combat violence. Two such programs were the Violence Intervention Partnership and Saving Our Sisters.

Peaceoholics achieved remarkable results. It sent 160 troubled youth to college, found employment for 361 D.C. citizens, and brokered forty-one truces between both male and female rival gangs. Ron has worked tirelessly for the last seventeen years to enhance the quality of life for youth and adults, especially those east of the Anacostia River where the majority of the poor reside. His personal sacrifices have helped others rise to become free and responsible citizens in the pursuit of happiness.

He was appointed to serve on the Ballou Senior High School PTSA (Parent Teacher Student Association), to the Mayor's Taskforce to Eliminate Homicides, and to Congresswoman Eleanor Holmes Norton's Commission on Black Men and Boys. Mr. Moten has helped various city, state, and national governments and universities develop strategies and implement best practices to move young people from a life of violence to peace, despair to hope, and from unskilled dependency to skilled self-sufficiency. These include Seattle, Washington, U.S. Virgin Islands, Georgetown University, and Johns Hopkins University.

He has traveled around the country promoting peace and devising strategies to positively engage young people. Mr. Moten is a skilled trainer in conflict resolution. His work has been widely recognized by both civic organizations, government agencies, police departments and by the offices of four different D.C. mayors.

Among the awards and recognitions Mr. Moten has received are the MPD (Metropolitan Police Department) Citizen Advisory Council

Community Partnership Award in 2006, the Delta Sigma Theta Award for Outstanding Community Service in 2007 and 2008, and the NAACP Outstanding Leadership Award. He was honored by Howard University School of Social Work and, in 2008, by the internationally known Search for Common Ground whose other honorees have included Muhammad Ali, John Lewis, and the Freedom Riders.

Mr. Moten also serves as an advocate for under-privileged youth, seniors, and returned citizens. He teaches empowerment through active and practical citizenship, not just being passive residents. Drawing from his own entrepreneurial ventures, Ron has taught and trained others to discover and use their skills to become the next generation of business-minded individuals once prevalent in our communities.

Some of Mr. Moten's entrepreneurial successes include starting a company called Reddoor Entertainment in 1997. Reddoor's profits funded on-the-job training for young people. Through Reddoor, he produced major events in Washington, D.C. and Atlantic City, which attracted stars such as Mike Tyson and Don King. Reddoor also used entertainment as a way to help the District of Columbia HIV/AIDS Administration educate youth on health issues. He also collaborated closely with other community organizations, educational institutions, and city agencies to promote health consciousness and nonviolence using well-known artists such as 50 Cent and Fat Joe.

Mr. Moten was blessed to receive valuable lessons from living civil rights legends who had worked with Dr. Martin Luther King, Jr. It was several of these icons who told him. "If you want to continue the work we started with Dr. King, you better learn how to drink muddy water." By drinking muddy water, they meant having to endure things and do things that are as distasteful and as demeaning as drinking muddy water. This was their way of saying that when you fight to uplift others and to build institutions for success for the less fortunate, you better be ready to suffer and not quit.

Table of Contents

Acknowledgments

I want to thank God for all he has done for me, for giving me the breath of life and the experiences and opportunities I needed to write this book. With all the muddy water I've had to drink in my life, I know it was God who took me through my trials, tribulations, successes, and failures to prepare me for my ongoing mission in life.

Thank you, to my parents, Arlene Moten and Ronald Starks. They went through a lot themselves and often took the wrong roads in life as a result of their drug addictions. Seeing the consequences of their self-medication saved me from the possibility of becoming a drug addict. I especially want to thank my father for coming back before it was too late to help me rear my children, which allowed me to help others.

I thank God for sending me the best grandparents in the world, Thaddina and Edward Floyd, who have been there for me through the good and the bad. To this day they are the reason I've been able to help so many people. They sacrificed everything; they worked night and day to take care of both their children and grandchildren, which is rare today with so many becoming grandparents at a young age. I don't know where the fabric they were made of comes from, but I am grateful for every bit of it that I inherited. That is what I want to pass on to my children and grandchildren in order to help recover what most of this generation has lost.

I am grateful to my Aunt Gwendolyn Haywood and her partner, Dovey Roundtree, who mentored me and gave me the drive to work hard and to expect nothing to be easy. Then there are my Uncle Tony and my cousin Michelle who were there for me when I needed them during my rocky up and down journey.

I thank my children for being so humble and understanding and for sharing me with others. The world does not often appreciate the sacrifices of the children of those who dedicate their lives to helping others. My two oldest boys helped me break the cycle of men in my family going to prison. My angel Yasmeen and my two little ones, Asanti and Asantawaa, give me something to smile about every day.

I owe a big thank you to my daughter Yasmeen's mom, Nicole, for being an excellent mother who has always been good to me even though we have gone our separate ways. She has married and I consider her husband a friend and we are raising Yasmeen as a team and family! Thank you, also, to Ronald's mother, Lashaun Morris, who has been a dear friend and had to raise our son without his father while I was in prison.

I give thanks to the few real friends that I had in the 1-4 Zone where I grew up including Muhammad & Darb. I would also like to thank the founder of Cease Fire Don't Smoke the Brothers and Sisters, a man who I often disagree with, but genuinely love. He shared so much with me; thank you, Al-Malik Farrakhan. I also owe much to my friend and attorney Rodney Mitchell who received only a few pennies to help me fight a vicious political system. Carolyn and Darnell are two other very special friends, really true capital letter FRIENDS. Thank you both so much, I don't know what I would have done without you in the last year as I was writing this book!

Each of the former Peaceoholics' staff deserves my thanks for being so committed to helping the people, especially Ms. Princess, Whali "Big Wax" Johnson, Aunt Carolyn Robinson, and Mama Jo Patterson who stuck with us to the very end. I also greatly appreciate Jeanie Shelton who was the landlady for our Peaceoholics offices. She not only gave us a below market lease, but when our funding was cut off, she let us stay long after we were able to pay. A word of thanks also to the seeds we planted like Maia and Duck who have grown beautifully and are doing great things through their own organization.

There were also many judges to thank for working with us including Judge Zoe Bush, Judge Milton Lee, Judge Anita Herring, and Judge Lee F. Satterfield. Then there are the everyday folk in the community and in all the government agencies who are the real change agents; this includes community activists Phil Pannell and Anthony Muhammad who was a mentor to me over twenty years ago when I was in D.C. jail.

I truly want to thank all the pastors who have stood by me. Of special note are Rev. Willie Wilson who kept me from being homeless in 2004, Rev. Tony Lee of Community of Hope AME Church, and a special thanks to Rev. Michael Bell of Allen Chapel AME Church who worked with me during my recent storm when many others backed away.

The media in a free country needs to be thanked whether they reported fairly or unfairly. Without them Ronald Moten and the work of Peaceoholics would not be widely known outside of my own community. I thank them all. There is a saying that goes, "Success has enemies." So, to all of those who became my enemies because of my success, thanks you for making me stronger.

I would also like to thank legendary Washington Post columnists Courtland Milloy, Colbert King, and Robert Pierre. It was Robert Pierre who told me I was a fool if I didn't sit my behind down and write a book about my story. Robert was also the first to do real stories highlighting the work of the Peaceoholics. I needed that encouragement after having put so much at risk to help others only to see Peaceoholics defunded by corrupt politicians. As I finish this book, many of them are already under investigation, indicted, or in prison. Others have resigned from office in disgrace. I tried many times to reconcile and resolve my differences with the people who attacked Peaceoholics and me personally, but to no avail. This book tells the truth about what really happened.

I continue to rely on the dedication of Patrice Lancaster who not only encouraged me to write this book but has also been a tireless campaign worker and all-round administrator for the numerous community and political activities in which I am still involved.

Dr. Jennifer Woolard of Georgetown University has been a great partner in the area of social justice and youth empowerment. She has been a true friend who asked tough questions to help us understand the value of what we were doing and how to do it better.

Charlotte Jacobsen has been a dear friend. We come from different worlds, but when there was something she did not understand, she always assumed the best and asked direct questions for clarity. She has always been there to help me get my message out to the masses. It was Charlotte who introduced me to Padma Venkatachalam, a professor at Montgomery Community College with a PhD from Howard University. Padma provided invaluable statistical research information for the section on Rebuild the Village Model®.

I am grateful to the civil rights leaders from whom I learned so much. Also, Phil Pannell needs to be recognized for being a straight shooting and principled Democrat who has always supported Peaceoholics and the children of D.C.

Most importantly, I thank the children and families who helped me redeem me for the damage I did to others and the community before I turned my life around.

Good editors are gold when it comes to writing a book. I must thank Rev. Edwin L. Jones, Sr., Geraldine Washington, and LaChett Landrum for the many hours spent on editing this manuscript. Thank you! Big thanks to Cha Ros-Estes for helping us get across the finish line.

Last, but not least, my publisher, editor, and friend Curt Ashburn and his family as he sacrificed and worked with me to publish and edit my book. I was dead broke and people literally stole from me in order to

Introduction

Learning to Drink Muddy Water

If you are going to continue the work we started with Dr. King, then you are going to have to learn to drink muddy water.

—Unknown Civil Rights leader

If my name is familiar to you, it is most likely because I was a co-founder, along with Jauhar Abraham, of the Peaceoholics in Washington, D.C. Naturally, my work with Peaceoholics and its eventual demise at the hands of unscrupulous politicians is woven throughout this book. However, *Drinking Muddy Water* is much more than just the history of Peaceoholics.

Peaceoholics certainly plays a significant part in what you are about to read, but not simply because of all the good we did for the people of this great city. My years with Peaceoholics are also significant because of the many hard life lessons I learned during those very successful, but also very turbulent times. Those lessons have resulted in both a personal and political transformation in my life that I believe speak to the current plight of all Americans and, in particular, to African Americans.

That transformation had its real beginning in 1991 when I was locked up as a result of a federal sting operation. I passed the jail countless times and for some strange reason, I never thought the day would come, that I would end up there myself. One afternoon while lying in my cell, the patrolling guard unlocked my door and told me to report to the Chaplain's office.

I had only been locked up for a month and had already been instructed several times to report to different administrative offices for processing and evaluations as a normal part of institutional intake protocol. I figured a visit with the Chaplain was just another part of the routine. I had no idea what awaited me. I entered the office and was greeted by a clergywoman. She told me to take a seat and begin to explain why I was there.

I vaguely remember her attempting to soften the blow of the news by gently saying, "Your little brother and his best friend have been kidnapped, robbed and killed. She then began to ramble off important details about the event, but to me everything went cold and dark after the word *killed!* I sat motionless for what seemed like hours but in real time may have only been a few minutes. I sat in that chair powerless to go back in time to help my little brother. He too had been in the drug game following in my footsteps.

That is when it hit me that there had to be a better way to live. I realized I needed to change the path that I was traveling. I was raised to be a better man than the one I was in that jail cell and I was determined to change. The changes could not wait until I got out of prison. I received my GED three months after entering Danbury. When I was transferred to Allenwood I enrolled in several History classes at Park Community College. Those History classes really opened my eyes for the first time to the basic outlines of my purpose in life. I was determined to pursue it at all costs!

After my release from prison, that determination led me co-found Peaceoholics with Jauhar Abraham. Jauhar had been kicked out of DCPS (District of Columbia Public Schools) in the third grade because his mother would not put him on Ritalin. At nine years old, he got into trouble with the police for being a lookout boy for the drug dealers on Kennedy Street. He was arrested and later released without any charges being filed. He was locked up again when he was twelve for strong-arm robbery. By his sixteenth birthday, Jauhar had moved to Maryland where he finished high school, but not without some close calls and barely avoiding going to prison. What eventually saved him was his mother's insistence that he enlist in the Army, a life-changing experience. Upon his return from the Army, Jauhar found that most of his friends were dead, locked up, or bums on the street.

These kinds of chaotic childhood experiences inspired each of us to do the kind of work you will read about in this book. We mediated gang conflicts, taught some of the most violent youngsters in the city to reject violence, and helped them find inner peace and purpose in the midst of incredibly turbulent and stressful lives. The work has been both heartwarming and heartbreaking, but the results had a positive impact citywide for many years.

We worked with more than one hundred neighborhood crews and gangs while with Peaceoholics. We are credited with saving hundreds of lives, laboring 24/7 in places considered by nearly everyone to be the most dangerous and frightening in Washington, D.C. At times, those neighborhoods had multiple hostile incidents jumping off at the same time. With needs so great, we could not stop every outbreak of violence.

Still, we managed to negotiate over forty truces, twenty-nine of them in one two-year period. The results of our efforts have been bitter sweet. The number of lives lost on the streets of the District of Columbia due to gun or other violence in just one year is mind boggling and all of them unnecessary. Many of those caught up in the violence that escaped death, found themselves in wheelchairs or otherwise physically and emotionally damaged for life.

Sadly, Jauhar and I have attended nearly three hundred funerals and wakes, the majority of them for young boys and girls whose lives had barely begun. Here, in the "most powerful city in the world," one hospital alone treated 4,003 victims for violent crimes from 2006 to 2010. 1,458 were treated for gunshot wounds, over 1,300 for stabbings, and 1,200 from other types of assaults. Over 2,700 of the victims were ages fourteen to twenty-five.

Each shooting costs the taxpayer from fifty-thousand to $1 million. You don't hear this on the news because the city does not release such data. Unfortunately, even if this information was released, people have grown so accustomed to the violence that many just don't care until it knocks on their front door. If that front door is in a poor neighborhood, little is done about it; if it is in an affluent area, it always gets outrage.

Through all of our successes and occasional failures, we learned what works and what doesn't. We know what communities need. We also know how to work with city officials to bridge the gaps and break the political gridlock that thwarts long-term solutions to the problems of violence in homes, schools, and neighborhoods. Our successes are many and widely celebrated; our failures were mostly mourned in private, but were magnified and adversely scrutinized and used against us by those who seldom lifted a finger to help anyone but themselves.

We were honored to have our work recognized by those in other cities and countries who are grappling with similar problems. We hired and trained more than 231 people in five years carrying an average of 60 staff and consultants on the Peaceoholics' payroll. Most had no skills for the current job market and 80 percent were *returned citizens*, a term that will be explained in more detail later, but is basically how we always referred to what most people call ex-offenders.

However, *Drinking Muddy Water* is not just about all the good work done by me and all the other great people at Peaceoholics. Unfortunately, it is also the story of corrupt politicians who used every means at their disposal, all their "politricks", to ruin our reputations and to defund our organization. When we refused to compromise our integrity by jumping on the bandwagon and opposing Mayor Adrian Fenty in his bid for a second term, we got caught in the politics of it all. We refused to choose sides other than the side of doing what was right. The powers that be, including then City Council Chairman Vincent Gray turned against us and succeeded in defunding the work of Peaceoholics. Eventually, we had to close our doors.

This is also a book about vindication. Within three months of Mayor Vincent Gray's administration coming into power, the truth started coming out that we had been the target of their corruption. It was revealed in the summer of 2012 that the mayor, officials in his administration, the former chairman of the City Council, and multiple council members were under federal investigation. Some have already been indicted and several have been convicted and sent to prison. I was convinced that the truth would eventually come out and that it would vindicate both me and Peaceoholics. Unfortunately, it is too late to save Peaceoholics and these sad scandals have further tarnished the reputation of our great city.

Drinking Muddy Water is also about redemption, my ongoing effort and lifelong commitment to make amends for my past and to keep the promises I made to myself when I left prison. I confess that I was a part of the problem. There was a time when I contributed to the destruction of my own community. Now I am deeply committed to reducing incarceration and homicide rates, to ensuring that our forgotten youth finish school and go to college, to promoting entrepreneurship, and to pounding away at the importance of family and faith. I want to help empower our communities to rebuild the institutions of family and faith that are historically the best way to combat violence and poverty.

Most people know very little about the world of gang beefs, murder, drug trafficking, and the constant fear of retaliation. This was the life that I lived and then fought against through Peaceoholics. The distance between the world to which I have dedicated myself to changing and the world of most Americans is one of the primary reasons that I wrote this book. I wish my world did not exist, but it does and it cries out to be healed and not used as just a political battlefield. It is time for the American eagle to soar again, but to do that, it needs black people to wake up and once again become as much of a force in the Party of Lincoln as we are in the Democratic Party.

I remember taking my first trip with Jauhar and his brother Dan Bradley on one of our many Civil Rights Tours. We had the honor of walking in the farm fields of Alabama and Mississippi with icons of the Civil Rights Movement such as Rev. James Bevel and Rev. Joseph E. Boone. We often went through swamp land or sat out back of the Civil Rights Museum located a block from the Edmund Pettus Bridge in Selma, Alabama facing the mighty Mississippi River. We sat at their feet and learned from them on the banks of the river where many of our ancestors were killed by the Klan and thrown into its muddy waters!

We cherished these walks and conversations with men and women who worked with Dr. Martin Luther King, Jr. to end segregation and to get black people the equal rights guaranteed by the U.S. Constitution. We took many of those trips and one of my favorite places to visit was Tuskegee University where we visited the grave sites of Republicans like Booker T. Washington and George Washington Carver. Then we rode around the corner and visited the house of the "Mother of the Voting Rights Act," Amelia Boynton Robinson, who is, at the time of this writing, one hundred years old and still teaching children in Alabama. We were so deeply impressed with her efforts in Alabama that we decided to fly her to D.C. to share her story with the youth in our organization as well as with the people in our communities.

We met civil rights "foot solders" like Pastor Gwendolyn Webb who marched for Dr. King as a child to end segregation under the guidance of Rev. James Bevel. She became our second mother and was always giving us wisdom and praying for us. These true American heroes taught us that the movement of black people then and the movement black people now should not be taken lightly, and that we better get used to "drinking muddy water" quick, fast, and in a hurry.

Lou Rawls had a song called "Drinking Muddy Water." It has a line that is right on point. He was referring to his woman leaving him for another man, but the line that I found out was true for the work of Peaceoholics and for my life to this day is, "I work for you like a Georgia mule, my friends all laughed and they called me a fool. Your kisses are as sweet as can be, but before I let you make a fool out of me, I'd rather drink muddy water." The kisses of corrupt politicians can seem as sweet as can be, but Dr. King and many others like him chose to drink muddy water rather than betray the cause of justice for personal benefit and comfort.

I learned so much about Martin Luther King, Jr. from those who knew him, things no history book will tell you. I also learned why many of them stayed down South rather than cash in on the movement as Jesse

Jackson and others have. I remember often being told to enjoy all of the good media and glory while it lasts, but to also get ready to drink muddy water. It is inevitable that when you are doing God's work, you are going to be tested and put through trials and tribulations. In many cases, the resistance to the work comes from those who you least expect it from.

The relationships and knowledge I gained as a result of those tours was a privilege from God that I will cherish for the rest of my life. I have included in this book many of the lessons we were taught like "The Bird's Nest" and "Hurt People Hurt People." One of the most powerful lessons I came to understand was how they utilized the strength of women and from that we came up with our own title for the lesson you will read later called "The Power of the Womb."

We took many of these trips year after year sending busloads of rival crews on these Civil Rights Tours. Many of the youth were in gangs and crews that had a history of beefing. We shared this idea with Terri Odom who was a top official at CSS (Court Social Services). We partnered with them for years to take children on probation on these civil rights tours. These were life-changing experiences, not just for the children and youth, but for me and the staff.

Those great but often unappreciated heroic figures helped clarify and explain to me my own life journey, past and present. They helped equip me with the love and forgiveness I would need for the battles ahead. Without love and forgiveness, it would have been impossible for me to continue sacrificing everything even when it came at the expense of my family. I learned from them that I was not alone, that there were men and women who suffered the same kinds of betrayal as I would experience and worse.

Through our work with Peaceoholics, Jauhar and I learned the importance of building institutions for success: family, faith, health, education, finances, judicial systems, entrepreneurship, and many more. It was here that I learned that one of the biggest problems of my people was that we get caught up in personalities and not principles. This continues to be one of the biggest downfalls in the communities I worked in. An enormous problem for me was that I was being enlightened by so much, so fast, that I was always busy helping others and not myself no matter how it appeared from the outside.

We also learned not to judge a man by the color of his skin but by his actions and deeds. We learned that many of these icons who walked with Dr. King are or were, like Frederick Douglass, Civil Rights Republicans. This is true for several of our recent and distant ancestors going all the way back to the fight for freedom from slavery. They kept and preserved those Republican principles and taught us to always support the best candidate and make sure the people were active citizens and not just passive residents.

Too many of them drank and drowned in muddy water for us to let those principles die. They learned to drink the muddy water of sacrifice to make our country what it is today; we can do no less. The question is: Are we willing to finish their work and finish their dream of bringing our country together in freedom, equality, opportunity, and individual responsibility for every citizen of the United States of America?

Finally, *Drinking Muddy Water* is about how a lifelong Democrat, an Obama supporter and community activist decided to become a Civil Rights Republican. By making that choice, I am rejecting the dependency culture of my own people and the entitlement mentality of the Democratic Party. I am also calling for the Republican Party to embrace their history as the Party of Lincoln to restore a balance in politics so that the American eagle can soar once again and, this time, take all the people with it.

It is time for the true Civil Rights Party to return to the proud tradition of Frederick Douglass, Abraham Lincoln, Nannie Helen Burroughs, and its ideals of freedom, opportunity, and individual responsibility for all. These are the sacred beliefs of our nation for which so many have died. They are enshrined in the Declaration of Independence, the Gettysburg Address, Dr. King's "I Have a Dream" speech and the words of Booker T. Washington who said, "You can't get something for nothing." They were lived out in flesh and blood by Sojourner Truth, the Buffalo Soldiers, Harriet Tubman, "the black Moses," and all the other heroes from the Underground Railroad to the Civil Rights Movement.

Civil Rights icon Gwendolyn Webb who walked with Dr. King as a child foot solder going to jail twice. She joined me at Union Temple for a youth event and spoke about the important part children played in ending segregation.

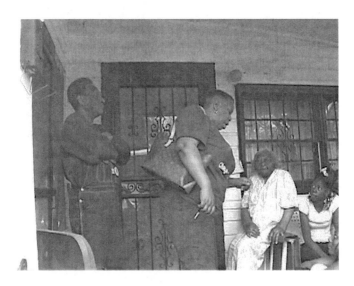

Civil Rights icons Annie Lee Cooper (seated) and Richard Boone (left) talk to D.C. youth on Peaceoholics Civil Rights tour.

In Tuskegee, Alabama with former rival gang members, Dina from Choppa City, and Monica Watts from Lynch Mob at the house of the "Mother of the Voting Rights Act" Amelia Boynton Robinson. This was just one of many life-changing Civil Rights Tours Peaceoholics conducted for hundreds of D.C. youth and adults.

Civil Rights icon Rev. James Bevel conducting a citizenship class at Peaceoholics' first headquarters.

Young men on one of our Civil Rights Tours reenacting "Bloody Sunday" walking across the historic Edmund Pettus Bridge in Selma, Alabama.

In Atlanta, Georgia with youth and adults on one of Peaceoholics' Civil Rights Tours. Here we are in the office of Rep. John Lewis (center). Congressman Lewis who marched with Dr. King gave a lecture on the Civil Rights Movement.

1

Red Ass Boy

Where It All Started

Without the lessons learned through the trials and errors of my life journey, I would be inadequately prepared to serve others who are hopelessly trapped in the valley of death that is the daily existence of urban America.

—Ron Moten

A little red boy was born in the Nation's Capital and resided at 801 Kentucky Avenue, SE with his mother, Arlene Moten, and grandparents, Thaddina and Edward Floyd. Life was fun and full of love during those times before the crack epidemic hit our great city in 1984. I remember my grandmother cursing a lot and being tough as nails. She would often go outside and fight for my uncles. She once took a knife from two men who beat her nephew. Then she did the beating and sent them spinning out in their pimped-out black Ford LTD.

All that changed dramatically when my grandmother became a Jehovah's Witness. From that time on, the hard, filthy-mouthed woman, who always gave tough love, changed her life in major ways. Suddenly, she became a gentle, passive woman full of love and wisdom. That transformation taught me an important lesson in life: never stop improving, never stop listening to those who love you and the Lord, keep learning from your mistakes.

My mother was fifteen when I was born. She raised my sister and me at my grandparents' house. She eventually married my sister's father when I was four. Then one day my stepfather assaulted my mother with a knife. Suddenly, my grandmother appeared with an iron in her hand and told him he better not put his hands on her daughter again. This led to the loving, but unstable, situation of my sister and me going back and forth between our mother's house and our grandparents' house.

My biological father tried to be in my life off and on, but his drug addiction was more powerful than his desire to be a father. I built up tremendous animosity towards him as I watched my mom struggle to raise us and deal with different men who were physically and mentally abusive to her. This abuse led her to have several mental breakdowns and trips to St. Elizabeth's Hospital for the mentally ill.

There were several times when I had what I call "kiss with death" experiences. One I think about often was when my mother was introduced to an ex-felon named William Marshall. He was six-foot-three-inches tall, sculpted like an African warrior, and was a black belt in karate. Initially, he was very loving and caring towards my mother and us. One day, however, he would not let my mom, my sister, and me out of the house. In an attempt to defend us, I yelled, "Leave my mother alone," but he refused.

My sister was somehow able to slip out of sight, call my grandmother and the police, and then find her way out a window and down the fire escape onto the street. I managed to escape out of the front door, but on my way downstairs, I heard a loud noise and a thump. I was anxious but was determined not to stop running until I found help. My mother was inside with him for a while longer. She too was later able to escape, but not before suffering multiple bruises and a dislocated shoulder.

Shouting at Marshall earned me a trip back to my grandparents' house while my sister stayed behind with my mother. I thank God for the family structure my grandparents provided. Although the only man that I have ever called Granddad was not related to me biologically, he always treated me with the same love as he did his own blood and I am forever grateful to him for that.

I would visit my mom's house every now and then until Marshall moved out. Two weeks after he left, we were watching a news report about a boy who tried to protect his mother from her boyfriend just as I tried to protect my mother. Only this boy was killed by the boyfriend who then committed suicide. The boyfriend's name was William Marshall who I had escaped from. That is when I realized that I had just had my first "kiss with death."

Twenty-five years later, I found out something about William Marshall that I will never, ever forget. My sister told my grandmother that Marshall tried to sexually assault her and that our mom knew and never reported it. That explains why my sister's relationship with my mother was distant and why there was so much tension between the two of them.

At the same time, I learned that my mother was also, allegedly, the victim of sexual assault. Her sexual abuse was at the hands of her biological father. My grandmother, who never tolerated any kind of mistreatment of her children, put a gun to my grandfather's head. He denied the allegations, however, he did admit to smoking weed with my mother and my uncle. Predictably, with my mom never having received any counseling for her abuse, this terrible family dysfunction repeated itself with my sister. I am delighted that my mom and sister have reconciled and now have a much healthier relationship.

Not surprisingly, my mother's life changed and she began to blossom after Marshall moved out of the house. She completed Wider Opportunities for Women and became an electrician. We were even featured with her on the front page of the Washington Post in an article about a single parent excelling against the odds in an electrician program for women.

I lived on and off with my grandparents for the remainder of my childhood. In 1976, with the assistance of two well respected black civil rights lawyers, Dovey Roundtree and Gwendolyn Haywood, my grandparents purchased a home in the Petworth community. Petworth was a predominately black neighborhood and, interestingly, the attorneys who gave their assistance were associates of the late civil rights leader Dorothy Height as well as part of our family.

The purchase price was about $38,500. The neighborhood is now predominately white homeowners and that same house is currently worth over four hundred thousand dollars. Many of my childhood friends moved out of the area because either they or their parents lost the family home. Many homes were lost by black families due to the effects of the crack epidemic and the destructive nature of addictions within the family. Some moved out to escape the plague of crime in the city or were tempted to sell and take advantage of higher real estate prices that were the result of the gentrification going on throughout the city.

My grandparents would never have been able to purchase this home without the kind assistance of Gwendolyn Haywood and Dovey Roundtree. Long before my transforming experiences with iconic civil rights leaders in the South, I was blessed as a child to have the influence of these two great women as part of my daily life. I have included a reproduction of the mortgage document and some biographical information for those who are unaware of my Aunt Dovey's historic accomplishments in the Civil Rights Movement.

Dovey Johnson Roundtree moved to Washington, D.C. in 1947. She was an attorney, ordained minister at Allen AME Church, retired Army captain, and community activist. She was mentored by such historic figures as Mary McLeod-Bethune, Dr. Martin Luther King, Jr., Thurgood Marshall. She played an important role in the Civil Rights Movement even arguing before the Supreme Court the case that opened interstate bus travel to blacks.

Directly across the street from Allen AME Church on Alabama Avenue is the Roundtree Residence, facility for seniors named in honor of Ms. Roundtree. I am so proud to have grown up with such a great person watching out for me. Even though I went through some years as a young man when I disappointed her and my grandmother, the seeds she planted in me as a child eventually took root and bore good fruit.

I frequently stayed at Aunt Dovey and Aunt Gwendolyn's house on weekends. They lived in what was called the Gold Coast on 16th Street directly across from Rock Creek Park. It was in their home where I was exposed to the many well-known people who came to visit them. I remember as a child being highly impressed by their quality of life.

It is interesting what we remember about our childhood. I always wondered why these two women slept in the same room. I thought only men and women slept together. Their relationship struck me as being odd, but no one, not even I, ever talked about it out in the open. Being gay was akin to being a crime at that time and everyone just kept silent. What was most important to me about them was that they loved me and I loved them back. Even this experience has come full circle in my life through my work with gay gangs as I learned early on to accept people for who they are even if I did not agree with or understand their lifestyle.

These strong women also taught me many business skills and how to hustle legally. They paid me to rake leaves and shovel snow. I also took on other odd jobs from their friends and associates. This is one of the reasons why, when we started Peaceoholics, we were committed to teaching the youth how to take the hustle mentality of the street and turn that skill into legitimate ventures. Youth simply need to be given the tools of success, encouragement to work hard, and the opportunity to show what they can do. Then there is no limit to who and what they can become.

I attended West Elementary School where I experienced one of the happiest moments of my life. I was not only selected to participate in the National Science Fair, but also won honorable mention. The finals and awards ceremony were held at H. D. Woodson Senior High School. That was a big day for me. When I think back upon receiving that award, I felt like I was the MVP of the Super Bowl. I was so proud to have my mother there to share that moment with me. As I walked across that high school auditorium stage, it seemed as if there were more than a thousand people there just to see me receive my award.

I often had to go to the Kingdom Hall of Jehovah's Witnesses where I learned a lot. During this time, there were some famous people who were Jehovah's Witnesses such as Stacey Lattisaw, Michael Jackson, and later, Prince. Every Saturday morning, I had to muster up enough courage to knock on the doors of strangers and get them to listen to the word about Jehovah God. Later in life I studied many religions and I now consider myself a spiritual person. I go to church, but I dislike it when formal religion separates people. I love God, Jesus, and all of the prophets and messengers. I have learned how to decipher the good in all and to apply the wisdom of the scriptures to my everyday life. I understand that there is only one God and we are all on our own unique journey to find him.

Alice Deal Middle School is where I became a certified class clown and troublemaker, but in spite of being a clown, I always managed to complete my class work. Every day I would hear coming across the loud speaker; "Ronald Moten and Roosevelt "Lump" Jackson, please report to the main office." By this time my mother was using drugs with my Uncle David Moten. David was like a surrogate father to me. The drug preference at the time was marijuana – then called sesse. Occasionally, I would steal from their stash and take it to school to sell and smoke. When their stash was low, I would take the seeds, crush them into dust, and persuaded my friends that we were smoking the best marijuana in the city. Even then I was a leader, just in the wrong direction.

I have many good memories of my time at Deal Middle School, but one very bad one, too. The administration said to me, "We will never let Ronald Moten walk across our stage." Although I did everything I was supposed to do in school academically, the staff believed that letting me walk across the stage would set a bad example for the rest of the students. So, they gave me an "F" in Physical Education, which meant I had to attend summer school. That was their way of letting me graduate while keeping me from walking across the stage.

It was one of the biggest disappointments in my life. Even though I had behavioral issues, I believe they did me a great disservice and injustice. Instead of exploring why I was acting out, they punished me by not rewarding me for my academic success. The same type of thing still happens today in schools all across America and it crushes our children's spirits.

During this time, I experienced another great disappointment. I discovered that my Uncle David was gay. He was a dearly loved surrogate father who was always there for me. He corrected me, bought me clothes, and filled the gaps between my mom and grandparents. Uncle David had a few girlfriends, what some call beards, but around 1984 when I was about fourteen he began to hang around a lot of men. He worked at a place called the Clubhouse, which my friends and I later discovered was a club for gay men.

Prior to learning about his relationship preference, I despised any gay man who looked at me in what I perceived to be a perverted way. I've always been heterosexual and a bit homophobic, but my personal love and respect for my Uncle David took away my phobia.

The root of my homophobia was in a childhood experience. While I was still an adolescent, I would often sleep in my grandparent's basement on the sofa bed. One morning I woke up both shocked and outraged because I felt someone touching me. It was George, my uncle's friend, who I later found out was Uncle David's boyfriend. He was touching my genital area. I jumped to my feet, picked up a dumbbell weight that was lying next to the sofa bed. I tried to bust his skull open.

He ran out, but not before he begged me, "Please, don't tell anyone! I knew the consequences he would have paid if I told anyone. I loved him so much that I thought it was best to stay silent. I've not mentioned it to anyone until now. My Uncle David and I remained close even though I knew his secret.

Three years after this event, my uncle died from spinal meningitis, the same disease that my paternal grandmother died from. Uncle David slipped into a coma after falling and striking his head on the floor in my grandmother's house. The most painful aspect of this was watching the EMS treat my uncle like a worthless piece of trash because they thought he was high on PCP.

The memory of how they treated my uncle still hurts. This harsh treatment still exists today in how poor people are often handled by medical personnel. Whenever I see it happen, I am reminded of what I witnessed with my Uncle David and it brings back the sad and hurtful memories of how they treated him. Here again, I was not able to help Uncle David, but all these experiences prepared me for my journey.

Just before my uncle's death in 1987, he and my mother started using crack. I witnessed firsthand the trickery of using recreational drugs and how they can seduce you into becoming addicted to harder drugs. I made a personal decision to stop my occasional use of marijuana and, after making that commitment to myself, I have never again used drugs. I will expand later in the book about crack cocaine and how the "War on Drugs" waged by our government resulted in the mass incarceration of our people. All I knew back then was that it was destroying the people I loved.

Shortly after my uncle's death, I began to learn more about my mother's physical and mental health problems. She never really healed emotionally from my uncle's death or from all of her abusive relationships. My mother and my Uncle David were key figures in my life and I wish their lives had been a little easier.

I have always loved learning even through all of these negative experiences. I had responsible and loving grandparents and a mother who tried her best. I learned how to hustle and flow from watching all the key people in my life: my grandparents, my mother, and from the civil rights lawyers and family friends, Gwendolyn Haywood and Dovey Roundtree. The common lesson I learned from each of them was simple: hard work pays off. I was fortunate enough to be exposed to that great work ethic, but a lot of children in urban communities are not. They have role models who just stay home and live off entitlement checks rather than being empowered and uplifted. This is a major factor in why many black youth lack the drive and motivation to succeed.

At the age of fifteen, I was working at Swenson's Ice Cream Parlor at Mazza Gallery. One day, a Dominican man named Louis, whose last name I never knew, walked in with his wife and kids. What caught my eye was not the fact that he was a family man, but how he showed his financial status by the amount of jewelry he wore. He must have had several thousand dollars in gold chains hanging around his neck and he had diamond rings on his fingers. His demeanor clearly represented the classic, highly paid street hustler. Mind you, this is around the time that the average urban black male's role model was not a father figure in the household but the Tony Montana character played by Al Pacino in *Scarface*. So, of course, with Louis fitting the Scarface profile, my movie role model became my reality. He had that kind of look.

Today, we see young black boys in the same situation, sagging pants, dreadlocks, plenty of weed, tattoos all over their faces wanting to be like Lil Wayne. What is sad is that not one in a million will ever get millions of dollars from a record like Common or KRS-ONE or have a movie like *The Great Debaters* that positively stimulates the minds of young Americans.

Even young men who were as lucky as I was to have hard working grandparents who had two jobs and who made sure I had everything I needed, were still susceptible to that "wannabe" syndrome. The desire to be like Scarface was just as powerful an influence on young men in impoverished, urban communities as the best role models in their lives. Many youth in these communities commit what I call "poverty crimes" due to their social and economic disadvantage combined with poor parenting. It's pretty easy then to look to the media, entertainment, even characters in movies like Scarface and Batman and be seduced by the "wannabe" syndrome. I'm not excusing the behavior, just describing the social influences on our young people.

Now back to Louis. I simply asked him, "Can I have a chance? You see I'm a hard worker and you can trust me." Remember, I was fifteen years old. Louis said, yes, gave me his number, and told me when to call him. Right then I started to daydream and thought I was about to be the next Tony Montana. This was during the powder cocaine era, right before the big crack epidemic. It was still a time in the black community when old heads would kick you in the butt and tell you to go to school if you asked them to get you into selling drugs. They would even give you money for having a good report card.

Most things were done behind the scenes except for places like Hanover which was run by a smooth drug kingpin by the name of Cornell Jones. Louis tested me with a quarter of an ounce of cocaine and then he gave me a half ounce, and then an ounce. I would go down to Hanover after Cornell's folks closed up shop. I had a friend named Bey Brother who was a runner down there and we would go together. I didn't really know what I was doing; I just had some good stuff that I was cutting with aspirin. Cutting with aspirin is a way to stretch the product so you can make more money. It was good for the snorter, however, we found out you could not cut coke with aspirin for those who wanted to put it in their veins because it would become thick and gummy like glue.

The Hanover trial and error experiment came to an abrupt end when our previous buyers returned with our gummy product in hand. They wanted their money back. Back uptown I went into the neighborhood where I soon got screwed by an old head by name of Baron Kelly. I kept my stash in Baron's house because I feared and respected my grandmother too much to put it in her house.

Well, as one would expect, the old head screwed me. Baron told me he had stashed it in his basement ceiling and that it fell from the ceiling to the ground. Yeah right, but what was I to do? Baron was ten years older and cut up like Hulk Hogan. I knew that if I did anything stupid, it would get back to my grandparents or Mr. Brown. Mr. Brown was my neighbor and mentor. He paid me to do odd jobs and always took me fishing. Mr. Brown died shortly after the episode with Baron. His death was a great loss to me and left a void no one else has ever filled.

Louis was mad after I explained what happened with Baron, but I was lucky because he was one hustler who understood that you couldn't get money from a corpse and you never give more than what can hurt you, so he just cut me off. This was bad news, but good news, too, because my little stint of being the first young guy uptown with cocaine gave me respect with the old heads up on 14th Street.

During this time, I was also a member of Gangster Chronicles, a gang started by Alley Cat, some guys from uptown, and a few other childhood friends. I was in a gang, but my grandparents had a rule that I had to be in the house when the street lights came on, so, I would sneak out of the house through a window. I will never forget the one time that my grandmother realized that I wasn't home and sat downstairs in a living room chair with the lights turned off waiting for my return. I came in and saw her sitting there with a two-inch leather belt. She tore my butt up. This is a true testimony to the fact that you can still have good parents and continue to do things that are displeasing to them.

We had fights, but we rarely used guns before the crack cocaine explosion. I only remember one of my friends being shot. It was Black Suede who was shot in the Go-Go at the Washington Coliseum (Go-Go was D.C.'s home-grown music created by the legendary Chuck Brown). They had to shoot Ant Man only because he was so good with his hands and never lost a fight. He was shot by a rival crew "The Hill Boys." There were many neighborhood gangs and crews back then; that's why my gang work with Peaceoholics was always natural for me.

A lot of things youth do today, such as flash mobs, we did too, except we were more discreet and there was less technology around to catch us. When we left shows at the Cap Center or the Coliseum, we would go to stores like the 7-Eleven and craftily steal by blocking the view of the clerks; there were no cameras as you see today in every store. During snow storms when everything in the city was closed, we used to break into stores in high end places like Georgetown and steal clothes. We got a rush from running into expensive stores, snatching an entire rack of clothes, and then running away. Stealing with your crew is nothing new. The difference now is that surveillance cameras are more prevalent, affordable, and sophisticated.

My last academic stop in D.C. was at Theodore Roosevelt Senior High School. I did my work, but I continued being a class clown. My favorite teacher was Mr. Perry Williams. I was in his science class. I received an "F" for the first quarter because I had not adjusted to learning material. Once I became more familiar with the information, I began to enjoy his classes. Mr. Williams was a very funny teacher and he made me want to learn. From the second quarter on, I did not receive anything lower than a "B" in his class. Mr. Williams also took notice of my improvement in his class. I started out the year with him saying, as only he could, "Mr. Mo-o-o-o-ten, if you say one more word in my class, I will zero you right off my roll," and in the next breath saying, "Why can't you all be like Mr. Mo-o-o-oten? He's one of my best students." You see, Mr. Williams not only had a sense of humor, but he stuttered, too. His classroom was connected to other open-space classrooms, so when he stuttered and said those things, his class laughed at him along with the other two classrooms nearby. I was saddened to find out that he later died from a brain tumor.

After a couple of years at Roosevelt, I was put out of school by a principal named Tony Upson. The irony of it all is that Mr. Upson was later removed as principal by DCPS for an alleged misconduct. He briefly played basketball with the Washington Bullets. He was often seen at Upshur, our local playground, where he would play a little basketball with the fellas. It amazed me that he put me out for my behavior problems rather than helping me address them given that he obviously was plagued with a few disciplinary issues of his own. I see teenagers treated like this today and wonder what those in authority think they are accomplishing. I wonder how statistics would improve if educators would take a little more time and apply a little more energy to encourage our youth to do better. America is in crisis with a 50 percent dropout rate in our urban schools. Tossing kids out of school is not the answer.

By the time I was seventeen, I was employed part-time and then full time at the Washington Hospital Center as an orderly. Let me be clear, I had to dress up a little bit to get the job. I also had a helping hand that guided me during the application process. The help came from a nurse who worked for a staffing agency called Nursing Services that had a job placement contract with Washington Hospital Center.

The nurse's name was Bobby. He said, "Ron, I can help you out, I see you are a hard worker." I asked, "How can you help me? I don't have the proper nursing certification or a high school diploma." He simply said; "We can fix that." Oh boy! We fixed it alright! Bobby took his certificate, made a copy, and then we typed my name on it and made another copy to make it look original. Then he taught me how to take vital signs on the job and the rest was history. Those tricks would never work today because of the Patriot Act. There are very few jobs that do not require an FBI background check and more.

I was a hell of a worker. I bought a car, a 1987 Toyota Camry, for which my grandmother co-signed. This made me the first seventeen-year-old guy in my neighborhood who was able to get his own new car through sheer hard work. I was making as much as twenty dollars an hour when rich people just wanted someone to sit with their loved ones. Sometimes, I would work twenty-four hours straight, which was against the law, but I wanted to do well in life and it also help my family who did so much for me.

All good things come to an end. My head nurse told me I had to choose between working directly for the hospital as an orderly or continuing to work as a contractor with the staffing company. Of course, I chose to stay with Nursing Services because it paid more. It was good for a minute, but then the Washington Hospital Center cut back its use of Nursing Services and that meant a reduction of my hours, too.

Now, here I am, a young guy with a car note and insurance payments, and not much money coming in. As if things weren't bad enough, I was dumped by a girl I was in love with, my true first love. Her name was K.K.; she was from the Caribbean island of Trinidad. K.K. had me going in circles. I later found out that she, allegedly, did Voodoo on me by cutting my hair and putting it in between her mattresses. I also left home around this time because I thought I was a grown man and my grandmother told me, "If you don't like the rules, there's the door." I took the door.

I was feeling let down by a lot of people. I was determined to make sure that those who turned their backs on me would regret it, especially K.K. She left me for her baby's daddy and that really hurt. I started out with only $150, just enough to buy a sixteenth of an ounce of cocaine. Within six months I had $150,000 cash and was buying kilos of cocaine. I still worked hard, only this time, it was illegal.

It was only a matter of time before it caught up with me. I was arrested and did ninety days on a youth study at Lorton and was given a youth act. This meant that my record would be erased once I finished my probation. I am grateful for the legendary Judge Eugene Hamilton who helped so many young men like me. I got to be a big boy in the drug game when I decided to reach out to an old head by the name of Gene Byrd. He was a very professional, progressive, behind-the-scenes drug dealer, who dealt with large quantities of drugs or, as we refer to it in the street, a lot of weight. He didn't deal with people on the street level, only with professionals.

I gained his respect from my brief stint as a drug dealer working with Louis. He recognized that I was young, but very mature. I would meet him at places like Takoma Station Tavern up town. Back then, Takoma Station was a really hot jazz spot with all the pretty, sophisticated ladies who had big coke habits. You would never know it though because it went through their noses. This was right around the time that crack was making its way into the Nation's Capital. I would take a drink of wine, flirt with the ladies, get my product, and leave. Sometimes, I would meet Gene at his paint shop; I learned so much from him. He was a really good guy who never took advantage of me. However, my relationship with Gene would eventually cost me.

One day, I took $50,000 to cop two keys (kilos) from Gene. This was the first time he ever invited me to one of his houses at the elegant Blair Towers. Once inside, he paced back and forth waiting for his shipment. I knew something was wrong because he had never invited me to his house, which was a no-no in the drug game. That was the first time I saw him snort cocaine. Someone knocked on his door and he pulled his gun out of the stash. When he looked out the peephole, nobody was there. I stashed my money on the balcony because I thought it was the stick up boys.

Gene later sent what some would call his flunky, Sidney, to check outside the door and see who was out there. Boom! In comes in the DEA (Drug Enforcement Agency), looking like ninjas with machine guns, telling us all, "Get on the floor and don't move," while they held guns to our heads. They asked me my age and I told them I was nineteen. They told me that I would be thirty-nine when I got out of prison. They asked Gene how old he was. When Gene gave his age, they told him he would die in jail and they told Sidney the same thing.

They looked at a picture of Gene's girlfriend, Monica Turner, on top of the TV. They asked him, "How does an ugly man like you, get a pretty girl like that?" Then the agent slammed the picture on the ground saying, "It must be the f**king drugs." This Monica, who Gene helped send through college at Georgetown University, is the same Monica who married Mike Tyson. As they were taking me to the car, I saw Monica coming back to the apartment with groceries and looking as if she was in a state of shock as the feds were walking me out in handcuffs.

At that point, the feds knew nothing about me. Ronald Moten's name wasn't hot, I wasn't in the system. I was released on a $27,000 cash bond. I paid it all myself rather than accepting my grandmother's offer to use her house as collateral. I was soon getting calls from Dovey Roundtree telling me and my grandmother that I was being watched and that I better be careful and leave the streets alone, but I didn't listen. Gene took a plea to ten years because he was set up by the Columbians he was buying from. That reminds me of a similar situation with my longtime friend Bobby Haynes-Bey. Bobby was also copping his supply from Columbians, but in his case, after serving a twenty-year prison sentence, Bobby was gunned down by two men on a motorcycle.

After Gene went in, I still had a need to keep my inventory stocked. I would go up to New York City whenever there was a shortage and cop from the cousin of two so-called friends of mine —
"Friendnemies" as I call them — Mike and Make-Make. On one of those trips, I was caught in Elizabeth City, New Jersey on the way back from New York after copping a quarter of a kilo of crack cocaine. They found the drugs stashed in the trunk of my car in two WD40 lubricant spray cans. I was mad because the only reason I got caught with the drugs was because, after the police pulled me over for "Driving While Black," they saw that I had a few colored bags in my car. They knew drugs had to be somewhere. They checked my car twice and found it the second time around.

Both my father and his father had done time in jail and so I was following in their footsteps. I was preparing to serve a thirteen-month jail term two states away from home in Bordentown, N.J. I was also preparing for my first child, Little Ronald, to be born.

I had a special friend named Chae Thomas who sent me letters and visited me in prison. Along with visits from my family that made my time pretty easy. In N.J., they prepared you for going home. I was in work release making fifteen dollars an hour. I was the man as I was the photographer for people on visiting day. I've always done well in institutions because I used my brain more than my hands. My entire time of incarceration I was only involved in three fights. I understood due process and made sure the law respected me. I came home with good intentions, but hung around the same people and was easily sucked back into the same lifestyle, which always produces the same results! This is a common practice of insane behavior that exists in our community and in my life at that time.

I hooked up with a friend who was a kingpin, Eric King from Kennedy Street. I got back in the game. I met Eric when I ran away from home and was living with a friend named Maurice Butler also called Moe. Moe was killed while I was in New Jersey. He was set up and shot in the head and burned inside his car.

I had a relationship with a girl named Lisa and she too was burned in a fire. It happened on the same day that I had arranged for a friend of her brother to connect with some of my friends to exchange coke for money. To this day, I still don't know what happened, but it's something that I have to live with for the rest of my life. She recovered from her burns and she lives a decent life. She is still beautiful, but she will live with some permanent scars. She was always a good person who just got caught up in a wicked game. As bad as I felt about this, you would have thought that this was the last lesson I needed to learn before I changed my ways, but it wasn't!

I took some time to regroup but eventually went back to hustling and that's when I reconnected with Eric King. We were like family. We would go to fights together in Vegas and play cards. We were like a tightly knitted family. I was probably the only person he felt close to that didn't work for him. Lump, Tap, and I were all friends working the same area but we all hustled on our own. We turned the middle class 14th Street neighborhood into an open-air drug market each of us selling a key of cocaine a day.

I had one-and-a-half fifty gram rocks (working "50's") with lines of people as far down the alley as my eyes could see. It was just like Hanover Street. I was dumping loads of cash under my mattress. My mother told me that she and my son's mother would steal from me, but they had a rule, "Just don't take the hundreds and fifties" because I would remember that. Everything was good, I had a BMW convertible RX7, gold, diamonds, vacations in the Dominican Republic, Versace, Gucci, you name it and I had it, all at eighteen.

My second close call with the "kiss of death" came by way of my so-called friend Mike. Mike knew there was a shortage of coke in D.C. He called and told me that his cousin, who I would cop from in New York City, was in town. He had keys for $18,000 and, since the going rate in D.C. at that time was $25,000, I said, "Hell, yeah." The previous week Mike and I were riding on 13th and Upshur Street with the top down on my RX7 when we saw this girl. We nearly crashed looking at her. Seems kind of a random incident, but it didn't turn out to be random at all.

Not long after that, I met Mike and his cousin at the house. I walked through the door with a bulletproof vest strapped tight. My .38 was tucked away on my hip and I had $36,000 in a Louis Vuitton duffle bag. We were on the main floor of the house. I heard someone moving around on the upper level and then they began to come down the steps. It was the same girl Mike and I saw walk down the street.

A street dude always knows when he's being set up so I turned to Mike and said, "What's up?" Mike asked, "Do you want her?" I said, "Hell, yeah." Of course, when you follow your crotch instead of your head, you lose all common sense — something Marion Barry or anyone with a sex addiction would agree with! I was told to go downstairs.

I proceeded down the steps with high expectations and very aroused. Out of nowhere, someone who looked like a monkey with twenty gold teeth in his mouth, put a gun to my head and said, "You know what time it is." He took my gun from my waist before I could get to it. We continued to the basement where I was stripped naked and tied up.

I saw them bring the yellow container of Prestone coolant into the room. At this point, I knew they were going to kill me because Prestone was said to eliminate fingerprints and evidence. I had to think fast; this was the first time since being a child that I could not control my urine. I thought fast enough to say, "If you don't kill me, I have another one hundred thousand dollars in my apartment, just please, don't hurt my mother."

My mother didn't even live with me, but I knew that this would be the hook and bait that might save my life. Of course, Mike's jealous and cruddy butt took the bait and hyped it. He said, "Yeah, he got it." They then argued over who would hold the money, should they leave it in the house or take it with them. They decided to drive me there in my car, a two-seater. One person let me drive while holding my seatbelt over me with a gun pointed at my side. The other four guys followed us in a taxi. I had orders not to drive on any main streets; I was supposed to take all back roads.

My first thought was to run into a pole and jump out, but I decided to go against what they told me and I took a main road, Georgia Avenue. I saw the police on the opposite side of the road at the light. I jumped out of the car and started jumping up and down as if I was doing jumping jacks and yelling, "They kidnapped me, they kidnapped me!" I ran over and jumped into the police car; the cops panicked and jumped out with their weapons drawn. The kidnappers jumped out of my car, dropped my bag (with the $36,000) in it, and ran. The cab carrying the other dudes drove off. I then jumped out of the police car, picked up my bag with the money in it, got into my RX7 and made a clean get away.

The last "kiss of death" came when I got a call from Eric King asking me to take a ride with his brother, his sister-in-law, and a driver by the name of George Younger. He wanted us to go to the car dealership to look at some cars. I was sitting in the back seat as we sat at a light on Kennedy Street. We were about to make a sharp right onto North Capitol Street when a station wagon pulled up parallel with our car and BAM! Glass windows began exploding and shards flew everywhere.

Suddenly a friend's beef with someone else became mine as the enemy hit him in a drive-by shooting. All the windows in the station wagon were down and the men in it fired semi-automatic weapons at us as they drove away. Our driver George Younger was shot so I put him in the back seat and drove to the nearest fire station. My shirt was soaked with George's blood. I was so dazed that when I looked at all the blood on me, I actually felt pain as though I was shot.

The EMT and Firefighter's laid us on the floor of the fire station to check for wounds. They found George's injures but didn't find any on me. Thank God I was not shot. I had a brief moment of relief and then George leaned over and whispered to me that he had a gun in the car. My first instinct was to scream, "Why the hell didn't you use it fool?" I got up and ran to the car like Speed Racer because I was on parole for the New Jersey charge and I wanted to stash the gun somewhere to avoid a parole violation.

By the time I returned to the fire station, the police were asking questions and showed me a picture of the innocent woman hit and killed by a stray bullet. Her name was Marcia Williams and her brains were splattered all over her kids who were in the car with her. More than twenty detectives took turns trying to get me to talk. I sat in a chair handcuffed to the floor while they fired questions and spit on me. I refused to talk and was released after a sixteen hour interrogation. When they let me go, one of the cops warned me that if they ever found out that I knew more than what I was saying, they would make sure the feds "got my red ass."

Within a year I was locked up as a result of a federal sting. I was set up by a guy who had no criminal record. I was selling this dude a half ounce every payday. He worked for Washington Gas. I don't know how they found him; all I know is the discovery said he was paid four thousand dollars to set me up with a DEA agent. It also said I sold the undercover agent twenty-five grams of coke a half a block away from my grandmother's house. The agent said that the next time he wanted a kilo!

I remember the day he said that he wanted a kilo. That statement raised all kinds of red flags in my mind. I walked back into my grandmother's house thinking, nobody goes from buying twenty-five grams of coke all the way up to a kilo in a week. At this point, I knew I was being set up. I rushed back out of the house and saw police cars everywhere. I hoped they were not for me. I turned back towards the house where my father and brother, Demetrius were waiting for me.

As I approached the house, I saw a white man sitting in his car reading the newspaper and I knew why he was there. He and dozens of other law enforcement officers tried to apprehend me but I ran straight into the house. They grabbed my father and brother as I flew by them. I was able to make it all the way into my grandmother's house and up to the roof. I ran about a block, jumping roof to roof and then into my friend Chris' house. His weird brother was in the shower and I explained to him what was happening. He told me to hide because the police did not have a search warrant. Moments later the police entered Chris' house from the roof in their riot gear. I surrendered with my hands in the air this time not asking for help, but asking them not to kill me! Once again, my name was in the Washington Post but this time the story was not about my mother's accomplishments but about a crime that I committed with a dramatic roof-top-chase.

So there I sat in D.C. Jail. One way that helped me cope with the idea of doing time was that I had a female friend who was in law school. She was allowed to have legal visits with me. They eventually turned into conjugal visits. I was able to get shoes, marijuana, and much more from her. A month later, while sitting in the D.C. jail, I got the order to report to the Chaplin's office where I got the news about the death of my brother, Demetrius "Meaty" Starks.

To many people my brother was just another statistic. He was one of more than 6,000 people murdered in Washington, D.C. between 1989 and 2009. Most of those were young black men and their deaths were the result of the drug game, gang and crew beefs or other forms of senseless violence.

While serving time, I was also told that a female named Renae with whom I had a one night stand was pregnant with my child, Tavon. Here I was in prison, my dumb ass being a player with no education, having all these babies and having the nerve to be angry at my dad for not playing a more significant role in my formative years. Tavon and my oldest son, Ronald, deserved to have a father at home with them, teaching and guiding them. I knew better. I wanted more for my sons than what I had. My dad was really not around much back then. At one point, while I was incarcerated in D.C. Jail, my dad was locked up there, too. We were actually being detained on the same block. That stayed in my mind. I was determined to do what was necessary to ensure that my children would never end up in jail.

I soon grew tired of drinking this kind of muddy water. It served no purpose but to destroy lives. This kind of muddy water could not be purified. It was destroying my family, friends and my community. This muddy water was unlike the muddy water the civil rights leaders had to drink. The muddy water they drank was for the purpose of sacrifice. They drank it so that others would have endless opportunities that many now take for granted. My muddy water was causing the end of opportunities not only for me but for my children. Drinking muddy water of my own making had to end.

I knew that God saved me for a reason and I also knew that there was no college, grad school, or theory that could have prepared me better for the work that I was yet to do than my life experiences, both good and bad. In October 1994, I touched down from the Allenwood FCI and saw my childhood friend "Lump" who told me about a group that was just formed called "Cease Fire Don't Smoke the Brothers." He was one of the founders with Al-Malik Farrakhan.

This was perfect for me because I already had in my mind that I wanted to do something positive. I wanted to keep the commitment I made in prison to give back to my community, to atone for the wrongs that I had committed against my neighborhood. I was also motivated by the fear of knowing that God had saved me for the last time and that I had better take heed to the purpose he had for me or my next "kiss with death" might be my last! The insanity was over!

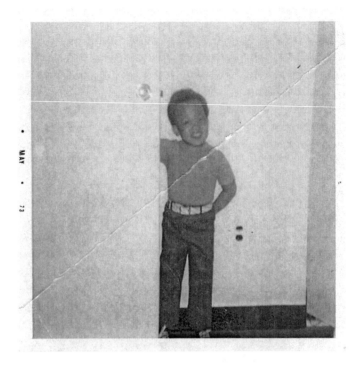

Me, Ronald "Moe" Moten, as a little Boy

From top left: my mom, Arlene Moten and my cousin, Arvette Winslow

From bottom left: Uncle Edward Floyd, my cousin Wendy, and me

With my father, Ronald Starks-EL, and my brother, Demitreus Starks

My grandparents and my son Ronald visiting me in prison at Allenwood Federal Corrections Institution at special Thanksgiving Dinner

My mother, Arlene Moten, and Uncle David Moten with my Uncle Edward Floyd at his graduation outside of Constitution Hall in Washington, D.C.

At age 18, me visiting with former girlfriend and her friend at her home before she was tragically burned.

With my mother at a Peaceoholics' fundraiser held at the Renaissance hotel in Washington, D.C.

My son Tavon Scott who I raised as single parent and my daughters Yasmeen and Asantawaa Moten

With my oldest sons, Ronald and Tavon in 1997

Me at age eighteen with my brother, Demitreus, and my sister, Michelle at a Maze concert

Me in Allenwood, Federal Correctional Institution with fellow Washingtonians in the rec yard

My brother, Demitreus (center), and my friend Clarence (left) were both killed in 1991 on my sister's twenty-first birthday and my friend Paul (bottom), who was killed in Ward 5's Trinidad community

In Las Vegas for the 1991 Mike Tyson – Razor Ruddock fight

In Las Vegas in 1991 with Eric King (left), a drug kingpin who was killed during my last stint in prison, and Heavy D (right)

Lesson One

Rules of the Game

Life in America is really a game. One of the concepts we teach our community and youth is that life is like the game of basketball. If you don't know the rules to the game, you will turn the ball over to the other team and commit fouls. Eventually you foul out and can't help your team.

Because so many of us don't know the rules to the game of life, we end up in one of the biggest businesses in America, the prison system, and that doesn't benefit us at all. It has a domino effect from generation to generation. While racism still plays its role in this, our ignorance and lack of understanding of the rules cause us to flood the gates of this thriving business, the prison-industrial complex. The mass incarceration of the black male population is fueled by both the misguided "War on Drugs" waged by both political parties and by ignorance on the part of our people about the rules of the game. Black women are now entering the gates at alarming rates.

The rules of the game in America are spelled out in the U.S. Constitution, so knowing what the Constitution says can take you a long way. It's a great document and knowing what is in it can be to your advantage. Just look at the life of Thurgood Marshall who led the fight against the segregation of schools in 1953 by making a constitutional argument before the Supreme Court of the United States. Fifteen years later he became the first African American to be appointed to the Supreme Court.

Blacks make up only 13 percent of the population in America, but we make up over half of the prison population. In my workshops with "returned citizens" coming home from prison, or with troubled youth from grade school to college, or with the educated black elite, not one has ever been able to quote the Thirteenth Amendment of the Constitution.

It says, "Neither slavery nor involuntary servitude, except as a punishment for crime whereof the party shall have been duly convicted, shall exist within the United States." Let me break that down for you. In simple English it means that if you commit a crime in America, you can be enslaved or forced to perform free labor in America.

Then I ask them to quote the Fifth Amendment which addresses due process, no one can answer that one either. It says, "No person shall…be deprived of life, liberty, or property, without due process of law." The Fourteenth Amendment also contains an almost identical due process clause.

Then I explain how they always end up in jail when they say the police violated their rights. I point out that in more affluent neighborhoods of D.C. like Georgetown, the residents respond differently when they are disrespected or treated wrongfully by the police. They don't make things worse by cursing out the police, which is what gets you smacked upside the head and locked up for disorderly conduct. No, they demand due process.

Most residents of Georgetown would file a citizen's complaint because they know they have the right to due process. They also know that if an officer gets more than six complaints in his jacket within a year, it is very unlikely that he will get a promotion. An officer with several complaints will chill out and respect the person and community that have a problem with his or her behavior.

Government dependence programs have made too many of our people expect to get something for nothing. Without an education, business, or trade skill in this competitive world, you will sit on the bench. And when you do obtain that education or job skill, you better practice to improve. Most youth have the attitude of NBA great Allen Iverson who didn't like to practice. When asked about it he just said, "Practice? Practice?" As if something was wrong with his coach asking him to practice with his team. Iverson is now retired and never won an NBA Championship, maybe there is a correlation. No one likes practice, but the difference between Michael Jordan and Allen Iverson is that Jordan practiced even when he didn't feel like it.

If you don't practice and learn the skills to acquire gainful employment and then, once you get there, practice to stay sharp and above your competition, you will eventually sit on the bench. The danger then is ending up like Javaris Crittenton, formerly of the Washington Wizards, a backup player who was involved in an incident with his teammate Gilbert Arenas in which they drew guns at each other in the locker room over a silly bet. Jarvis was cut from the team, but they kept Arenas, why? Arenas had superior skills. Since then, Jarvis' life has gone in a downward spiral from an NBA bench rider to recently being charged with murdering someone in a drive-by shooting in which he killed an innocent mother in Atlanta, Georgia.

Javaris Crittenton, another black man who either did not know the rules or refused to play by the rules. He let his God-given talents go down the drain. These rules are not rocket science; they are just rules that every citizen and child in America should know. However, we can go into every high school in urban America and, I can guarantee you, 90 percent of the students do not know the Constitution of the United States of America. Thurgood Marshall knew what was in the Constitution, he knew the rules of the game and he never stopped developing his talents. Now his name will be remembered as long as there is a United States of America.

If we don't educate the people, they will never stand up and truly be "WE THE PEOPLE," they will be institutionalized into legal slavery and continue to destroy our community as everybody pays the price for this ignorance of the rules of the game. Whatever color, whether rich or poor, educated or uneducated, we must master the rules of the game. We need to have insight into enduring principles of the Constitution of the United States of America. It is critical to develop life skills including basic common sense because, especially for blacks, if you don't know your history, someone else will write it for you and it will cost you your freedom.

Almost one hundred years before Thurgood Marshall argued and won the landmark *Brown vs. Board of Education* decision making segregation in schools illegal, the Democratic Party, led by Stephen Douglas, was celebrating the *Dred Scott vs. Sandford* decision that upheld the Fifth Amendment rights of slave owners by categorizing slaves as property. That is Democratic Party history; it is fact.

Three years earlier in 1854, the anti-slavery Republican Party was formed. It was so committed to anti-slavery that Democrats called them Black Republicans. It took the election of the first Republican president, 700,000 American casualties in the Civil War, the assassination of Abraham Lincoln, and the passage of the Thirteenth Amendment to the Constitution to reverse the *Dred Scott* decision. It is that kind of contrast in the histories of the Democratic and Republican Parties that has inspired me to become a Civil Rights Republican.

Yes, I am aware that Republicans have some sorry episodes in their history also, but there is one big difference: Democrats don't truly honor the U.S. Constitution; they are constantly either ignoring or changing the rules of the game. I can forgive the past, but when the powerful keep changing the rules, it is WE THE PEOPLE who suffers. It does not matter if it is your local city councilmember ignoring the rules of ethics and fair play in favor of pay to play, the Obama Justice Department choosing to enforce some laws and not others, or President Nixon covering up the Watergate break in. Local or national, Republican or Democrat, no one is above the law. The rules of the game are in the U.S. Constitution and they apply to everyone.

The fact is that Michael Jordan could not have won even one championship if the other team was allowed to ignore or change the rules of the game when it was to their advantage. Learn the rules of the game, play by them, and demand that the politicians of both parties do the same!

2

Peaceoholics Part I

Keeping My Promise

I am ready to act if I can find brave men to help me.
—Carter G. Woodson, Civil Rights Republican

People coming out of prison are often called ex-offenders or ex-convicts. I not only refrain from using that terminology, but was part of a group that, along with Yango Sawyer, a great community activist and others, came up with the name "returned citizens." Words are powerful and we decided on this name because we never heard anyone call Martha Stewart or Paris Hilton ex-offenders or ex-convicts, so why should we or anyone else be identified by those negative labels? Many people tried to take credit for coining the term "returned citizens," but God knows where it came from. I am proud that the District of Columbia has adopted "returned citizens" as its classification of formerly incarcerated citizens.

Cease Fire Don't Smoke the Brothers is where Al-Malik, a reformed "returned citizen," introduced me to Jauhar Abraham. Jauhar and I both worked as youth organizers for the Million Man March for whom we organized youth in the District, Maryland, and Virginia along with other youth around the country. We were working to bring as many youth as possible to the historic march in Washington, D.C. When I look back, I really appreciate the opportunity to work at Cease Fire in its beginning stages because it clarified my purpose in life. It was a natural fit as my previous life experience taught me to relate, organize, and confront issues in my community that others seemed to have problems addressing.

I stayed with Cease Fire until 1997, pushing Al-Malik Farrakhan around in his wheelchair as we agitated, advocated, and fought for the people of D.C. We even cleaned up our 14th Street Petworth neighborhood known as the 1-4 Zone. This was the same neighborhood that I had earlier helped infest with drugs. Now, here I was running a drug dealer named James Jones out of the neighborhood. We had helped get him out of prison and then he had the nerve to come back to our neighborhood to sell drugs again. In fact, he ended up calling the police on us. The police came and harassed us, as if we were the drug dealers, but all I was trying to do was to keep my promise to make up for the damage I had done to my people and the community.

We later called Commander Monroe with whom we had a good relationship and he told the police to let us go. In the process, we were threatened by a guy named of "Joe Slimmy" who was about six-foot-four inches and 260 pounds. I caught him on 14th and Crittenden (one block from Cease Fire headquarters). He popped off with his mouth; I hit him with a right hook and then caught him on the way down with a UCF style knee to the jaw knocking him out. Then Al-Malik rolled up in his wheelchair and smacked the daylights out of him, waking him up.

This is how serious we were about cleaning up our neighborhood. I do not advocate unnecessary physical violence, but at the time, I had not been mentored in the ways of nonviolence. I was just drawing on what I knew from the streets. After that we were threatened by James Jones, Joe Slimmy's drug supplier. We went down to them on Parkview Street and let them know that we were changed men, but the reality was that they didn't want any trouble from us. We didn't have any more problems out of them. Later you will read about citizenship vs. snitching. This is what I tell guys in the street who don't believe that law-abiding citizens have the right to call the police when they see brothers and sisters committing crimes and destroying our communities.

There is a ridiculous double standard. When a drug dealer has his car stolen, he is all about calling the police so that a police report is created for insurance purposes. No one ever calls that snitching, and it isn't. But if you see that same person selling drugs to children on the corner and you call the cops on him, then you are called a snitch. Why is it called snitching when a law-abiding citizen is looking out for the welfare of children in the community and it isn't snitching for a drug dealer to call the cops about a stolen car. There is something terribly wrong when a drug dealer's stolen car is more important than the children in our village. We always taught our youth that reporting crimes is how they exercise their rights as citizens; it is not snitching if you are running the streets or part of the illegal activity.

Working with Cease Fire Don't Smoke the Brothers was an irreplaceable experience. While working with Al-Malik, I had the chance to absorb so much profound wisdom from one-on-one conversations with people like Winnie Mandela, Marion Barry, Jim Brown, and Stokeley Carmichael. I will always be grateful to Al-Malik for that opportunity.

As a reward for our labor in helping organize the Million Man March, Al-Malik, through his relationship with the Nation of Islam, arranged for me to have dinner with the Minister Louis Farrakhan. I also spoke on the same stage with him at Howard University leading up to the Million Man March. I was there to mobilize the students. This was big for me because many in my community do not agree with many of Minister Farrakhan's religious beliefs, but they do respect him as one of the few leaders who speaks out on the real issues affecting African Americans.

Al-Malik and I had some disagreements because I'm a very vocal person and when I would see something I didn't agree with, I would speak out. One of the lessons that I learned was that our elders in the African-American community need to do a better job of supporting our youth as they grow and preparing them to fly for whatever the reason. It's important to pass the baton because in a real village the youth always come back and support those who planted the seeds in good soil so they could grow. I promised myself that I wouldn't follow in their footsteps by treating the young people who I mentor in negative and hostile ways when they decide to move on.

I am grateful that during this time, then District of Columbia Mayor Marion Barry wrote a letter to me about the great job we were doing to address the needs in our community by working with gangs and troubled youth. Below is a reproduction of his kind letter.

Until this letter was written, MPD Warrant Squad (Metropolitan Police Department) raided my grandparent's house several times, looking for me on parole violation warrants related to my old New Jersey charge for which I had just been released. In spite of some of the political disagreements I have had with Marion Barry, I continue to have a good personal relationship with him built on mutual respect. The text of the letter reads:

To whom it may concern:

On February 28, 1995, I met with 50 young rivaling gang leaders, members and Mr. Al-Malik Farrakhan, who was instrumental in gathering these young men to my office. Under the leadership of Mr. Farrakhan and my guidance, these young men drew a truce between themselves to stop the killing, crime, drug involvement and related violence that had once plagued their lives.

February 1995, was truly a most moving, inspiring and impressive day to remember. Along with witnessing the profound peace agreement also came the existence of **Cease Fire Don't Smoke the Brothers, Inc.,** (Cease Fire) and my first meeting with Mr. Ronald Moten. Truly, history was made on this day.

It is because of these events that occurred in February 1995 that I am compelled to write on behalf of Ronald Moten. Not only is Mr. Moten one of the founders of Cease Fire, he has become one of the organization's most serious, dedicated and dependable members. He now holds the position of spokesperson for the organization.

Ronald Moten's efforts, as spokesperson for Cease Fire, have been profound and effective as they relate to problems facing our youth-at-risk. Mr. Moten has responded to these critical situations and has resolved issues without incident. The message he delivers along with the positive action he exhibits, ring loud and clear. His words touch many hearts and help to turn their lives around. Mr. Moten's message of peace, justice and love is spoke before many diverse groups.

In my meetings with Mr. Moten he has shown sincerity, compassion and devotion. I have been able to call on him without hesitation, knowing that whatever the circumstance, he will respond in a positive and responsible manner.

In light of the above, a critical situation that must be resolved has been brought to my attention. Mr. Moten is being sought by the State of New Jersey. Please understand it is crucial that the jurisdiction requesting his presence know the dynamic impact Ronald Moten has made on our population of youth-at-risk. Also, it is crucial that the New Jersey jurisdiction be aware of the impact that his absence (if required) will have on this community. It would be a travesty to not allow the continuity of his efforts to give back to the community and provide guidance to the present and future youth-at-risk generation.

It is important to state before closing, that six months prior to the official founding of Cease Fire, Mr. Moten was very instrumental in its planning and development stages. He was steadfast on a path of constructing positive change in his life. Further, for the past 18 months, Mr. Moten has remained on parole in an outstanding status while under the Federal Parole Department. His parole has gone without incident.

If you should need assistance in resolving this issue without the incarceration of Mr. Moten or request further information please contact Phyllis E. Anderson, my Executive Assistant at (202) 727-XXXX. I appreciate your immediate attention to this urgent matter.

Sincerely,
Marion Barry, Jr.
Mayor

THE DISTRICT OF COLUMBIA
WASHINGTON, D.C. 20001

MARION BARRY, JR
MAYOR

March 12, 1996

To Whom It May Concern:

On February 28, 1995, I met with 50 young rivaling gang leaders, members and Mr. Al Mali Farrakhan, who was instrumental in gathering these young men to my office. Under the leadership of Mr. Farrakhan and my guidance, these young men drew a truce between themselves to stop the killing, crime, drug involvement and related violence that had once plagued their lives.

February 1995, was truly a most moving, inspiring and impressive day of to remember. Along with witnessing the profound peace agreement also came the existence of **Cease Fire Don't Smoke the Brothers**, Inc., (Cease Fire) and my first meeting with Mr. Ronald Moten. Truly, history was made on this day.

It is because of these events that occurred in February 1995, that I am compelled to write on behalf of Ronald Moten. Not only is Mr. Moten one of the founders of Cease Fire, he has become one of the organization's most serious, dedicated and dependable members. He now holds the position of spokesperson for the organization.

Ronald Moten's efforts, as spokesperson for Cease Fire, have been profound and effective as they relate to problems facing our youth-at-risk. Mr. Moten has responded to these critical situations and has resolved issues without incident. The message he delivers along with the positive action he exhibits, ring loud and clear. His words touch many hearts and help to turn their lives around. Mr. Moten's message of peace, justice and love is spoken before many diverse groups.

In my meetings with Mr. Moten he has shown sincerity, compassion and devotion. I have been able to call on him without hesitation, knowing that whatever the circumstance, he will respond in a positive and responsible manner.

In light of the above, a critical situation that must be resolved has been brought to my attention. Mr. Moten is being sought by the State of New Jersey. Please understand it is crucial that the jurisdiction requesting his presence know the dynamic impact Ronald Moten has made on our population of youth-at-risk. Also, it is crucial that the New Jersey jurisdiction be aware of the impact that his absence (if required) will have on this community. It would be a travesty to not allow the continuity of his efforts to give back to the community and provide guidance to the present and future youth-at-risk generation.

It is important to state before closing, that six months prior to the official founding of Cease Fire, Mr. Moten was very instrumental in its planning and development stages. He was steadfast on a path of constructing positive change in his life. Further, for the past 18 months, Mr. Moten has remained on parole in an outstanding status while under the Federal Parole Department. His parole has gone without incident.

If you should need assistance in resolving this issue without the incarceration of Mr. Moten or request further information please feel free to contact Phyllis E. Anderson, my Executive Assistant at (202) 727-2980. I appreciate your immediate attention given to this urgent matter.

Sincerely,

Marion Barry, Jr.
Mayor

cc: Chief Judge Eugene Hamilton
    D.C. Superior Court

I decided in 1997 that it was time for me to move on from Cease Fire. One major reason was the financial hardships I was experiencing because there was no money in the movement. To no one's surprise, Brother Farrakhan's style did not make it easy to raise funds. On top of having no money, I was locked up for a couple of hours when my son's mother didn't show up for a child support hearing in front of Judge Diaz.

That was the last straw for me. I started a company called Reddoor Entertainment and was doing street promotions for people like Kelly Swanson and Don King and large parties where stars like Mike Tyson and the singer Monica appeared. I lived off that income while working in the community for years without a dime from the government. I can remember my grandmother saying, "You are out there helping the world, but you can barely help yourself."

It was up and down, but a good learning experience. I did a lot of street promotions for my buddy John Day at the HOBO Shop. HOBO stood for Helping Our Brothers Out and was a line of sportswear. I worked with a lot of boxers like my friend and local D.C. hero WBA Champ William Joppy. I introduced them to John at HOBO and they wore his clothes in the ring, which gave him exposure all over the world.

John made Joppy a fancy outfit with a robe that had Reddoor Entertainment and HOBO on it. William wore the robe for his historic HBO fight with Felix Trinidad in New York City. This outfit was so extraordinary that John started making clothes for other champs, Three from D.C., Joppy, Sharmba Mitchell, and Chop Chop. I am proud to have joined John Day in giving birth to a revolution of marketing in the boxing ring. Our style of marketing John's clothing changed the whole marketing game in boxing. Before we came along, it was boring and most boxers did not get paid for wearing those Everlast boxing outfits into the ring for a prize fight.

This exposure helped John's already lucrative business explode. HOBO was already booming in the D.C. area, but the exposure on HBO made it explode. HOBO took over the urban clothing market from Virginia to Baltimore, Maryland. I used those same marketing and promotional skills later on to market the work of Peaceoholics. I found that if people didn't know what you were doing, you couldn't get funding. I have also passed my entrepreneurial skills on to the youth from the gangs and returned citizens who need to have their hustling skills re-directed.

John was later introduced to Baltimore's Hasim Rahman who was cool with Joppy. They both had the same managers, Steve Nelson and

Stan Hoffman. This led to John and me meeting Rahman and Don King for breakfast while in New York City for the Joppy-Trinidad fight.

In 2002 Jauhar and I worked together at a charter school called Village Learning Center Public Charter School where I was a Health and Physical Education instructor. We became enemies for a short time. To this day, we rarely get along, we aren't enemies, but we don't dress alike, think alike, or act alike. Some call him Martin Luther King, Jr. and refer to me as Malcolm X. I later found out that Malcolm X is my biological cousin on my father's side. Jauhar and I mended our relationship for the greater good, which allowed us to begin the great work of Peaceoholics. Most people do not understand that Dr. King was listened to because the establishment could not deal with the alternative, which was a man whose motto was "by any means necessary."

It is important to note co-founding Peaceoholics with Jauhar only happened because of two elders from Penn Branch in Washington, D.C., Dr. Donald Johnson and a Moorish American named Bradford-El. These wise men initiated a mediation that showed us how we could accomplish more together than separately. Since we both wanted the same outcomes for our communities, joining forces made sense.

On a personal note, I want to thank Dr. Johnson in particular. I lost out on a lot of personal growth and maturity when Dr. Johnson and his wife moved down South in retirement. I learned so much from him. He once told me, "If they do not pay you for your work, they don't respect you!" I have never forgotten that.

The Peaceoholics organization was born because Jauhar and I got tired of being consultants for people who were just putting band aids on a gunshot wound and had no real understanding of the people. In fact, most of them were just in business for the paycheck. We believed that we were born to serve our great city and beyond having learned such valuable lessons through our life experiences and through trial and error while working with others.

The actual decision to start Peaceoholics came in the midst of our work at Ballou Senior High School in Southeast Washington, D.C. I could not get anyone to give us startup capital for Peaceoholics. Fortunately, my uncle had gone through some of the same things Jauhar and I went through as children. To his credit, he changed his ways before he ended up incarcerated. He went on to become a senior manager at Lockheed-Martin where employees are encouraged to give back to the community. That inspired him to jumpstart our ambitions with a generous donation. As usual, when somebody believed in me and gave me an opportunity, I made the best of it.

The following stories are examples of Peaceoholics' many successes and a few of our less successful attempts, even outright failures, to make things better for our beloved city. As you read these stories, it is important to keep one thing in mind. The point of this chapter is not to glorify myself or Peaceoholics, but to demonstrate what can be done in our communities when leaders put the people first.

With Cease Fire Don't Smoke the Brothers and Sisters, Inc. where I started my activism

In NYC, doing street promotions representing D.C. and Reddoor Entertainment with my two sons and WBA Champ William Joppy. Standing beside me is my friend and mentee Chi Ali of the Suttle Thoughts Go-Go- Band.

WBA Champ William Joppy showcases the HOBO shop and my Red Door Entertainment brand for his May 12, 2001 bout with Felix Trinidad at Madison Square Garden shown live on HBO.

In a hotel with NFL Hall of Fame legend Jim Brown after a Cease Fire Don't Smoke the Brothers and Sisters meeting

Me speaking to the youth leaders of the Million Man March at its headquarters in 1995. .

With Eric Tap, Cease Fire founder, Al-Malik Farrakhan, and Winnie Mandela in Mayor Marion Barry's office.

Receiving my first award with Cease Fire Don't Smoke the Brothers from Public Allies Inc.

Ballou the Untold Story

Ballou Senior High School was a once proud Southeast, D.C. school. Even though the majority of its students were from some of the city's poorest neighborhoods, many found a path to success such as Gina Adams, now Senior Vice President of Government Affairs for FedEx, Curtis Etherly of Coca-Cola, and Mike Rawls, CEO of D.C.'s famous Goodman Basketball League and a Homeland Security officer. When the pride and spirit in the school disappeared, many fell to the wayside. They can be found in America's prisons, on street corners, and cemeteries.

Once pride and dignity began to erode, conditions were tolerated that would not be at all acceptable in more affluent schools. On any given day, you could walk into the building and see trash throughout the hallways as if you were in a D.C. back alley. Students were having sex in the hallways. Intruders from rival neighborhoods would sneak into the building to help their friends fight other students. Getting in was easy because, even when the doors were locked, Ballou students would open them from the inside and let their friends enter.

The school's test scores were miserable, not surprising given the fear created by the daily violence. There were twenty-three rival gangs in the school although we did not use the term gangs. We called them Neighbors with Needs, but the reality is that they were gangs and they created an atmosphere of chaos and terror. There was a complete failure of leadership. We needed a Joe Clark who turned around the infamous Eastside High in Paterson, N.J. as shown in the inspirational film.

No one knew when or what would bring all this chaos to a head, but everyone knew it was inevitable. The tragic day turned out to be Feb 2, 2003. The Barry Farms vs. Condon Terrace beef had reached an all-time high and resulted in Ballou Senior High School star quarterback J-Rock being killed in the hallways. He was killed by T.J., also a Ballou student and promising rapper from Barry Farms, a rival community.

Both communities are in Southeast, D.C. public housing complexes where there are many homicides. Too many of our children are killed by other children who are then locked up. This made national news and changed the way school security was handled in D.C. and throughout the country. These types of incidents have become a pervasive reality in America's schools.

Two days after the murder, Mayor Anthony Williams arrived at the school for an emergency community meeting in Ballou's auditorium. Over three hundred parents and community leaders were present. Peaceoholics had come to the school periodically to deal with the beef, but the old school bureaucrats thought we were a threat to their authority and treated us like new kids on the block. They gave us a hard way to go because, in their eyes, we were not endorsed by the right people in their bureaucratic world. However, on this day, all that changed.

One of the community leaders attempted to facilitate the event in front of a hostile crowd. He was a pastor and had worked with the school and with us in the past. When the meeting began, a parent yelled, "Why do you all have him on the microphone? He had sex with my daughter!" He wisely passed the microphone to Jauhar and we managed to bring some order to that meeting, which marked the day that Peaceoholics became a catalyst for bringing order out of Ballou's chaos.

Unfortunately, nothing was accomplished at that meet as it became a much needed venting session for parents. What the crowd did not know was that Mayor Anthony Williams was sitting there with a check for more than two hundred thousand dollars for the school which he never had a chance to present publicly. All of the politicians that day just sat and took the verbal beating from the community. They knew they would survive politically if they just absorbed the blows and do nothing. This was not Cleveland Park; most of these angry parents would not attend another meeting or exercise their right as citizens to vote. You would think that a murder would keep them involved, but you would be wrong.

Only fifteen parents showed up two days later at a PTSA meeting. This was a dose of reality to me as I began to grasp the size of the challenge we were taking on. You are fighting steep odds when the hellfire of a meeting like this is followed by silence. It was a lot easier to get parents to line up at six in the morning on the day the new Jordan's come out than to attend a PTSA meeting days after a student at their own children's school was murdered.

The first casualty of the murder was Ballou's principal. He should have been replaced long before this, but people in neglected communities often fight for those who abuse them. The abuse becomes addictive and an illusion of love. This man was allegedly having personal relationships with teachers, stealing from the school, letting athletes pass to the next grade that never came to school or who could barely read. There were seventeen programs in the school to help the students, but none of the students, parents, or teachers knew anything about them. Still, it took a murder in the school hallway to get rid of an incompetent principal.

It made me sick that people fought for this guy. Their attitude was that as long as he was one of our own, this stuff was acceptable. The

D.C. Public Schools Superintendent tried to get a strong black male principal to take the position and bring some order to this prison-like school. Nobody would step up; I guess no strong black men were crazy enough to risk their good names and reputations with all eyes on Ballou.

Thank goodness there was a strong black woman named Vera White, a master educator who knew "the power of the womb" (see Lesson Two) and was willing to leave the regional office and step up to the plate. She brought in another bright lady named Dr. Deborah Evans. Ms. White was initially a little standoffish, but soon after they arrived, they heard that we had been called to help by ERCPCP (East of the River Clergy and Police Community Partnership) who had a great relationship with Mayor Williams.

We recruited other "returned citizens" (ex-offenders) who we helped organize and teamed up with volunteers. Most help coming in from the outside could only be counted on to be at the school when the television cameras where there. Our team stayed in the school all day whether there were television cameras or not. We worked with the communities and beefing neighborhoods in the evenings. We brought calm to an atmosphere that was worse than what I had ever seen even in the D.C. jail, one of the wildest atmospheres on the planet.

Talking strategy with famed activist and Ward 8 D.C. Board of Education representative William Lockridge after the J-Rock shooting at Ballou.

Once things got better, reality set in. I got a call from Dr. Evans telling me that DCPS was bringing in the fingerprint machines to fingerprint all of us and we could not return to the schools until we had clearances. I was mad and felt used. I had no problem with the fingerprinting because that was the right thing to do. The problem was that the government asked organizations like ours to hire "returned citizens" and now was making it impossible for them to participate. I had seen this kind of road block used before and, at that point, I knew they had no more use for us.

Here we were trying to encourage parental participation and had to tell parents who were ex-convicts (returned citizens) that they could not be volunteers. When they told people like Kenny Barnes who had a twenty-year-old marijuana charge that they could not return to the school, I knew what that meant for the rest of us. However, I refused to accept this and, because of the positive results from the work we had already done, we were eventually cleared to be in the school.

Some others who had the time to deal with the long process would also be approved. Understandably, most could not afford the time it took to get through all of the red tape of getting a clearance. This kind of clearance was normally not required by the D.C. government where the most you had to get was a police clearance from MPD. The police clearance only goes back ten years and only shows D.C. crimes.

How We Helped Turn It Around at Ballou

Mayor Anthony Williams and Councilmember Marion Barry called a press conference in front of the school and I walked the halls to find something positive about Ballou to present to the community. I thought of the Ballou Marching Knights band and I asked Dr. Evans to let them perform at the press conference. There were two problems. First, the bureaucracy, second, the band did not have anything presentable to wear.

One of those was in my control. I got John and Angie Day of HOBO and Curt Bone from Alldaz to make Ballou band members some clean shirts to wear under their Ballou sweat jackets. The regional office made a game-time decision and let them perform and the band made the news. After that, I helped the band more and more to bring back the old school pride.

Band Director Darrel Watson, his staff, and all of the Knights alumni knew what the old Ballou spirit was all about. They worked tirelessly and we helped them put together the Battle of the Marching

Bands to give them continuing exposure. I used all my marketing skills, but it was a story by Courtland Milloy in the Washington Post that helped them raise eighty thousand dollars to compete at Disney world. Ballou alumni from Coca-Cola and FedEx got their companies to contribute and the Ballou pride was back full force.

Ballou High School marching band practices to play at press conference after star quarterback J-Rock is gunned down in school hallway.

Mr. Watson and his great staff did a wonderful job with the band. They also performed in the Macy's Thanksgiving Day Parade and participated in competitions throughout the country. The Ballou Marching Knights also went with us to support teams from other schools who had no band such as the Roosevelt girls' basketball team. In 2013, the band played at President Obama's second inauguration.

I helped sponsor the basketball team on a trip to New York to play a number of nationally-ranked teams including the number-one-ranked Christ the King. The girls lost by two points with the Ballou band inspiring and created an atmosphere like you feel during NCAA March Madness. I will never forget it and neither will the girls from Roosevelt. Most importantly, it was one more thing that put Ballou in the positive spotlight. The sense of pride that was restored by the success of the Ballou Band created a movement to bring back D.C.'s rich history of marching bands to most D.C. high schools under the leadership of Mayor Adrian Fenty and the City Council.

With Ballou's basketball team in California on one of many trips I helped sponsor for the nationally-ranked team whose members all lived in impoverished communities in D.C.

Another part of turning it around was working with J-Rock's mother, Ms. Richardson, and Ms. Pearlie, T.J.'s mother, who asked the youth not to retaliate. Ms. Richardson also asked the boys to keep it in God's hands. We took both families out to dinner at Cranberry's, which is now a TGI Fridays, to start the healing process. Both women were very spiritual and powerful. Maurice Benton, Ms. Pearlie's other son, whom she asked me to mentor, later got shot. He died five times on the operating table. As I called the family together and asked everyone to pray, the doctor told us that it didn't look like he would survive, but we prayed and he lived.

Maurice "Moe" Benton, who is like a son to me, asked his hood not to retaliate because of what he had learned from our teaching on nonviolence and forgiveness. We had the great civil rights leaders to thank for teaching us those principles. Moe often spent the night at my place until I lost my house in Hillcrest. We are still close and I pray for him as he is dealing with complications from his injuries. He lost all but two inches of his intestines and five surgeries later underwent a new procedure called a full intestine transplant at Georgetown University.

Our successful intervention at Ballou was not an isolated event. The lessons we learned and the healing that grew out of that conflict resulted in a model for reconciliation that we used in a variety of ways in many different settings. For example, years later a few old heads came home from prison and helped us all but eliminate neighborhood conflicts. We also dealt with the same problems within institutions such as DYRS (Department of Youth Rehabilitation Services) where a beef between two crews shut down the whole compound.

Some said we did the miraculous by bringing about a truce between these two crews. We had these guys hugging and walking back to their units crying. We were told nothing like this had ever happened there before! Our Rebuild the Village Triangle connected the dots with the communities, schools, churches, and the D.C. Jail because these issues and conflicts are all intertwined. We had to be entrenched in all of these institutions to be successful.

We did what we called cross-fertilization activities with many of the twenty-three hoods who were beefing with each other. We held intramural basketball games making them play with each other. We worked only with the staff that were all about the children and ignored the ones with wrong priorities and were there to just get a check. We walked the halls to prevent trouble before it started. For example, we stopped a student who was about to set a fire. He was not just being malicious, he did not know how to read and setting a fire meant he could avoid the embarrassment of having to read out loud in his next class. It was sad to see so many children socially promoted in elementary and middle school and were now in high school without basic academic skills.

Ballou's new principal Ms. Karen Smith did wonders for the school and gave us lots of freedom as long as we ran things past her first. For example, I told her there was a way to bring prayer back into school and not get in trouble for violating church and state laws. We started a Prayer Club in the school at 7:30 AM every morning. Students that were normally tardy everyday would get there early for a good breakfast and to hear ministers like Rev. Tony Lee of Community of Hope AME. It is no coincidence that the atmosphere in our public schools began to change for the worse when prayer was prohibited. That one liberal Democrat policy helped destroy one of our most important institutions.

On April 11, 2008 the Washington City Paper wrote that Peaceoholics might have found its targeted audience. "This group wasn't our best behaved," Principal Smith said after the breakfast. This is what we did best, go after the worst. These students who were always tardy got spiritual uplifting and were on time for their 8:45 AM classes. They got a good breakfast which helped them in school. Nothing like starting the day with positive thoughts and knowing that no matter what happened before you got to school, God has your back.

Rev. Tony Lee from Community of Hope Church speaking at one of our many Peaceoholics' prayer breakfasts at Ballou Senior High School.

At Peaceoholics' 2008 Change Agents Awards at Lincoln Theatre with change agents Ms. Bojoli and Daniel Bradley.

What is sad about this is that our people let a liberal Supreme Court impose its social values on us by removing prayer from our schools. That ruling is as contrary to the beliefs of most Americans and of almost all African Americans as was the *Dred Scott* decision. Whenever there is a conflict between black values and far left values, Democrats seem to choose against black values.

The same thing is true with school vouchers and abortion. Regardless of which side you take on these issues, it is clear that liberal Democrats and their obedient media darlings are liberal first and American citizens second. Democrat politicians assume, correctly, that blacks will vote for them by habit. Once something is habitual, the person does not have to think anymore. We need to turn our brains back on again! We have to face the reality that we have been sheep led to political slaughter whenever Democratic Party policies come into conflict with the beliefs of our historically conservative black community. When will we wake up!

Prayers, Redemption, and Setbacks

The school was taking a lot of steps forward, but there were always a few steps backwards along the way. One setback was a shooting outside the school. Dee Dee, a young man from Barry Farms had been put out of Anacostia Senior High School and did several stints in DYRS. He was prescribed Ritalin and thrown back into society for two years with no social worker or DCPS representative checking in with him to make sure he was going to school. Eventually, he started self-medicating, he was smoking PCP and committed horrific acts of violence with two high-profile drive-by shootings. One was in front of Ballou, in which four people were shot. Two of those shot were our mentees, a boy and a girl from 1-Duce who was beefing with Barry Farms.

The other shooting was a drive-by in which Dee Dee shot some guys from Washington View. The people who ran our juvenile justice system have never been held accountable for their role in this, but that's the norm! We worked with the school and various agencies to get things working the right way. Acts of violence of this kind were normal to most people east of the river in the Nation's Capital. We have learned that youth are resilient and so this was not really mission impossible. All we needed was a school administration, community leaders, and police who were willing to put the students first.

Ms. Smith resigned after a few years of great work because promises were not kept to the students. The constant lack of support will burn out even the most committed people. Fortunately, People only remember you for how things are when you leave and she is remembered well.

Mr. Branch, who was her assistant principal, took her place. I respected him so much because he was faced with a tough decision as the politics kicked in and people tried to get us removed from the "New Ballou" after we got things turned around. He knew we were there when things were bad and he did not buy the rumors about us. He heard from teachers and students that the school is safer with Peaceoholics around. He went with us to squash beefs in the streets with Gadget, a young leader we trained to be a youth intervention specialist.

Gadget later worked in the John Wilson Building as a Fellow for a City Council member after we helped him see the light and turn his life around. An envious friend, who also smoked PCP, later killed him right before his graduation and his death rocked Southeast D.C. and the Wilson Building. I remember speaking at the funeral on the same stage with the great Stevie Wonder when he performed at Gadget's funeral at Allen Chapel AME Church. This was also the first black church attended by Barack Obama after he became president.

We always called Mr. Branch on Monday mornings to let him know who fought in the Go-Go clubs where the bands played over the weekend. He would hold them until we all could get together and squash the beefs. I was voted vice president of the Ballou S.H.S. PTSA. I also transferred my son to Ballou because I knew things had changed that much and Ballou was now just as good as any school uptown in my book. I got Mayor Fenty to remodel the whole gym, the library, and the computer lab. When Ballou's basketball team was ranked #2 in the Washington Metropolitan Area, I helped sponsor and raise money for the team to go to tournaments all over the country including California.

The Washington Times quoted Mayor Fenty as saying, "This season, the Ballou Knights men's basketball team has surpassed its reputation as one of the best teams in the region becoming a force to be reckoned with nationwide." This was after a great second place finish in the Mission Prep Christmas Classic in San Luis Obispo, California. They defeated national powerhouses Pasadena High and Los Angeles Prep losing only to Taft in a nail biter by three points. The Ballou boys defeated Lake Clifton the previous week. Lake Clifton was ranked fifteenth in the nation at the time.

I am grateful for the help I had in making these tournament appearances possible. The people who helped me do this were good black business men whose businesses were empowered by Fenty administration policies. After qualifying for and receiving contracts to do perform service to the community, they gave back to those same communities by supporting things like these trips for the Ballou basketball team. These trips were about more than basketball, they gave those who participated an opportunity to broaden their horizons and to see that their dreams could come true.

My childhood friend Jenkins Dormu was the head coach; both of us went from being members of a gang called the Gangster Chronicles and drug dealers as youths to lifting up our beloved Ballou as men! With the help of my friends Mike and Kharima, I also brought Stevie Wonder to the school where he brought his spirit and agreed to help.

It was fun and the place was packed. Everyone laughed when I tried to sing and Stevie said with a smile, "That's enough Ronald." I guess I didn't sound so good. We also brought Ballou Alumni Sugar Bear to one of our PTSA meetings. He was the leader of the Go-Go band that had two number one hits. The first was "Doing Da Butt" featured in Spike Lee's soundtrack for the movie "School Daze." The second was "Taste of Your Love." That meeting had one of the biggest turnouts ever. It is a disgrace that it takes celebrities to get parents involved, but you also have to face reality and do whatever it takes for the children.

In my role as Ballou Senior High School PTSA vice president, I brought in Stevie Wonder to help and motivate attendance by parents. Here I am singing for Stevie!

While then D.C. City Council Chairman, Vince Gray, was calling me a crony, Mr. Branch was saying that Peaceoholics reduced police lock ups of his students, helped raise test scores, and reduced violence at Ballou. Then out of nowhere, Gray showed up at Ballou for its graduation, a place he had given no love even though he lived in the "Gold Coast" of Southeast D.C. Of course, the only reason he came was because he was running for mayor. Two years later, he returned to Ballou's graduation because his administration was up to its neck in scandals. Corrupt politicians like Vincent Gray always run to the poor for cover. Oops, bad move this time, they booed the heck out of him!

Ballou and my alma mater, Roosevelt Senior High School, will always have my heart. I also have special feelings for H.D. Woodson and Wilson Senior High Schools. When students at H.D. Woodson started assaulting teachers and taking the keys to the elevator, the assistant principal asked us to come in and help. We also assisted at Wilson where the SW and Uptown Youth got into major conflicts. I am looking forward to the day when I am back in a position to finish what we started, cleaning up the schools and helping to make them safe places of proud academic achievement.

The Lynch Mob – Choppa City Beef

For four years before we brokered peace between these two communities, Woodland-Lynch Mob could not attend its own neighborhood school, Anacostia Senior High School. The school was located in Choppa City and students from Woodland-Lynch Mob who wanted to attend school there had to bring guns and hide them outside.

Students were assaulted on buses and those stories would often be run on the news. In one case, gunfire erupted and the bus driver ran off the bus leaving it stranded. Day Day Sams from Lynch Mob drove the bus full of his Lynch Mob friends to safety. There was also a girl from Winston Middle School who was whipped and pulled out of the window of a bus causing her major injuries.

Additionally, I want to note that children from Woodland, Choppa City, and 3-0, all from Winston Middle School, did not feel safe. They had been shot at and were afraid to go to school. Winston was the feeder school for Anacostia which had the same problem. We were instrumental in resolving the issue of students being afraid to attend at both schools.

The following was written by Lynch Mob member Chauncey Anderson during some bad times in D.C. By bad I mean, for example, forty-four youth who were part of the juvenile justice system were murdered in 2005 and 2006. Not one of them had a high school diploma. Chauncey's speech will give you some valuable insight into the impact that Peaceoholics had on young people caught up in violence. I have reproduced it exactly as it was written.

The Choppa City and Lynch Mob beef was a big deal in the District of Columbia. Choppa City is not an average neighborhood because it consists of several streets on and off of Good Hope Road such as 16th and W Street and Green Street and has several hangout spots where members of this crew gather. Lynch Mob, which is Woodland Terrace and Langston Lane, is just like your ordinary hoods. It's very similar to the projects in cities like New York and Philadelphia. I know more about Lynch Mob because that's where I grew up. A lot of people in D.C. like to label neighborhood figures as gang members just because we often get into fights and shootouts, but that's not the case.

When two neighborhoods consider themselves beefing, it is supposed to be violence whenever and wherever these two hoods may clash. Well that's how the beef between Lynch Mob and Choppa City was. It all started some years ago at the Unifest, which was a big event held every year on ML King Jr. Avenue that consisted of food, fun, games, and entertainment that brought lots of neighborhoods together in one small area.
A girl from Woodland was hit by a boy from another neighborhood with a toy hammer he may have won at a game stand. She went back and told the guys from Woodland and they went on a search for this boy. They ran into a group of boys that had that same toy hammer and argued each other down that these were the group of boys they were looking for. Since one of the boys from Woodland couldn't be persuaded that this group with the hammer actually wasn't the group they were looking for, he started the fight off and when one fights, we all fight.

Guns were drawn, fists were thrown and bodies dropped, but not by gun fire. This fight lasted for a while and then stopped, but in actuality it never stopped. It turned out that those weren't the boys responsible for hitting the girl with the hammer. It was another neighborhood, but it was too late to take back the fight that had already happened.

No matter where we were something usually always happened between Lynch Mob and Choppa City whether we fought, started shooting, or just passed a few words. I remember numerous occasions when Choppa City caught my neighborhood at a disadvantage. Anacostia High School was both of our neighborhoods' school so no matter what, we had to see one another. Youth from my neighborhood had to deal with this violence because they had to attend school. That's where the beef actually started, inside the school. I had the opportunity to go to a top school because of my grades, but every day I came home I heard about my friends fighting Choppa City.

This beef caused my whole neighborhood to be kicked out of Anacostia High School and this caused a lot of them to drop out. This one neighborhood beef caused my friends to end their education and limit their future. The school didn't care where my friends went but they couldn't stay in the school. This didn't end the beef; it was still fights at the clubs, bus stops, in the streets, and even on the buses.

That specific incident on the bus caused the Peaceoholics to get involved because it wasn't just the boys, but the girls were just as wild. The Peaceoholics started gathering the girls from Choppa City and Lynch Mob to talk with them and try to direct them into a nonviolent and successful life. They started showing progress with the girls and soon got them to end their grudges.

This was a big thing to me because I never thought this beef would end. Once they got the girls squared away, they started grabbing at the boys in the two hoods. The boys were much more complicated than the girls because they went through so much in Anacostia that they didn't even want to hear the thought of squashing anything.

The Peaceoholics got me and a couple of my friends to meet with them. We only went for the free food, but once they started talking to us things changed. None of the guys knew what was happening until it was too late. The Peaceoholics were getting to us. Even though it took several meetings, dinners, and retreats, the beef got squashed and, because it was so big in the city, the media got involved. The beef was squashed but something really simple could spark it back up.

The girls gained much more than the boys from squashing the beef. The main girls' Choppa City and one girl from my neighborhood are all in college. The girls took more advantage of the situation than the boys. Its only two boys including myself that still participate with the Peaceoholics. The only thing I hope is that everyone did in fact learn a lesson and will look back at this history when they need to see where they've come from.

It is gratifying to see that so many of the boys and girls from the gangs have made it. Some had to hit the brick wall first just like I did, but we had given them what they needed to find success. The seeds we planted often did not begin to sprout until they had hit rock bottom.

We all make a lot of bad decisions when we don't know or ignore the rules of the game, but a few encounters with the kiss of death or attending enough funerals for your friends, you start making better decisions. Even after all these years, they still come back and thank us and tell us they will never forget the lessons we taught them.

Chauncey Anderson Speaks Before the City Council

The City Council was now on a witch hunt to bring down Peaceoholics. They did not give a damn whether or not we were helping the children. The following is Chauncey Anderson's testimony before the City Council thanking Peaceoholics and asking the council to save the organization that saved him.

Good evening ladies and gentlemen my name is Chauncey Anderson. Lots of people know me as "Whokid" but that's a long story so I'm going to skip pass that chapter. I remember my first couple of visits to the Peaceoholics office. It was so many girls at the office I couldn't keep myself away, even if it was just to walk in and out. As I progressed, becoming an employee at the office, a go to guy for Moe and Jauhar, and a senior in high school, everything started to change. I was always down City Council testifying and at every press conference speaking on whatever issue there was.

I was like a real adult staff, but I was in a little kid body. Peaceoholics was literally my life which is why I'm here speaking in front of you today. When my mother moved away from D.C. and went to "live like da rich folk" like Plies would say, I could've rolled out too but I stayed. Sure I would've loved to live in a big house with a big yard and my own room like all kids in the hood dream of, but I was almost eighteen and I needed my own life.

I continued to be a part of Peaceoholics because I knew Jauhar would support me as long as I did the right thing. He was like the father I never had that I always wanted. Aside from Peaceoholics I still hung around the old neighborhood. Moe and Jauhar told me from the beginning that if I stayed with the program some of the people that I thought was my friend wouldn't seem so friendly anymore. All because I refused to point out an ex-rival from another neighborhood I found myself having problems in my neighborhood.

Moe and Jauhar didn't lie about my friends not really being my friends but I didn't think it would be like that. Even though I soon got rid of those problems there shouldn't have been any in the first place. I still continue to visit but it's not the same as when I was in junior high and early high school.

By me being in Peaceoholics, I was able to open my eyes in many ways. I learned about friends being snakes and experienced it firsthand. I learned about gentrification and saw people I know personally be forced to move from their homes. I learned about conspiracies and saw big numbers of people in my neighborhood disappear. I learned about Title 16 and how young teenagers are being charged as adults for crimes other than murders.

I learned about the Constitution, specifically the 13th amendment which basically states that you can be legally enslaved if you are convicted of a felony in the US. I learned about and watched the Children's March and saw how the children ended segregation but in school we're taught it was the doings Dr. King. I met and saw so many important figures to name a few, the Minister Farrakhan, Rev. James Bevel, and by me attending the civil rights tour I had the opportunity to meet some of the participants of the Children's March.

I went on so many trips that I lost count and met a big number of adults and youth through the program. Peaceoholics has impacted so many people's lives that it would probably ruin them if the program was to cease. They shouldn't even have to ask for funding. The work that they do should speak for them. This fund raiser should just be for fun every year.

To end this I just want to thank all the Peaceoholics staff for their support but I want to give special thanks to Moe, for going with me to court when I was in trouble and for helping me out every time I needed him, Jauhar, for all the tough love and extra cash that kept me afloat, Dan, for being there that night when I was about to ruin my life and all the rides and trips we took together that kept me out the streets, Mike, for allowing me to stay with you and be a part of your family, and Wayne and Mrs. Princess for your speeches and advice that I could always count on. Without the help of these people I know I wouldn't have made it to today so thank you all.

And thank you all for listening.

The truce lasted for six years, 2006 to 2013. No disrespect to the Guardian Angels, but this is what we consider success. Imagine how much money this saved the city and improved the quality of life for everyone. Real change comes from fighting crime by changing people and creating institutions for success.

The challenge of maintaining the peace is finding ways to pass the message on to the next generation of leaders. Unfortunately, once Peaceoholics was gone, this did not happen and the beef reemerged. The youth of Choppa City in Anacostia now call themselves the Cruddy Mob. I am still at work challenging the young adults from both communities who we helped go on to college to come back and be mentors to the new crop of leaders.

It is important to note that Peaceoholics not only worked with the high school gang members but with the children in the feeder schools including Malcolm X Elementary School. This is significant because a June 2013 article in the Washington Examiner revealed that violence is up 33 percent in D.C. elementary schools. I know a lot of people had a beef with me personally and with Peaceoholics as an organization, but no one ever questioned whether or not we were effective. Mayor Gray, who would later called me a $10 million crony, praised our work with gangs in the following letter.

Dear Mr. Moten and Mr. Abraham:

I write to indicate my support for the Peaceoholics [sic] and to congratulate you for all the work you do on behalf of our youth, especially those at great risk. I know that the Peaceoholics [sic] depend in substantial part on the generosity of private citizens and the business community in order to sustain your important services. Consequently, I want to urge those who you may approach for support and extend a helping hand and provide vital resources in order to permit the continuation of your important efforts.

I know firsthand the value and importance of your work by virtue of the excellent intervention you provided at the Winston Educational Center in order to address vandalism that had occurred at the Hillcrest Recreation Center. Your approach with the young people was direct but sensitive, firm but understanding, and clear but extraordinarily caring. In short, it worked.

You are to be commended because there are so few organizations that focus their efforts in the way the Peaceoholics [sic] organization does. Yours is a message that resonates with youth, helping many find a path to constructive activity, in lieu of violence and misdeeds.

I wish you the best of success and, once again, strongly urge those to whom you reach out to wholeheartedly support your efforts. If I can assist further, do not hesitate to contact me.

Sincerely
Vincent C. Gray
Councilmember – Ward 7

I have included a photo copy of this letter in case he denies writing it. He seems to have conveniently forgotten a lot of things since he turned on me for being affiliated with Mayor Fenty.

COUNCIL OF THE DISTRICT OF COLUMBIA
THE JOHN A. WILSON BUILDING
1350 PENNSYLVANIA AVENUE, NW
ROOM 506
WASHINGTON, DC 20004

VINCENT C. GRAY
COUNCILMEMBER
WARD 7

TEL: 202-724-8068
FAX: 202-724-8097
VGRAY@DCCOUNCIL.US

May 23, 2005

Ronald Moten
Jahuar Abraham
Co-Founders
Peaceaholics

Dear Mr. Moten and Mr. Abraham:

I write to indicate my support for the Peaceaholics and to congratulate you for all the work you do on behalf of our youth, especially those at great risk. I know that the Peaceaholics depend in substantial part on the generosity of private citizens and the business community in order to sustain your important services. Consequently, I want to urge those who you may approach for support to extend a helping hand and provide vital resources in order to permit the continuation of your important efforts.

I know firsthand the value and importance of your work by virtue of the excellent intervention you provided at the Winston Educational Center in order to address vandalism that had occurred at the Hillcrest Recreation Center. Your approach with the young people was direct but sensitive, firm but understanding, and clear but extraordinarily caring. In short, it worked.

You are to be commended because there are so few organizations that focus their efforts in the way the Peaceaholics organization does. Yours is a message that resonates with youth, helping many find a path to constructive activity, in lieu of violence and misdeeds.

I wish you the best of success and, once again, strongly urge those to whom you reach out to wholeheartedly support your efforts. If I can assist further, do not hesitate to contact me.

Sincerely yours,

Vincent C. Gray
Councilmember - Ward 7

I mourn the fact that violence has returned in neglected pockets of the city. It now exceeds the levels of violence that we were addressing when Peaceoholics came on the scene. For example, from 2007 to 2013 at least forty-two Ballou students have been killed. Can you imagine the outcry if even half that number of students were killed at a Montgomery County, Maryland public school?

I wonder if the corrupt politicians who brought down Peaceoholics ever read stories like this and have even the slightest regret that Peaceoholics is not in our schools today helping our children. Once again it seems like scoring political points was more important than the welfare of our children.

With Jauhar Abraham and former gang leader "Poo" from Choppa city at her graduation from Winston Salem University. She also attended graduate School.

Female Gangs Form a Truce

Photo By Victor Holt

From Left: Meme, Dina and Monica in 2005. After the truce, the girls spoke at Youth Truce Day started by Peaceoholics and former Mayor Anthony Williams in Washington, D.C.

Former Choppa City and Lynch Mob boys, who once lived to kill each other, are peacefully together learning citizenship at Mayor Fenty's Inauguration with Marion Barry and me.

Hall Monitors for the City

A successful hall monitor in a school is a person who has a relationship with students, staff, parents, and the community knowing all of its secrets and hiding places. We spent years in relationship building and understanding the problems of broken institutions as well the challenges of neglected communities.

In an October 2009 article about our work, the City Paper wrote that Peaceoholics always knew what was going on or were on the scene before the police. One reason for that was that we got calls from youth in gangs who told us they were about to get into shootings or fights. They knew we would not do anything to indicate who had tipped us off. We would just show up out of nowhere to intervene. That way, no one was labeled a sucker or snitch.

In a few cases, we needed backup from the police. The police trusted us and let us handle various situations and were glad to stand by to provide backup if things got out of hand. This kept people out of jail because beefs would be handled without police involvement. In most cases, situations were resolved without anyone getting hurt and, most importantly, innocent people kept out of harm's way.

We often sent staff to teen Go-Go's. Teen Go-Go's were dance clubs (not strip clubs) for teens where D.C.'s home-grown Go-Go music was played. One of these was run by an irresponsible club owner. Fights were causing people to be shot leaving the club. In the past, this was also how a lot of innocent people got shot, but we would see who was beefing and worked on getting people home safely.

The club was on the Maryland side of the line and we had MPD out to make sure when children crossed to the D.C. side that there would be protection for them. Then we would notify principals of the schools we had relationships with and tell them we needed to come to school on Monday to work this out so it would not start up again in the school.

A tragic example of the community trusting us more than they trusted the government or police happened in the Washington Highlands neighborhood. A woman had killed all five of her children and let them decay in her home for months. Two Peaceoholics leaders in the community, Jauhar's brother Dan Bradley and a young man named Mike let us know there was a horrific smell coming out of the house. We called the top brass in MPD who found the dead bodies.

We had hundreds of situations like this all over the city. We were flying around like bats out of hell trying to fix everything. We were even called on during severe snow storms to help the city clear the sidewalks for children to go to school and for seniors to get out of their houses or have food delivered. Amazingly, some people even criticized us for this. Calvin Woodland Foundation helped us in these snow removal efforts.

The media also had us on the top of their call list whenever anything was going down on the streets. They not only knew that we were working on the majority of things that were happening in the city, they also knew that we were getting positive results and playing a major role in changing the culture of violence. We were mentioned positively in over forty newspaper articles, news video clips, and talk shows.

Anwan "Big G" Glover: From Hobart Star to Hollywood Star

Back when I was first released from Allenwood FCI, I was a twenty-five-year-old young man looking for some fun. My old childhood friend Lump said we were going to the Ibex to see Big G. This was the spot where everything and everybody who was anybody went every week. There were always long lines going around the block and a lot of excitement.

This was before the fun ran out at Ibex after a cop named Brian Gibson was shot and killed outside the club on February 1997. That incident shut down Ibex marked the beginning of the decline of fun Go-Go spots. When someone got killed after a Go-Go, the band was blamed even if it was totally uninvolved. This limited the clubs that would invite them to play.

I remember the first time I saw the tall and slender Big G also known as Anwan Glover who played Slim Charles on HBO's The Wire. He was the lead talker for Backyard, D.C.'s famous Go-Go band and radio personality on 93.9 WKYS. He was telling the crew at a club to put the spotlight on the butt cheeks of the hundreds of women fighting to get to the cage to show what they had. He created excitement wherever he went and it did not help that Big G did not like the police. They weren't crazy about him either and had it out for him often threatening his life. He would use his public platform to say screw the police in a more direct way than Easy-E and NWA did it straight out of Compton.

I developed a personal relationship with Big G through my friend Lump, aka Swamp Dog, as we both worked with him through Cease Fire Don't Smoke the Brothers. Big G had the whole city saying, "Cease fire; don't smoke the brothers!" He gave much love to the Petworth neighborhood we grew up in called the 1-4 Zone. We were part of his extended family. Big G put his hood, the Hobart Stars, on the map and they were a force to be reckoned with on the streets of D.C. Big G was a straight-up gangster and not a studio gangster like many people in show business, such as Chris Brown, Drake, and Lil Wayne.

As a promoter, I kept in contact with Big G, often getting his band to play at places like Club U who wouldn't normally take a chance on booking the Backyard Band because of what happened at the Ibex and other isolated incidents. For the most part, G got control of his crowd and served as a positive role model as we fed into him. Jauhar and I started working together when I left Cease Fire. We continued to work with Anwan "Big G" Glover. It was not easy; it was nothing to ride up on him and find he was hiding three handguns and a sawed off shotgun under a long trench coat.

Everyone had Big G's back and he owned uptown love just as Tupac had the California love. Still, that did not stop G from getting shot over thirteen times. One of those times was at a club called Millennium where Jauhar and I were the first ones to promote a Go-Go music concert. On that night, Big G performed on stage and was shot in the testicles and elsewhere on his tall, lanky body. In spite of his reputation, G has a big heart. Our goal was to get him to use his heart in the right way and to make it out of the hood in one piece without spending the rest of his life in jail.

Fortunately, he had a strong woman, now his wife, and a manager who was a great father figure. We all had our angles and strengths working with Big G. We helped him help himself by getting him to help others, which is the best cure in the world. Big G traveled with us to the Virgin Islands to talk to youth as the Bloods and Crips infiltrated their Islands like they tried to do in D.C. Fortunately, we were successful in stopping this effort in the Nation's Capital. We were getting phone calls from inside and outside of America for our assistance.

He also worked with us in the schools speaking to children and helped us broker truces in the same type of conflicts he was once involved in. This work helped him see the light as we participated in bringing about a truce between Choppa City and the Lynch Mob at the now closed Market Lounge Go-Go. We brokered a peace agreement between the leaders from both sides before the Peace-Go. We wanted Big G to finalize it in front of their peers so that over one hundred members from both sides could see that it was real. We wanted them to know that they could do something they had never done before, party together in peace. We did these free Go-Go's with rival neighborhoods and the Washington Post wrote a story on what we called Peace-Go's.

Big G Marching with Peaceoholics and over two-thousand youth and young adults in Peaceoholics' annual Atonement Day March in celebration of the Million Man March.

In order for youth to attend, they had to take a class on the Children's March where we showed them that there was more power in peace and unity than in a gun. We had to do only a single mediation at

Peace-Go's and never had a fight breakout. I am proud that we were able to take D.C.'s own Go-Go music and associate it with nonviolence and peace. I know Chuck Brown, the godfather and originator of Go-Go was proud of what we did.

Jauhar helped Big G with a portfolio as he traveled back and forth to New York auditioning for various roles as an actor. People told G what he was not going to do and we told him not to give up on his dreams. We helped him any way we could and he helped us as he matured into a worldwide superstar after landing a role on HBO's The Wire.

As Big G's role on the program expanded, an old gun charge became a problem. The Legal Times called on George Pelecanos and Simon to drop him from the show. I asked then Ward 4 Councilmember Adrian Fenty to write a letter in support of Big G who he knew from when G would shop in the Fenty family shoe store, Fleet Feet. Fenty asked me if he would regret writing this letter and I assured him he would not. I was right; Big G showed his appreciation and gave Fenty his staunch support during his reelection campaign for the mayor of the District of Columbia and with his work with D.C. youth.

With Anwan "Big G" Glover (center), who starred as Slim Charles on HBO's The Wire. We were in front of the city council and mayor's office leading Concerned Citizens United protest.

However, Big G would have one final test when his brother was murdered. He had to decide whether he would give into the natural response to retaliate or if he would practice the way of nonviolence he learned from us. His brother, who was still in the streets, was killed and this was a tough one. I knew it would take everybody including God to get Big G to do what he knew was right.

Outside Go-Go Music club having serious conversation with Anwan "Big G" Glover.

Our prayers were answered and Big G has moved on to get roles in a few movies and to make appearances on shows like Law and Order and HBO's Treme. Big G used his street credibility and his fame from the Backyard Band and hit television series "The Wire" to help us with a campaign to put the code on the streets that only suckers and cowards do drive-by shootings. It worked because no one wanted to be called a coward because they all wanted to be Scarface.

We have many stories like this one, but of less well-known people. Big G just happens to be more high profile than most. This is a young man who I really love and know he will fulfill all his dreams and aspirations. God still has him on this earth for a reason. To this day, people try to pull this brother into the streets, but he knows he has a purpose in life to raise his children and give back to his community. He has a son who was shot during a robbery attempt, but is now on his way to becoming a college basketball star. I would also like to give a shout out to the Blonde Angel that helped Big G throughout his trials and tribulations!

The 1-7 vs. the Girard Street Nightmare

We found ourselves called upon once again by Councilmember Jim Graham, who I considered my friend. They did not accept violence in

Ward 1 especially when people were hit by stray bullets affecting the daily lives of people who were not involved with gang and crew activity. At the time, Ward 1 had the most homicides in the city; and Ward 2, according to APRA data, had the most drug use per household, but because of the income and education levels, the public perception was better than the reality.

One of the beefs that helped increase the homicide rate in Ward 1 was the Girard Street 1-7 beef. We were called because we were the ones who were getting results with these types of children. Ironically, Ward 1 had several organizations, one that had an annual budget of over ten million dollars, yet they failed to conduct even one real gang mediation.

An LAYC (Latin American Youth Center) worker called and asked me to show them how we do our outreach and engage urban youth. I would have gladly trained them, but they would not compensate me for my time. I want to be clear that LAYC does some things very well like educating children in general, but not those who are gang and crew affiliated. And yet, some people consider LAYC as the specialists in gang work and intervention.

We often encountered situations in which other individuals and organizations stole Peaceoholics' ideas and data, but could not get the same results. Thanks to the policy of bulldozing of low-income housing, the decline of the drug game, and the work of other good organizations we were able to bring a stop to the cycle of violence. We did miracles with a lot of loving hearts.

This is not to say that we were always successful. Jauhar, Walter, Al, Whali, and I sat in a Silver Spring, Maryland Ruby Tuesdays watching the leaders from 1-7 and Girard Street arrive. I was thinking, "We are about to do it again, another beef bites the dust!" Things could always be heated, but these guys were very mature. They did not talk much. Normally, this type would not come to the table if they were not intent on resolving the matter.

So, there we were at the table and one side is ready to squash the beef, but then, out of nowhere, one of the leaders jumped up and went off. He stormed out of the restaurant and screwed up the whole thing. This was a very complex conflict. There were many homicides and a lot of violence that made the youth fearful for their lives to the point that they did things like carry guns on Metro buses and trains. What we thought would be a home run turned into a long fly ball. We put in a lot of work with some success, but in the end it was a failure.

Even in the midst of disappointment we were able to get leaders from both sides moving in the right direction. Walter, our outreach and workforce development specialist now works for a nonprofit in Ward 1. We got another leader a sheet rock apprenticeship. He started off making twenty dollars an hour and eventually bought a car and much more, legally! Then we got a leader from the other side into Benedict College where we had previously enrolled many leaders from other crews.

Unfortunately, one of the failures was a youth who we placed in an internship in Ward 1 Councilmember Jim Graham's office. The intern eventually shot a rival 1-7 member and is now serving an eleven-year sentence. Every life matters. Even when you have done everything humanly possible, you still pray for miracles and it hurts when life does not work out for someone you tried so hard to help.

We were very successful for two of the four years we worked on this beef before deciding to give it up. Neither the community nor the government cared about the beefs as long as they did not affect them directly. Sometimes even the best players are forced to fold a winning hand. In September 2010 a funeral was held for Ashley McCrae at Walker Memorial Church near 13th and U Streets. Ashley was a young girl who grew up in the community where 1-7 was active. She was killed near Lynch Mob (Woodland Terrace) by Day Day Sams, a leader who left the gang life and helped us bring about the Lynch Mob - Choppa City truce. We had enrolled this young man into an electricians program and he was able to find work. We thought he was ready for change and would soon be on his way to being another of one of our success stories.

He was said to have been playing with a gun and accidentally and fatally shot Ashley. We were the only people in town who knew her funeral could be a catastrophe because all the crews who were beefing like 1-7, Girard, 3500, Hobart, CTU, CHV, LeDroit Park, and Garfield loved her. Unfortunately, I was now just a volunteer with Peaceoholics and in the Islands on a much needed vacation.

The Peaceoholics staff we had trained tried to get many of the various crew members to stay home and called me to let me know it might get ugly. I made phone calls to MPD to get them to cover the funeral and make sure no one would get hurt, but I could not reach the person I trusted. My staff did not talk to law enforcement because this work is all about relationships and you cannot trust everyone and very few in law enforcement when it comes to these issues.

When it was all over, I got a call saying it was like Armageddon out there. My staff had to hide behind trees during a shootout. 1-7 and

Girard overturned a truck with the driver shot dead and a second victim hospitalized in critical condition. People said you could smell the smoke in the air and hear helicopters everywhere. All of this, mind you, was at a funeral. Most of those involved are now in jail on charges of conspiracy and homicide.

RIP Badge we gave out at Lucki Pannell's vigil. Lucki was killed on her front porch by a stray bullet fired during the gang beef between 1-7 and Girard Street that turned violent again after the Peaceoholics program was ended.

Whali "Big Wax" Johnson and youth in the mayor's luxury box at Wizards game which we used to bring about peace.

The majority of those involved in the violence resulting from this beef did not come from impoverished areas of Wards 7 and 8. Many of them had more a support system within their families and the community. They just got caught up in the spider web of the streets and got stuck trying to escape. Some of them did not believe the stove was hot when we told them to stay away, but they touched it anyway.

This is one time the antidote did not work to the degree we were accustomed to, but trust me when I tell you, it could have been a lot worse. There could have been four years without any time out. I am proud to say that we provided some relief for two of the four years, but sometimes you win the battle and lose the war. When it came to 1-7 vs. Girard, we lost the war. On the positive side, our good work was recognized and, besides Walter, two more of our best outreach workers were hired in Ward 1 to continue to work with these youth. One worked with the Columbia Heights Shaw Strength and Collaborative and the other with the Department of Recreation.

Gay Gang Goes from Gallery Place to Peace on the Runway

"Check It" is America's first documented gay gang. They have been held responsible for a wave of violence and theft in the stores at Gallery Place Metro in downtown D.C. Their weapons of choice were mace and knives. They committed many heinous crimes such as making people drink bleach. They have also seen one of their members run over by a car driven by a rival gang member, which we referred to as Neighbors with Needs. What started as a group of twenty gays uniting to protect themselves from bullies, eventually turned into a gang of more than two hundred members who themselves became bullies.

Check It members are mostly LGBTQ (Lesbian, Gay, Bi-sexual, Transgendered, Queer) youth. It originated in Ward 5's Trinidad neighborhood and is now in all eight wards and Prince George's County, Maryland. As a direct result of my work, these youth made a decision to turn over a new leaf and renounce all illegal activity. On September 27, 2011, the Washington Post published an article on Check It's remarkable turnaround. As a result, several community organizations, as well as the media and MPD have responded to help me "adopt" these young people.

A turnaround of this nature is a long process, but the leaders of Check It have taken giant steps with positive reinforcement from the community. Some of these former gang members are being trained as entrepreneurs and have branded their own line of fashion clothing called Turn It Up. MPD allowed the Check It youth to use their gym to practice for a fashion show. One young man is being trained to box and dreams of becoming the first openly gay boxing champ. Many received their first job with the help of partners like the Far Southeast Family Strengthening Collaborative. This is what can happen when communities, businesses, and government agencies wrap their arms around disadvantaged youth.

The pain in the lives of the Check It members is obvious in everything they do including their highly successful fashion shows. The pain comes from having been hurt by others and there is more pain when they react and hurt others in return (See Chapter 8, "Hurt People Hurt People"). The fashion shows are outlets to tell their stories and start the process of healing within and as a form of redemption.

One segment of the show is titled "You Don't Know My Story." These stories were chilling and the whole room got silent out of disbelief! "I'm a gay male who was stabbed and died twice on the operating table," "I'm a female who was shot three times by an AK47 while standing on my front porch watching my friend get shot down and killed before my eyes," "I was neglected by both parents who abused drugs," "I'm a beautiful female who at the age of thirteen started stealing cars and, at the age of fifteen, started selling drugs to support me and my sibling. At the age of seventeen I was charged as an adult for armed robbery," "I was raped and all anyone wants to know is why I am gay."

We later partnered with Vitaminwater and Gibson Guitar Showroom in Chinatown to allow these gang members to perform in front of the businesses they had terrorized. They showcased the progress they had made and told their stories. It was a huge success and the high point of the Check It transformation.

They are on the road to recovery and redemption. I hold them accountable for their actions every day, but we must also continue to create avenues and runways for success. We found other outlets for them to share their stories like speaking forums with other youth.

Our work with this group started with Peaceoholics outreach workers Whali, Dan, and Aunt Caroline working with the girls in 2006. Years later when the gay gang leader was locked up, he said we didn't show them the same love that we showed the girls. I was no longer working with Peaceoholics and was dead broke, but I could not turn my back on them and went back to square one. In January 2012, the same film company that produced the HBO documentary on Marion Barry started following the core group of Check It leaders. Their story will soon be told in a documentary called "A Bad Thing Gone Good."

Teaching "Check It" crew about responsible citizenship outside the U.S. Capitol.

Check It Members Kevin, Erica, Tray and Skittles with District of Columbia At-large Councilmember Phil Mendelson.

Check It performs "Beat It." Though I label them a
D.C. crew, law enforcement labels them a gang.
Check It is America's only documented gay gang.

Check It members hold a press conference to launch
Turn It Up clothing line.

Chuck Brown – D.C.'s Irreplaceable Legend

Washington, D.C. has produced many music legends including Marvin Gaye who is known throughout the world. But I believe it is Chuck Brown who for many reasons is the most important for our identity as a city. I can personally attest to the greatness of Chuck Brown who has touched the world and four generations of Washingtonians. Chuck Brown did not just make a known style of music popular; he was the lone creator of a unique genre of music called Go-Go. I can't think of any other artist who can legitimately claim to have single handedly created an entirely new style of music.

Chuck Brown after his induction into the Go-Go Hall of Fame with Jauhar Abraham, and others.

What makes Chuck Brown more incredible is that Go-Go music built an underground economy that annually generated millions of dollars for our city when we were in bleak economic times. This form of music created a blueprint for youth who attended area schools such as Sugar Bear of EU Sugar Bear who attended Ballou and released "Doing Da Butt", the biggest Go-Go hit ever and was number one on the *Billboard* charts as well as Little Benny and James Funk who were founding members of Rare Essence. And don't forget D-Floyd who attended Duke Ellington School of Performing Arts.

This blueprint produced revenue for thousands of musicians, promoters, sound technicians, and security. It generated business for restaurants in Georgetown which depended on the crowds in the Go-Go clubs. Clothing stores were flooded every weekend and, whenever there was a big show, it would be like holiday shopping in malls and local stores. Go-Go was the only thing that brought nightlife to the now rejuvenated and popular U Street after the riots when nobody wanted to go there. Go-Go could survive anywhere and it did until it was no longer needed. Chuck Brown was truly a statesman who brought together the haves and have-nots and a spokesman for those who needed a second chance in life.

As a teenager I remember being with Leroy, a saxophone player, rapper, and Chuck Brown's right hand man on stage. Leroy and I slipped out of the side door of the Masonic Temple on U Street, NW into an alley to meet Chuck. It was in that alley where I first saw Chuck using crack cocaine. Crack is responsible for destroying many lives in my community. He used it with a lemon chaser that he squeezed after a shot of Hennessey.

I don't know if Leroy ever freed himself from the monkey that was on both of their backs, but Chuck did. He took pride in going back to tell ordinary people in his home town that failure does not have to be the end of dreams. He was always telling people that if he could learn how to play a handmade guitar in Lorton Prison and later shake off the drug habit, then we all could. This motivated tens of thousands of fans to get clean and go back and counsel others. It also motivated me and many of the 60,000 formerly incarcerated "returned citizens" who learned from their mistakes and returned to be of some value to our communities.

At a time when many Washingtonians are experiencing hard times, I encourage you to develop the talent that God gave you just as Chuck Brown did when he picked up that Gibson guitar and made the hit "We Need Some Money." Chuck went on to use his talent to take care of his family and leave his mark on this earth!

In 2008 Jauhar Abraham and I co-produced the first of many Go-Go Hall of Fame Award Shows at the Washington Convention Center. We wanted to honor Chuck Brown, his life, and his music. Chuck Brown and the band Rare Essence were the first inductees honored in front of more than three thousand people.

Little Benny was like a son to Chuck Brown. Benny was inducted into the Hall of Fame in 2009. He passed away unexpectedly shortly after his induction. I was honored to coordinate Benny's funeral at the Washington Convention Center where he had just become a member of the Go-Go Hall of Fame. Many dignitaries and more than seven thousand fans paid their respects.

Afterward, I wanted to do something special for the memory of this Go-Go icon. I suggested to Mayor Fenty that he name that alley out the side door of the Masonic Temple after Little Benny. The mayor graciously agreed and that alley with so many memories, both good and bad, is now Little Benny Way. I will always be grateful to Adrian Fenty for acting on my suggestion.

Chuck Brown himself died in May 2012, but because of the politics I could not help with his home going. However, I must say that Mayor Vincent Gray did well with the event. He was helped by people like Brooks, Douglas Jemal, the Go-Go community, and Cherita Whitting who was like a daughter to Chuck Brown. Over 12,000 people paid their respects at the Washington Convention Center where I had the privilege of inducting the one and only Chuck Brown into the Go-Go Hall of Fame.

Many well-known artists tweeted about Chuck Brown's passing including Snoop Dogg, Santana, and Jill Scott who collaborated with Chuck on a Grammy-nominated song. Many celebrities in the music industry flew into town as we lay to rest the Godfather of Go-Go who was to D.C. what Elvis was to Memphis, and, in some ways, much more!

Given the worldwide fame of Elvis, that might sound like an exaggeration, but I am not talking about the level of fame they brought to their respective cities, but the fact that Chuck Brown involved in many things including our efforts to stop the violence in our D.C. neighborhoods. I feel like we were the godfathers of stopping violence, but like Dick Gregory told me, "When the universe chooses you, sometimes you don't leave any footprints behind."

I also tried to save Go-Go venues in 2007 by organizing the Go-Go community. We marched in Prince Georges County, Maryland to the County Council and executive building where they were about to vote on a bill that would put Go-Go out of business in the county. We were heard by legislators at the session, but a corrupt and now convicted and imprisoned politician named Jack Johnson stopped our efforts.

Johnson was allegedly extorting money from the clubs that refused to sign an agreement created by our anti-violence network, the Go-Go community, various law enforcement agencies, and D.C. and Maryland government officials. The agreement included D.C. MPD, PGPD, the Executive Office of the Mayor, the U.S. Attorney's Office, the Maryland States Attorney, clubs, bands, promoters, Forty-Days of Peace, and the Violence Intervention Partnership. Just add aiding and abetting the death of Go-Go to Johnson's long list of misdeeds.

Me and Jauhar with Go-Go Coalition at emergency meeting with PG County Council members after our march to save Go-Go music and allow Go-Go bands to play in the county.

But neither Jack Johnson nor anyone else could keep us from using music created by Chuck Brown to produce stop the violence songs, citizenship videos, voter registration initiatives, HIV/AIDS testing and much more at a time when politicians had turned their backs on Go-Go ,D.C.'s home-grown music. We used Go-Go music to help others and destroy the culture of violence in our neighborhoods. This was the exact opposite of the reputation Go-Go had from the violence that often haunted clubs like the Ibex. It just shows you that most things can be used for both evil and good. We even shared our model with other cities so that they could use their music to address local issues.

Unfortunately, Go-Go is under attack in the very city where it was created and made famous. For example, the majority of clubs in D.C. that play Go-Go have been shut down. It seems that when there are incidents in clubs that play other types of music, the club is closed temporarily, but Go-Go's are shut down forever.

Ironically, bands like TCB played at campaign events for both former Mayor Adrian Fenty and current Mayor Vincent Gray. Now the Gray administration considers TCB and other similar bands too dangerous to play at clubs such as Fur nightclub in D.C. Apparently, those bands are good enough to be used to get votes, but not to entertain the people who voted for him. On top of that, Vince Gray grandstanded to get a Chuck Brown memorial park, but put it in a neighborhood where outdoor music, including Go-Go, will not be allowed.

Me with Chuck Brown.

I loved Chuck Brown and I promised his family that I will keep working to preserve the music he created and the memory of the love he always had for his hometown fans. I will also want to help preserve the bounce beat spinoff of Go-Go developed by the younger generation of D.C. Go-Go artists. I invite anyone reading this book who loved Chuck to support my efforts to keep Go-Go music, clubs, and the Go-Go Hall of Fame alive and well.

I want to thank WKYS for starting the first Go-Go awards at Constitution Hall. Jauhar Abraham and I were honored by them with an award and did a skit at the awards ceremony with the band Critical Condition. The skit was done to their song called "Stop the Violence in the Street." Jauhar and I have since taken over the awards and also created the Go-Go Hall of Fame. We are currently planning our fourth awards show to be held in 2014.

Chuck Brown (left) with his Go-Go Hall of Fame award at the Washington Convention Center. The Go-Go Hall of Fame was created by Jauhar Abraham and me with the support of various Go-Go legends and scholars such as Preston, Nico "The Go-Gooligist" and Kato from Take Me Out to the Go-Go magazine.

The week my friend Chuck Brown died, the Washington Post asked me to share some of my thoughts about how his music and life affected his home town. The following appeared in the Post May 20, 2012:

What made Chuck Brown even more incredible is that his creation, Go-Go music, built an underground economy that generated millions of dollars during bleak times for our city. The blueprint he created produced income for hundreds of musicians, promoters, sound technicians, graphic designers and security guards. Aside from Ben's Chili Bowl, Go-Go was about the only thing that brought night life to now-rejuvenated U Street NW after the riots. Go-go could survive anywhere.

Mr. Brown was also a spokesman for those who needed a second chance in life. He came back from prison and personal struggles to teach ordinary people that failure should not be an option. He inspired fans to get clean and go back and counsel others. It would also motivate me and many other formerly incarcerated "returned citizens" to learn from our mistakes and return to our community to be of some value.

At a time when many Washingtonians are again going through hard times, I encourage everyone to pick up their own tools and gifts the way Chuck Brown did. We each have a gift like Chuck did. He used his to leave permanent footprints on this earth, because the beat he created will never stop.

The Adair Sisters: All They Needed was an Assist

There was a shooting on the front steps of Anacostia Senior High School and another star football player Devon Folk was dead. This was a very sad day because he was not involved in any gang beef and he had supportive parents who were engaged in his life and school. We worked at the school for years with no funding. We watched principal after principal come and go, yet each one failed to revive the spirit of Anacostia High.

This is the school where Willie Stewart became a football coaching legend. He won championships and produced great college and NFL players. He was a tough coach for tough kids in a tough neighborhood. One non-football statistic tells you all you need to know about the challenges he faced as a coach: in twenty-nine years, twenty of Coach Stewart's players were shot, four fatally. Bill McGregor, a legend in his own right at DeMatha Catholic High School said about Stewart, "It's not about wins and losses with Willie; it never was. It's all about the kids he's saved."

Anacostia High is also where Glenn Harris became a great baseball player. He went on to play at Howard University. Since his playing days, Harris has been a successful sports broadcaster and sports talk television host in his home town.

But this was also the school where the Choppa City-Lynch Mob beef had incubated. It was during that time that two tall, soft spoken girls who everybody loved brought back the pride and grace that was once the hallmark of Anacostia Senior High School. Jazmine and Jessica Adair were star basketball players. When they played, the gym was packed. The boys' team hardly drew any fans, but these two girls were not just tall, they were two of the best female basketball players in the country.

We met them in the Law Academy run by Ms. Thomas who at the time was one of the few white teachers who dared to care about what was happening east of the river. She had no agenda other than what was best for the students. She was there night and day helping our children and often called us to talk to troubled youth and motivate those who didn't have support. She was very humble and focused.

One day I got a call from Jauhar telling me we better get together because something had broken out between Anacostia and rival Roosevelt Senior High School, my alma mater. I had joined with HOBO Shop to sponsor work at Roosevelt. That meant we had relationships with both schools. We stepped in because the coaches also had bad blood between them, which did not help the situation at all.

All this happened right before the girls' City Championship game. Police and school officials were ready to take action which would have stopped the teams and their star players from participating. We were able to work things out by bringing the girls on both teams together around the dinner table. After that we developed a closer relationship with the Adair sisters and Sharell Kyle, a guard on the team. They came from dysfunctional families, and without the support of Coach Frank Briscoe and Peaceoholics, the chance of them making it was little to none.

The Adair sisters courageously survived some very difficult times their senior year. Home was not the easiest place for them and there were many nights of tears when we had to act as the father figures. When Jauhar and I were not available, staff like Dan, Big Six, and others were always there for the girls. My focus was more on Roosevelt High because those girls had a lot of issues as well. Roosevelt beat Anacostia two years straight and one of those years they also went on to upset the heavily favored St. John's College High School in the City Title Game. St. John's had Merissa Coleman, who went on to play in the WNBA.

We continued to mentor groups of girls, not basketball players. We also got Jazmine and Jessica Adair assistance with their SAT's. Their hard work both on the court and in the classroom got them full rides to George Washington University on academic scholarships. They were instant stars as double trouble on the basketball court and as vital players on a team that reached the Sweet Sixteen in the NCAA Tournament two years straight. Since they had lost to Roosevelt in the DCIAA Championship and the City Title game, making the Sweet Sixteen was their first great team accomplishment.

Jessica was drafted in the third round by Phoenix of the WNBA, but did not make the team. She worked hard to lose weight and was picked up by the Minnesota Lynx where she won the WNBA Title. She was a scrappy "sixth man" star who the fans loved. Now she was ready for prime time.

Jazmine returned to give back to the community by coaching at Ballou and teaching at her alma mater, Anacostia. Sharell Kyle graduated from Trinity College where she played basketball. She came back to get trained by Peaceoholics before she had to leave due to our budgets cuts. We were sorry to lose her, but glad to see she got hired by internationally known Sasha Bruce House.

Jazmine and Jessica Adair after college.

The Adair sisters holding Peace Pledge at Peaceoholics'
Youth Truce Day held at Freedom Plaza in 2005.

We continued to work with students in Anacostia and get great results as well as reduce violence. We also got people such as Washington Wizards star Gilbert Arenas to donate hundreds of pairs of new Adidas shoes and jerseys for us to give to students who were trying to make their mark in life just as the admired and inspiring Adair sisters did. Nothing is more gratifying than having so many girls come to us and say that they never would have made it without the help of Peaceoholics.

Nightmares at Kennedy and Deanwood Rec Centers

History also shows what happens to communities when organizations are caught in the middle of a nasty political battle. I will give you an example of a situation that exist to this day, only blocks away from D.C.'s premier economic development initiative, the Shaw community.

In September 2003 after our city invested millions of dollars and opened a world-class recreation center called Kennedy Recreation Center which is within walking distance of three communities that have been beefing and inflicting violence upon each other for more than a decade. Today, these communities are surrounded by million-dollar homes and multi-million-dollar developments that have exploded faster than D.C.'s rookie sensation RG3, Robert Griffin III.

Years later, the politicians did their normal photo op's, ribbon cuttings and fake truces at the facility, but there would be countless shootings and murders around the recreation center with bullets even hitting its walls and windows on several occasions. They even shot through a church window one block away during a Sunday service; thank God the stray bullet didn't hit anybody. The new communities were established in the midst of this dangerous beef and nobody thought about doing cross-fertilization or an intervention before developing the recreation center and other amenities.

Residents continue to fear for their safety while our do-nothing leaders wait on the bulldozers of gentrification to solve the problems for us. Many residents feel that the new recreation centers and other amenities are not truly for the people who have lived and worked in the communities for generations. It seems these nice new facilities are being held in reserve for the highly anticipated new residents from among the 11,000 new citizens that are moving into the District of Columbia.

In 2007, we partnered with the Columbia Heights Shaw Collaborative to facilitate a truce between conflicting communities: 7th & O, 5th & O, and LeDroit Park. We were close to a temporary cease fire brokered by respected great outreach workers such as Al and Whali. Unfortunately, the mission would not be completed as city officials injected politics and partnered with Alliance of Concerned Men who were quoted in the Washington Post saying, "Mayor Fenty made it rain for Peaceoholics." Homicides returned after a fake truce that followed with a press conference photo opt for politicians and the cycle of city leaders making promises that they would not keep continued and so would the violence. We would never accept that so we did not participate in that fairytale and we moved on because your reputation means everything.

Now fast forward to the story of the Deanwood Recreation Center. The city put $30 million into a world-class recreation center in Deanwood under Mayor's Fenty's leadership. It opened with a great big celebration as the candidates Mayor Adrian Fenty and City Council Chairman Vincent Gray were jockeying to take credit for this dream facility. Both wanted to claim this success story that happened on the side of town that has been neglected for so long. The center is not far from the house of Marvin Gaye and where streets like Nannie Helen Burroughs Avenue are named after great black leaders. Nannie Helen Burroughs, a Civil Rights Republican, started her historic school for girls back when blacks were a self-reliant people.

Deanwood Recreation Center

The Deanwood Recreation Center is one of the projects that members of the corrupt seven, such as, Harry Thomas, Jim Graham, and then Chairman of the City Council Vincent Gray would use to help beat Mayor Fenty for a second term. They did so by making it look like Fenty gave city contracts to his alleged cronies. For example, Omar Karim, won the contract to develop Deanwood and now has a $100 million lawsuit pending against the city, Metro, and former Metro board member Jim Graham for malicious intent.

Ironically, the only contracts that were ever issues in D.C. were the ones won by friends of our mayor who were black folks, which were the small minority of over 50,000 government contracts given out every year in D.C. government contracts. This is all newspapers like the City Paper seem to find, almost all the time. For some reason some people can't see this, but let me move on to the next story because today that argument would be called race baiting.

City Paper "honored" me in their annual "Best of D.C." edition by naming me "Best Savior and Best Villain" in 2011. You will read more about the campaign tactics in the chapter called the "A Mayor's Old School Ass Whoopin'." Deanwood was a world-class facility. It looked like something out of Michael Jackson's Neverland, but from the moment it opened violence erupted just like it did with Kennedy Playground. Three beefing neighborhoods would eventually be involved in shootouts outside the recreation center with bullets going through the windows. On the inside the three gangs had identified territories in the pool area as if they were fish such as the territorial Red Devils and Paraná's. This was months after I resigned from the Peaceoholics.

After my departure I was trying to help Mayor Fenty win reelection. Months later the Peaceoholics phone would ring and the developers of this great project called and asked Peaceoholics to help them solve the Deanwood problem. That gave me a chance to see if the model Jauhar Abraham and I created could work without us being involved. I was an informal advisor, but did little work, except when a great outreach worker name Al brought some of the guys to meet me. I gave them motivational speeches and guaranteed that whatever Al told them the Peaceoholics would do, would happen.

With a sharp young Stanford graduate, a past intern hired to take my place who had experience with us as a intern with former Deputy Mayor Brenda Donald Walker, she was also a LeDroit Park resident with a genuine love for the community, our captain Whali, a Ward 7 legend with street credibility and Walter, our workforce development specialist who we trained, Angel with our GED program and it all worked together to get the results that people deserved. Results like these can only be accomplished by touching the youth, their families and the institutions that are connected to their lives.

Other successful strategies include hosting community events to bring the government to the people and empowering leaders from rival gangs to be part of the solution threw learning how to practice citizenship. The project would cost over two hundred thousand dollars and was worth every bit of it because what good is a $32 million facility when everybody it was intended to serve couldn't use it because of the fear of being gunned down or bullied by a rival community. This project hired five people and funded our youth peer mentor training program in which gang leaders were given stipends to be mediators while we engaged them in education and employment opportunities. It also funded a GED program inside the recreation center, take children from rival communities on cross-fertilization trips, and much more.

Most importantly, it showed me that we created a model that worked and now could work without me. It takes more than just the right model; it takes the right people being trained properly. We carefully selected the ones we mention above and we were willing to put a young graduate from Stanford University in a very responsible position within Peaceoholics. In spite of being very young, she had great maturity and did a great job for us. Three years later in 2013, the City Paper wrote a critical article about this project, not on the good work we were doing but on the money we were given to do the work.

They took a typically short-sighted view of the problem and the costs. It's amazing how the wisdom of someone who lived over two hundred years ago can still be so relevant today. Benjamin Franklin said, "An ounce of prevention is better than a pound of cure." In other words, if you aren't willing to spend some money up front on an ounce of prevention before these young people turn violent and commit all kinds of crime including homicide, then get ready to pay for a pound of cure after the damage is done.

First, let me say that there are two three kinds of prevention. The best is what we were doing at Peaceoholics and which is outlined in detail at the end of this chapter under the heading "How We Did It." This is what the City Paper thought back then was a waste of money. I wonder what they think now that Peaceoholics and other good organizations have had their funding cut off and most of the prevention being done is option two, police presence, and three, incarceration.

Police presence is expensive. Millions of tax dollars have been spent to put police cars on both corners of Kennedy Recreation Center 24/7 every day for the last five years and the conflict still exists. The result is that the recreation center is only used by a part of the community. That, to a great extent, is due to defunding organizations like Peaceoholics that used to help to significantly limit violent crimes by changing the hearts of at-risk youth.

My grandfather called it closing the barn door after the horse is already out. Listen, it costs the city up to a million dollars for every violent crime. Included in the violent crime category are homicide, rape, robbery, and aggravated assault. The following table is from the Vera Institute of Justice. It uses the actual costs for violent gang crime in Los Angeles, California. The same approximate costs would apply to every city when adjusted for population. The costs listed are police hours, courts and prosecutors, juvenile and adult detention and probation, institutional and parole rehabilitation, prevention, apprehension, court costs, incarceration, and victim costs.

The bottom line of this cost analysis is that each homicide costs up to $4.4 million and the average cost of all violent crimes is $667,000. That's for *each* crime in case the people at City Paper can't understand the numbers. Now do you think that what organizations do for a fraction of the cost of just one violent crime is exorbitant? The cost of the ounce of prevention that the taxpayer paid for Peaceoholics to address violent crime was a bargain compared to the cost for the cure after the crimes were committed.

Funding Analysis Cluster
Vera Institute of Justice

Figure 3: 2006 Marginal Resource Operating Costs

Resource	Manslaughter/Murder	Rape	Robbery	Agg. Assault	Property
Police/Sheriff	$32,597	$6,631	$6,631	$6,631	$5,531
Courts and Prosecutors	$161,288	$7,169	$1,919	$1,919	$1,919
Local Juvenile Detention	$39,329	$39,329	$39,329	$39,329	$39,329
Local Juvenile Probation	$2,497	$2,497	$2,497	$2,497	$2,497
Juvenile Rehab, Institutional	$45,396	$45,396	$45,396	$45,396	$45,396
Juvenile Rehab, Parole	$10,088	$10,088	$10,088	$10,088	$10,088
Local Adult Jail	$22,076	$22,076	$22,076	$22,076	$22,076
Local Adult Probation	$3,572	$3,572	$3,572	$3,572	$3,572
Adult Corrections (Prison)	$23,828	$23,828	$23,828	$23,828	$23,828
Adult Corrections (Parole)	$3,572	$3,572	$3,572	$3,572	$3,572
Victim Costs (Monetary)	$1,422,982	$8,610	$3,254	$2,019	$6,608
Victim Costs (Quality of Life)	$2,640,460	$88,221	$8,056	$10,963	$87
Total Justice System Costs/Crime	$344,243	$164,158	$158,908	$158,908	$157,808
Total Victim Costs/Crime	$4,063,442	$96,831	$11,311	$12,982	$6,695
Annual Number of Crimes in LA	244	32	2015	4176	152
Justice System Costs	$83,995,342	$5,253,049	$320,200,108	$663,600,819	$23,986,853
Victim Monetary Costs	$347,207,671	$275,535	$6,557,485	$8,430,947	$1,004,475
Total Victim Costs	$991,479,832	$3,098,593	$22,790,718	$54,214,398	$1,017,663
Total Justice System Costs	$1,097,036,170				
Total Victim Monetary Costs	$363,476,113				
Total Victim QOL Costs	$709,125,091				
Total Victim Costs	$1,072,601,204				

Out of dozens of articles in the City Paper mentioning Peaceoholics or Ronald Moten, only one or two painted a positive picture without sarcasm or sensationalism. In fact, the most recent article was about the Deanwood developer, but they put *my* picture on the face of the article as if it was about me. As I indicated earlier, I was not even part of the Peaceoholics when it was working on the Deanwood project.

When I asked the writer Alan Suderman about this, he said "they probably should not have used my picture and he did mention the violence went away." But what he won't say is that our city is changing everyday with over 11,000 new people moving here every year and none of them know about my work over the last seventeen years in D.C. so their impression given in their articles will be the last thing they remember. It is as if the city gave these thugs money for nothing while the fact of the matter is others who do nothing get ten times over what we got and produce no results.

This kind of irresponsible journalism tarnished our work, sacrifices, and accomplishments. In my eyes Suderman was a great reporter and he probably did not have total control over the final content. Life is often unfair or unjust to people, organizations, or developers who are just trying to do the right thing while others who don't care or are trying to take all the credit go untarnished. It was Omar Karim and Keith Forney who were part of the development team for Deanwood and Peaceoholics and helped turn a potentially devastating start into a dream fulfilled for everyone in the community.

Washington, D.C. Then and Now

The current boom in gentrification, wealth, real estate development, and being a "recession-proof" government town often inspires Mayor Gray to brag about us having a world-class city. That is true at one level, but we still have some of the same things happening in D.C. that happen more routinely in places like Chicago and Detroit. It wasn't too long ago that D.C. was known as "Dodge City" and "The Murder Capital," a title that has now been claimed by Chicago.

Cities like Detroit have many more eyesores and less hope than we had in D.C. at our low point. However, don't be fooled, we still have pockets of poverty and many of the same self-destructive behaviors that have always plagued us. One change is that the growing economic divide has turned us into the "Robber Capital." Murder seldom has an immediate financial benefit, but muggings and burglaries have instant payoffs.

Fortunately, organizations such as the Peaceoholics, helped reduce the violence to the lowest rates in over forty years through the development and implementation of effective violence prevention models. History shows that these models work, particularly so when city leaders are supportive of these groups regardless of political affiliation. It is now nearly two-and-a-half years since my departure from the Peaceoholics. I left in an attempt to save the baby that Jauhar Abraham and I brought into this world as co-founders.

Many things have changed in the city I love so much during these two short years. When I left we had helped reduce crime and homicides as well as uplift people others had given up on. Other groups who wanted to help did not know where to begin and that is the expertise we brought and that I still bring to the table.

Horrific crimes are still committed, but murder rates are about the same, the lowest we have seen in many decades. However, other factors are left out. Over the last few years, the type of crimes has changed among our youth and young adults. In some cases, the drug dealers are legal merchants who sell a legal drug called K2 to our children out of gas stations and corner stores.

This is happening because the children don't have the money to buy marijuana, PCP, or pills, but can afford K2 and almost nobody says a damn thing. First, K2 is legal; second, there is at this moment no test for it. If you go to Home Depot to buy a can of spray paint, you have to show an ID to prove you are twenty-one, but an eight year old can walk into a corner store and buy K2 with no ID at all.

The exceptions are people like community activist Phillip Parnell and nonprofits like D.C. Voice, who use D.C. youth to do stings on these stores and the Far Southeast Family Strengthening Collaborative. It is amazing how the recent uptick in the theft of cell phones has gotten so much more attention than the drug game that produced so many beefs, drug robberies, homicides, and people paralyzed from violent crimes. It is interesting that a replaceable cell phone seems to outrage people more than the corpses of young black men we used to see almost daily on the streets of our Nation's Capital.

The recent spike in phone robberies touched a more diverse group of people and to Chief Cathy Lanier's credit she did something big. She got legislators from around the country to require phone companies to make stolen phones worthless which kills the black market that caused the crimes in the first place.

What we all know is that the youth will find some other illegal activity until we act to address the social and economic issues that created their problems. Until then, bulldozer gentrification that, according to former Commander Rodney Monroe, was eliminating homicides, continues to this day and is on steroids.

One of the causes of this is a HUD (Housing and Urban Development) program called HOPE-6. HOPE-6 was supposed to be just a small part of the overall HOPE (Homeownership and Opportunity for People Everywhere) program as originally conceived by President George H. W. Bush's HUD Secretary Jack Kemp. The problem is that HOPE-1, -2, and -3 have been gutted and HOPE-6, the Bulldozer Act, is responsible for tearing down almost 100,000 units of housing and displacing about 80 percent of the low-income residents. That is not what Secretary Kemp had in mind, but that is how both parties are using it. That is quite a homicide reduction policy.

This only served to empower developers and destroy the people Secretary Kemp wanted to help. The same was true of his Enterprise Zones. This policy was designed to help people start new businesses. The idea was to make it easier to start small businesses where they are most needed, in the low-to-moderate income communities.

Bill Clinton came along and changed the name to Empowerment Zones. Sound like a harmless change, everyone wants to be empowered, right? This is often the Democrat MO; keep the name almost the same, but turn the program into one that benefits special interest groups. What Clinton did with Empowerment Zones was make it easier for Friends of Bill or friends of Democrats who had connections to start businesses and crowd out the average citizen. This policy fits right in with the corruption of District of Columbia politics and is a prime reason why we need a balance of representation in both the Democrat and Republican parties in our cities. The answer is in the balance, not in 90 percent of African Americans belonging to one party.

Will our city continue taking this short cut while people fight to build tall buildings and at the same time not rebuild equal numbers of homes for people who have been here for six generations? As a prime example, look at D.C.'s H Street corridor or the Petworth neighborhood where my grandmother still owns her house, but only a few longtime Washingtonians still remain. I'm so tired of all the tricks of the trade such as using the words affordable housing. Yes, all housing is affordable to somebody, but not the ordinary people that government is supposed to serve and empower. I want "work force housing" to be a phrase used to describe an affordable housing program for anybody who wants to get off their behinds and take advantage of the opportunity to own a house or start a business without being penalized or paralyzed.

It is true that some types of crimes are down, but partly because the people who were here when crime was prevalent, are gone. The businesses that kept H Street alive when nobody wanted to be there were pushed out and not built up to enjoy the good times that are coming with the streetcars that were not installed for them. However, robberies like the one at Grace Deli on H Street that claimed the life of June Lim, a beloved Asian merchant, will occur more frequently.

The people we worked with are forgotten even more as the face of the city changes with no plan to empower the have-nots. Our work at Peaceoholics still contributes to the city because most of the truces remain intact. In addition, many of the people we helped have used what we were blessed to give them as a trampoline and springboard to a better life rather than as a safety net or the spider web of low expectations so many of us get caught in! But I can also say that we had a few workers and many youth who went back to what they knew best once the services we provided such as mentoring and employment were eliminated. Our work provided life-changing experiences that helped youth and returned citizens. Now, so many of the good works we began have been destroyed in the name of politricks!

It is my hope that people of all races will meditate upon the words of the great Civil Rights Republican Frederick Douglass. It applies to all of us: "Where justice is denied, where poverty is enforced, where ignorance prevails and where one class is made to feel that society is an organized conspiracy to oppress, rob and degrade them, neither person or property will be safe."

The following is an interview transcribed by Michael Finley, MFA in Film from American University, with Dr. Jennifer Woolard, professor at the Georgetown University Psychology Department & Center for Social Justice where she also does research on adolescent development, psychology and law.

Dr. Woolard explains her observations and studies the work, impact, and contributions of Peaceoholics' "Rebuild the Village Triangle in One Model," which was successful in uplifting communities and the lives of thousands of D.C. youth and young adults who had no hope and whom others had given up on.

FINLEY: Tell Me a little bit about how you came to know the Peaceoholics and Ronald "Moe" Moten.

WOOLARD: I came to D.C. in the fall of 2002 at Georgetown University and was very much interested in becoming involved in community-based work that was being done around juvenile justice and intervention with a particular interest in working with grassroots organizations or folks who were mobilizing and organizing people around communities and issues of intervention and change. So I talked with some folks from DYRS and they suggested that I get in touch with a couple of people and one of those people was "Moe" of Peaceoholics. I called up and had an initial meeting and the partnership blossomed from there. In spring of 2003...Moe and Jauhar were already doing that work....

One of the things that was really impressive was that they were focused directly on engaging youth through empowerment and education and really saw youth as the key to intervention and social change. So their approach wasn't one of adults doing things for youth, but partnering with youth and empowering them to be able to make the kind of social changes they wanted.

FINLEY: Can you give some type of specific examples?

WOOLARD: Some of the activities they engaged in to empower youth included a curriculum to teach youth about civic life in Washington D.C.; teaching them about the history of government and community engagement, teaching them about local government, all with the idea that these youth could be the ones to go to a City Council meeting or hearing and testify about issues that were important to them and their communities and the type of policy changes they wanted, rather than having adult leaders speaking on behalf of you. So they were really empowering and educating youth to how the system works...so adults would have to listen and engage with them....

FINLEY: Is there a specific segment of the population when we say youth, or is there a specific demographic or should I say group that this was targeted more towards?

WOOLARD: One of the things I found interesting as a community psychologist is that they are interested in engaging the whole community, and so they really take a holistic approach to understanding communities and understanding social change. For example, they engage in community fairs where resources would come in and they would be able to organize, they had community councils and their neighborhood councils would involve adults and the youth....

FINLEY: How is that as a different or novel approach from traditional methodological approaches to these things?

WOOLARD: Well, I think there are some tendencies in some individual approaches to take a very individualistic approach. So the idea is the youth who is at risk of engaging in delinquency or criminal behavior is targeted and then the problem is located within that youth, the intervention focuses on changing that individual, and then the intervention presumes the positive changes in that individual will create positive changes in that kid's life. The Peaceoholics' approach, I think, takes what I would call an ecological approach which recognizes that youth are not in a vacuum; they are located in a family, however they define family or they may be lacking some important family ties of that family situated in the neighborhood and that neighborhood situated in a larger community. So affection, you just can't focus on just one piece of that ecology and expect all the others to change. You've got to be aware of all those other components when you're trying to create the circumstances for the outcomes you want, positive development for the youth, reduction in crime and so forth.

FINLEY: Do you have any sense of how they developed this methodology? Was it something that was given to them by somebody else or how they went about crafting somewhat of a new approach to address these types of issues?

WOOLARD: So I spent a lot of conversations talking to Moe and Jauhar and others about their approach and trying in a sense to unpack their brain and get them to articulate what it was that they were doing. Because they were so involved in the doing of "it" right, so I think one of the challenges for any nonprofit like that is to really take the time and resources to put down on paper what you are really doing. Naturally, there is some reluctance to do that because it takes away from the time of actually doing the work. So in many of those conversations it appeared to me that this approach they were taking grew organically out of their own experiences of their own lives, and of the kids they were working with, that pulled on history of the Civil Rights Movement that pulled from a very Afrocentric approach to understanding community and youth development. And that all of those pieces were coming together in a synthetic way but it was based on their day to day understanding and experience with those kids. So it was kids with their interactions in schools, kids with interactions with their communities and so forth and so it really emerged out of what I would call the "lived" experience of youth in the District. This was not an academic piece, it was based on the experiences kids were having and I think in that way it was quite responsive to the circumstances that the kids and their families faced.

FINLEY: Do you think this methodology was more effective than the traditional approach?

WOOLARD: I think that any methodology like this that takes an ecological approach to understanding kids in their environment and their community is a more effective approach than one that focuses solely on the individual. Approaches that understand that behavior is a function of a person and their environment...I think is a more effective way than saying there is something internal to a kid's personality that needs to change — then magically all other circumstances are going to change with them. So I would see this community-based approach as a more effective way to try to change kid's lives and changes neighborhoods than ones that focus on individual youth.

Go to www.ronmoten.com to see the entire interview.

How We Did It: Rebuild the Village Model

This chapter detailing the story of our efforts to change the culture of violence and revitalize the neighborhoods of the Nation's Capital could have been three times longer. Besides demonstrating that Peaceoholics was an enormously successful organization, I also wanted to lay a ground work to answer two questions: Can these results be replicated in other urban communities and, if so, what core principles and strategies did we use?

The answer to the first question is yes. It is not easy, but it is possible and it is worth the effort. As you will see in the next chapter, "Politics Kills the Promise of Peace," the support of both the community and the local government is essential.

The second question is answered in two parts. First, the following document entitled "The Peaceoholics Rebuild the Village Model®: Violence Reduction and Community Revitalization" is an overview of the model we developed to address the issues of the urban community of Washington, D.C., which is common to those of other major urban communities.

Second, I am committed to seeing this model implemented anywhere that there are people with a desire to change the culture of violence in an urban community. I am available for consulting and for any opportunity to speak to those dedicated to saving our youth, caring for our returned citizens, safer neighborhoods, developing responsible citizens, and creating institutions for success. Contact me through my website at www.ronmoten.com.

PEACEOHOLICS AS CONDUCTORS OF PEACE

CONDUCTOR	PEACEOHOLICS
Conductor knows every instrument has its identified role.	Peaceoholics is aware of the identified role of each village.
Conductor must assess and recognize which instrument is off and redirect it.	Peaceoholics must assess and recognize any abnormalities within a specific village.
Conductor must reinforce the standards that will hold each player to a level of accountability.	Peaceoholics will continue to help reinforce the standards to hold each village to a level of accountability.
Conductor will continue to move towards achieving the goal of producing harmony.	Peaceoholics will continue to move towards achieving its goal to produce peace.

Upon completion of training, participants will be able to:

- understand the significance of the Fight Core Principles of Peaceoholics
- apply the Core Principles readily to various circumstances, and articulate the meaning of the Core Principles
- embrace and develop an innate understanding of the core principles, which will develop character
- identify and eliminate barriers to applying the core principles
- develop values & morals, which inspires dignity

The Peaceoholics Rebuild the Village Model: Violence Reduction and Community Revitalization

Mission

The mission of Peaceoholics is to promote a peace-minded community, transforming youth into crime-free and drug-free productive members of their communities. Our efforts in support of youth are directed at understanding problems such as school violence and developing solutions to them so that every young person has an opportunity to develop in an environment that is safe and secure, free of fear and conductive to learning.

History

The Peaceoholics was incorporated in 2004 by Ronald Moten and Jauhar Abraham following requests from area schools, politicians, court services, community activists, youth, families and clergy members for volunteer efforts to address crisis situations in local communities. The organization was founded to serve as an advocacy organization for youth and families, to respond to and address escalating youth violence in Washington, D.C. and to develop prevention and intervention services that meet the needs of the youth found in the gap between adult detention and death. With a staff of twenty and an annual budget of 1.8 million, Peaceoholics has touched the lives of over 10,000 youth and families in Washington, D.C. and surrounding areas.

Core Principles of Peaceoholics

- History
- Culture
- Pride
- Respect
- Education
- Family
- Community
- Character
- Citizenship

Our efforts have crystallized under our *Rebuild the Village: Violence Reduction and Community Revitalization Model.* Our intervention efforts are a springboard for long-lasting changes that the residents themselves must sustain through capacity building, community empowerment, and self-sufficiency.

Our model is a proactive customized strategy to be employed in troubled communities experiencing violence, crime, fear, and deteriorated social conditions with an absence of individual leadership and/or institutions. The concept behind rebuilding the village was to create a programmatic approach to establishing or reestablishing the spirit and reality of a safe and nourishing community. It seeks to connect members of defined neighborhoods into commonly identified and reinforced communities and thereby build social capital within these communities.

The Peaceoholics have demonstrated a unique and highly effective capacity in violence intervention, mediation and prevention among youth and young adults in a variety of diverse communities and neighborhoods.

From 2007 to 2011 there has been a fall in crime in the District of Columbia as shown in Table 1.

TABLE 1

Crime	2007	2008	2009	2010	2011
Homicide	181	186	143	132	108
Forcible Rape	192	186	150	184	172
Robbery	3,985	4,154	3,998	3,914	3,756
Aggravated Assault	3,566	3,609	3,295	3,238	2,949
Burglary	3,920	3,781	3,696	4,224	3,849
Larceny/Theft	16,476	18,787	18,012	18,505	20,124
Stolen Auto	7,323	6,191	5,299	4,864	4,339
Arson	63	51	55	49	61
Total	35,706	36,945	34,684	34,655	35,358

Source: Metropolitan Police Department. District of Columbia.

Based on the lessons learned through years of experience and preliminary analysis of our pilot "Rebuild the Village Model®, we start with the premise that much of the youth violence in our communities is directly rooted in the dysfunction and disconnect in these communities. The problems in our urban neighborhoods might seem insurmountable, but through faith in people and in a higher power, hope for a better future, and love for each and every person we encounter, we have been blessed with tremendous results.

The first principle is to have faith in a higher power and in the people around you. Faith in God helps get you through the inevitable hard times in this kind of work. If it were easy, everyone would do it and be successful; we have found it to be difficult, but rewarding work. It is important to have faith in people because most of us respond positively when someone believes in us.

The second principle is hope in a better future. Hope is the reinforcing motivational drive that inspires and sustains our resilient nature, to endure and overcome challenges in life. The third principle is love. Love the greatest healing and unifying force known to man, an omnipotent and sufficient power, capable of transforming lives of individuals and communities. With total commitment and through the judicious employment of these three principles, Peaceoholics addresses many of the needs that we find among the youths and families in these communities.

The residents of these communities, like the majority of the homicides victims, are largely of African descent. Building on their unique cultural heritage and their strong propensity for survival, we rely on the holistic approach to healing: Given the correct remedies, the community like our body, has within its own make up, the ability to heal itself of most deadly conditions. In instances where more intense or specialized responses are required, Peaceoholics provides referral through joint efforts with our collaborative partners, or known service providers with whom we have working relationships.

Ours is a long-term commitment to communities; not a one-time workshop. We recognize that violence prevention and citizen participation cannot be thought of as a one-time event that would protect community members for prolonged periods of time. We, therefore, take a long-term, sustained approach to helping communities and youths create long-lasting social change. All of these efforts connect to and are part of our Rebuild the Village Model.

The Triangle in One Method

The success of these efforts is attributed to what we call the "Triangle-in-One Method". Through this model Peaceoholics engages and services youth and families in three major areas: the Community, the Schools, and the Juvenile /Adult Justice System & Other Institutions.

The utilization of this process has provided information gathered in one area of the triangle to help assist in the de-escalation of incidents in one or both of the other.

For example, mentoring and working with a youth who is detained and maybe involved in violent behavior in the community and/or schools can be used to get that youth to positively influence his/her peers to come to a mediation or intervention in order to resolve these issues. In other instances it may be vital information about something that is brewing that can help in the prevention of violent acts.

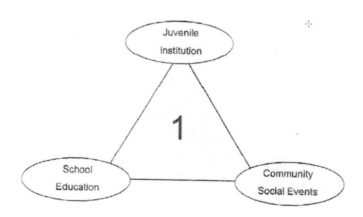

Juvenile Institutions

While working with **juvenile institutions** we develop relationships with the all the youth, but particularly those in the rival communities. We identify leaders and give them a blue print to use their leadership skills in a positive way to help transform into positive behavior, health and safe environments. In order to succeed in our efforts we must be familiar with issues that lead to conflicts that cause danger, injury or homicide. This work endeavors to promote a dialogue between rival crews, gangs or neighborhoods by going to the REAL LEADERS when conflict arises in society. In addition, we help develop an education plan for the youth and try to get youth to understand the consequences of their actions and who it affects. Once given a blue print, which is normally accepted, the youth realize that the consequences of their actions are much greater than previously thought.

School Environment

Although some improvements have taken place in the last few years, the students in the District are still below the national averages in many areas. The D.C. Comprehensive Assessment System (DC CAS)[1] data given below shows somewhere between 51 and 59 percent of our students are below proficient levels in reading and math. We consider this to be morally criminal with a per student budget of over $18,000: highest in spending and last in results.

Table II

Percentage of DCPS students who scored **proficient or advanced** on D.C. Comprehensive Assessment System.

Grade Level/Subject	SY 08-09	SY 09-10	SY 10-11	SY 11-12
Elementary Math	49%	43%	42%	46%
Elementary Reading	49%	44%	43%	45%
Secondary Math	40%	44%	46%	46%
Secondary Reading	41%	43%	44%	42%

Many studies have shown that learning is a social event and to improve students' chances for academic success, educators must strive to form meaningful personal relationships with students. In the **school environment** we develop relationships between youth and faculty with

---

[1] This annual assessment measures students' knowledge and skills in the Common Core State Standards in reading and math. It is taken by students in grades 2-10 and is administered in the spring. The DC CAS is managed by the **Office of the State Superintendent of Education (OSSE)** . DCPS is responsible for administering the assessment in DCPS schools.

relationship building techniques. For example, we have sponsored the thirty Days of Peace - a series of school activities through which youth and school staff build social skills and learn to work with each other to attain a common goal.

We develop activities with rival crews to be on teams with each other. We give out raffle tickets to youth who come to school on time and give away a prize at the end of the day. It is critical to identify youth leaders of crews, gangs or rival neighborhoods and impress upon them that there is a benefit to changing their behavior to being positive and productive.

We then train the same youth leaders of crews, gangs and neighborhoods to be youth intervention specialist. In order to change youth behavior, you must know the root cause of the negative/ violent actions they demonstrate. Cross-fertilization is very important before and after a truce of rival crews, gangs or general confrontation. You must let go of what happened yesterday.

Community and Social Institutions

The third part of our triangle is made up of **community and social institutions**. We determine who are the community partners and motivate them to work together as a collaborative so they may heal the family and the community as a whole. We also make sure government entities understand the importance of grass roots to nurture the relationships and to insure they get the services the government has to offer.

Projects such as beautification and youth engagement motivate youth and families to take pride, appreciation and ownership in their communities. We educate parents and guardians in their responsibilities towards their own children without it appearing that we are talking down to them.

The "Triangle-in-One Method" also depends on partnerships in these three key areas. For example, in a given community a partnership between its community-based organizations, churches, mentoring programs, and volunteers, is absolutely essential and key to building a strong referral base. This collaborative helps connect the youth with all services that they need in order to improve their opportunities for success.

Similarly, partnerships in the public school system are essential because violence from the community often spills over into the schools. It is critically important to work as a team with public school officials in order to both diffuse and prevent violent activity and negative behaviors. Finally, a strong relationship with the courts, detention/treatment centers, and local and state law enforcement agencies is vital to success. Just as important as gathering information from youth in the three areas of the triangle is the sharing of critical information with the partners to ensure the success and effectiveness of the process.

We are confident that our techniques and strategies can be scientifically demonstrated as a solid "model" to be replicated in other locations, be it School, Community, or Institution. The below listed bullet points represent standard developmental stages to be employed in our design and implementation process of customizing 'The Model" according to the unique characteristics of a given community, school, or institution.

- Assessment / Resource Mapping & Work Plan Design
- Violence Intervention /Mediation & Prevention
- Adult & Youth Leadership Development / Community Empowerment
- Community Institution Building & Sustainability
- Effective Evaluation and Replication

Assessment, Resource Mapping & Work Plan Design

In this phase we identify community resources with the goal of increasing motivation and engagement among community members. We follow our established Rebuild the Village Model® to identify formal and informal community leaders, even "potential troublemakers with influence who, once involved, create the tipping point for substantial community change. Specific activities include:

- the identification of current needs within the neighborhood (e.g., specific populations, behaviors, social and human service needs);
- the prioritization of current needs;
- the identification of existing community/agency resources and possible school-community linkages (e.g., Big Brother programs, Legal Aid, parenting resources, shelters, mentors, service dubs and organizations interested in developing programs).

A neighborhood-specific needs assessment and survey would allow us to identify barriers, crime trends, community temperature, and services to better gauge the best strategies to support young people and families living in these communities. This will also allow the collection of accurate on-the-ground data that will be used for planning, quality service delivery and interventions to ensure adequate resource allocation.

The assessment process specifically focuses on understanding the neighborhood, school, or institution from the residents' point of view, rather than the point of views of the government or institutional leaders. We identify key stakeholders and figure out who the leaders are within the local community. We then work to develop a community council that works to identify community needs from the community's perspective.

An important starting point is the identification of the reasons we enter the community. The reasons might include crisis intervention, an invitation from leaders and/or residents, or requests for prevention services. Regardless of the starting point, our goal is to pull all key stakeholders together and motivate them to work as one to identify and solve problems. We examine short-term and long-term outcomes, how to we make an immediate impact as well as commit to long-term initiatives.

As we work with the community to develop a work plan, we continue to broaden our community base. Even from these early stages we are already thinking about who will be able to move the plans forward once Peaceoholics phases out. Our goal is always capacity building within the community. We try to identify the "natural" leaders in the community who may or may not have formal roles in community leadership.

It is important to identify both positive and negative leaders - all of the folks who need to be around the table to solve community problems. By pulling together all the players, we make sure we are all playing the same tune (the conductor and orchestra analogy). We are also able to hold folks accountable, and empower the community to hold itself and government agencies accountable for their actions.

Violence Intervention, Mediation, and Prevention

Our violence prevention work takes a holistic approach to youth and their families. We recognize the importance of mediation and prevention activities that span the school, community, and corrections environment. The current approach of focusing on youth who fight in schools is insufficient. Simply suspending a youth without an alternative place for him or her to go while suspended or without initiating mediation activities will not work. When youth are suspended there should be a community space where youth are required to be present so that they can be engaged academically and supported socially.

We also propose that mediation activities will begin for youth while they are in corrections institutions rather than waiting until they are released. Studies conducted over the last two decades almost unanimously indicate that education in prison programs reduces recidivism and translates into reductions in crime, savings to taxpayers, and long-term contributions to the safety and well-being of the communities to which formerly incarcerated people return.

We work with probation and other agencies to increase supervision of youth/adults that are released back into the community. We will also ensure that a plan is instituted so that we can decrease recidivism and the potential threat to the community. Both for youth under suspension and those in institutions, we must have mediation services throughout so a plan can be created for next steps upon release and/or return to school.

Positive prevention efforts for all youth are critical. The "Peace-go" youth dance was created by the Peaceoholics organization in the fall of 2006 to create a positive alternative to youth attending "Go-Go" dances that have a long history of violence. The "Peace-Go" is not just a dance it is an ongoing process. Youth must first attend a training on nonviolence; where they will see videos depicting the harsh realities of the effects of violence, and upon completion must sign a contract stating that if they participate in any way in an act of violence or instigating an act of violence their information will be given to law enforcement officials and they will be prosecuted to the fullest extent of the law.

After signing this contract the youth will then receive an ID Card. This card is the only way a youth can be admitted to this event. This process ensures that only youth who have completed the training and signed the contract will be in attendance at this social event. The bands and performers must also attend a training showing how their lyrics may insight violence before they are allowed to perform at the "Peace-go."

Adult & Youth Leadership Development & Community Empowerment

Hackman and Johnson[2] have identified ten conditions necessary for collaborative public ventures. Their list includes "(1) good timing and a clear need; (2) strong stakeholder groups; (3) broad-based involvement; (4) a credible and open process; (5) committed, high-level, visible

---

[2] (Hackman, M. Z., & Johnson, C. E. (2009). *Leadership: A communication perspective* (5th ed.). Prospect Heights, IL: Waveland.2009. (p. 293).

community leaders; (6) formal support; (7) an ability to overcome mistrust and skepticism; (8) strong leadership of the process; (9) celebration of ongoing achievement; and (10) shift to broader concerns"

Our ultimate goal is to gradually reduce our direct involvement by empowering the community to utilize their newly enhanced skills. As we move through the three-year plan, we will assist existing community leaders to develop their skills and improve their capacity. Community members will identify, plan, and carry out community-building events.

Our "planned obsolescence" is specifically designed to foster increasing responsibility and direction among community members, ultimately empowering them to stand on their own without much direct assistance. Our program will endeavor to identify, educate, train, and then encourage its participants to be good citizen leaders who work to effect needed changes in the community through their efforts with public and private agencies and organizations.

These cross-fertilization efforts take youth out of the neighborhood to connect with youth from other communities. By seeing these other communities, youth can reduce the feelings of isolation and territoriality that lead to violence.

Community Institution Building & Sustainability

Once engaged in the community, we focus on training and capacity building. Training involves working directly with stakeholders as well as cross-training government agencies such as DOES (Department of Employment Services), Mental Health, Court Social Services, Court Services & Offender Supervision Agency (CSOSA), Department of Youth Rehabilitation Services, Parks & Recreation Roving Leaders and neighborhood schools with which we have good working relationships.

We conduct cross training with the police and the community so we can bring about some understanding and sensitizing for both parties. Through better engagement we support and empower community members and police to develop trust, enhance communication, and build partnerships to solve and prevent crime.

We connect with those in the religious community who want to get involved but don't know how to start. We explain how those churches can be utilized as safe havens, locations for truces and negotiations, and other activities. This is an important resource. As stated by the former HUD Secretary, "In acting as catalysts for community development, religious institutions possess four unique strengths:

- They often have a longstanding presence in their neighborhoods, and tend to remain as a source of community support after other institutions have left distressed areas.
- They have traditional missions of charity that extend beyond their congregations.
- They can leverage other resources. "Inner city religious institutions are seldom well-off financially," writes the Secretary, "but they do have resources in their inherent strengths as institutions and in their linkages to the outside world. Most important, their leaders typically represent a rare source of organizational skill."
- They can provide nurturing and support, especially for youth in distressed neighborhoods."[3]

Specific people identified from each of the government agencies will be connected to those communities so people can feel like they have a relationship with someone with the agencies. We are already in many of the institutions, and have partnerships with many of the agencies that are critical to the proposal's success.

Effective Evaluation and Replication

Our program evaluation is based in the Assets-Getting to Outcomes model developed by the Search Institute. This framework considers "what's right with children and youth and building from there, not viewing them as problems to be fixed" (p. ix). The Getting to Outcomes evaluators develop capacity within the client organization to understand and implement evaluation components themselves.

It is a data-driven approach to planning and implementation, defining data broadly to include traditional survey and numbers-oriented methods with qualitative methods such as in-depth interviews and focus groups.

Process measures (how well are we doing what we intended to do?) will track the number of interventions, mediations, community events and attendance. Outcome measures (what impact did our efforts have?)

---

[3] *Higher Ground: Faith Communities and Community Building.* Secretary Henry G. Cisneros. Available at http://www.huduser.org/periodicals/rrr/churches.html. Accessed on 6/11/2013.

will include the percentage of residents reporting greater neighborhood safety, the placement of at-risk youth into programming, and other relevant outcomes.

Training Curriculum

Our training efforts focus on three critical tools: substance abuse, prevention, and intervention. Substance abuse issues are critical to every area we describe. The distribution, consumption, and/or lifestyle involvement associated with substance abuse must be addressed. We have adopted a scientifically-based prevention curriculum.

Citizenship and Empowerment

Our youth leadership training curriculum includes workshops and trainings using our existing curriculum, attendance and participation in community and government meetings, and work for community change. Far too many violent crimes remain unsolved because of a culture that connects victims, communities, and perpetrators of crime through a 'community of silence."

The code conveys two fundamental beliefs: (1) that banding together to protect the "hood" from those who would destroy us is necessary for survival and (2) that if you provide information you will meet an unfortunate end. We have also developed interventions to educate people about the difference between snitching and making your community safe.

Core Principles

The Peaceoholics core principles include history, culture, pride, respect, education, family, community, character, and citizenship. This curriculum will ensure that participant's experience an elevated conscious as they learn the nine core principals of Peaceoholics. Character is the ultimate goal. Character is directly related to and dependent on the participant's knowledge of their history; appreciation for culture; enhanced dignity; respect; education; love for family, honoring the community, and citizenship.

Lesson Two

The Power of the Womb: A Divine Gift

Throughout my life I watched women who have an inexplicable power. These women can cast a spell over men and use this power to their advantage and to conjure up all kinds of evil deeds. I later learned this power could also be used for good and that it was given to women as a gift from God. It was this power that was used to do good for people during the Civil Rights Movement. We were told by several civil rights icons that have now passed on that the movement would not have succeeded without the women who nurtured it through by the "power of the womb."

We make this lesson about the power of the womb a priority in our teaching our youth. We have come to realize we cannot change what is going on in our world, especially in the black community, if the women do not use this power in a positive manner. Real change cannot be made without the positive power of the womb for life, not for death, for good, not for evil.

One of the problems I see is the black woman has been beaten up and used so much by our men that some have lost their dignity and forgotten their equal and rightful place and their God-give purpose on this earth. When women lose their sense of identity, so do men. The power of the womb is a divine gift from God. God has given women this power and this power is especially important in our urban communities that are hurting so badly. The black family is matriarchal. Even in two-parent homes, the woman holds the power and nourishes the family and the wider community, the village.

We are in desperate need of this unconditional nourishment that has kept our villages together through many horrific times. The divine gift of the power of the womb which is the instinct for women to give life and nurture is so powerful that even slavery could not destroy it. Unfortunately, there are powers at work among our people that are influencing our girls and women to use the awesome power of the womb to tear it down and not to build it up. Three of the most powerful influences have been crack cocaine, sex outside of its divine purpose, and destructive lyrics in some popular music.

A heartless slave master of the soul came to America around 1984 called crack cocaine. This was the first drug to feminize drug addiction. Crack breaks down the maternal instinct in women and destroys our village. It destroys the nurturing instinct in women and, in turn, destroys the fabric of our village. It influences women to misuse the power of the womb by turning it to the evil desire for the next hit

This breakdown in the maternal instinct hit an all-time high, or should I say an all-time low, during America's crack epidemic and the women enslaved by it lost all morals and principles. Crack was the first drug powerful enough to make women abandon their children. To our shame, many men have abandoned their morals and families for much less, leaving the women at home to take care of the children. But crack changed all of that. Crack is straight from Hell and the dealers work for the devil himself.

Women on crack lose their sense of the divine power of the womb to create life. I know of women who in the 1990's sold their bodies and some who even had sex with dogs as heartless men laughed at women who would humiliate themselves for a rock! I know of a sister who would prostitute herself for a Gucci bag or some big doorknocker-sized gold earrings that stretch her ears out of their original form, but when the crack hit, all she wanted was that rock. No humiliation is too deep as long as the payoff is a nickle bag of the drug from Hell.

Crack is not the only thing that causes women to misuse the power of the womb. Sex just for the sake of sex outside of its divine purpose is also destroying the fabric of our communities. This causes hostility from the betrayal of relationships, social ills resulting from single-parent homes, and the rampant spread of disease and mental health issues. The same power of the womb intended by God to be used as a positive force can also be used to manipulate men and degrade the woman.

The attraction of a man to a woman was meant to be for the creation of new life, not for destruction of her soul, the family, and the whole village. I described earlier how my own desire to have sex with a particular woman was used to set me up making a drug purchase that almost cost me my life. God spared me but I know too many men who lost their lives being lured by the desire for the womb. The awesome power of the womb can lead to the tomb.

I used to work with a star basketball player at an area high school who gave rookie NBA player Josh Shelby fits when they played against each other in Baltimore. That's how good this young man was and I helped sponsor road trips for his team to travel and get wider exposure. Unfortunately, he had a girlfriend who dropped out of college and decided she wanted him home with her. She caused him to miss road trips and the opportunity to showcase his talents. This was so baffling to the coaches and school because between this youth's mother who was also part of the problem and his girlfriend they could have easily used the power they had to encourage this young man through college and into the NBA. That's how the power of the womb can make the difference when it is used to help or to harm.

When some of our girls want to date a man, their mothers will only give their permission based on whether he or his parents have money. This teaches our daughters that their place in life is to be nothing more than upscale prostitutes. This also pushes young black men into the streets to make fast money to please these young women. All this comes from mothers misusing the power of the womb and teaching their daughters to look at men for material things more than their character and potential.

We teach our youth and parents that girls should not bring home any boy who won't show his report card. A man who is out of school better be able to demonstrate he either has a job, has skills that will eventually help him obtain a job or start a business! Jauhar drives the girls crazy with this but they get it. They learn to respect, protect, and use the power of the womb positively rather than use it to manipulate others.

We know if we can teach our girls this simple principle, it would eliminate all the harm of foolish rappers like Lil Wayne whose degrading lyrics help destroy our children to the point our dropout rate of fifty percent would decrease dramatically, maybe as low as 20 percent. The influence of rappers is powerful but not as powerful as the womb.

Sometimes female entertainers give mixed signals not realizing the power of the womb that they have to influence young girls who idolize them. For example, in 2006 City Councilmember Kwame Brown spent ten thousand dollars of his own money to arrange for some of the girls from rival gangs, Choppa City and Lynch Mob, to meet Beyoncé in person before a show at the Verizon Center. The girls were very inspired because Beyoncé gave them encouraging words about the power of hard work to overcome any negative circumstances.

Almost six years later, my fifteen-year-old daughter, Yasmeen, handed me her head phones and said, "Dad, listen to this mess by Beyoncé." That was the first time I heard Beyoncé's "Bow Down Bitches." Here is the woman who just had a baby girl, had sung at the inauguration of President Obama and was praised by the First Lady after her flawless Super Bowl performance. I am proud that it was Yasmeen who came to me to point out these lyrics that disempower women. Unfortunately, a lot of young girls will just accept the negative message and bow down as they are told.

We teach our girls about civil rights icon Dorothy Height who used the power of the womb to get all those competing male egos to get behind Dr. King to lead the 1963 March on Washington. The jealousy and envy of Dr. King by some of the other leaders threatened to derail the historic march before it began. This was the same jealousy and envy that we learned was the root of the first recorded homicide. Who knows, if Dorothy Height had not used the power of the womb behind the scenes the March on Washington might never have happened. What a tragic loss that would have been. We make sure our girls know the real power behind that pivotal moment in history!

I also saw this firsthand when Linda Cropp was the chairwoman of the City Council. She knew how to deal with all of the cocky, self-serving male egos. She stood by her principles and knew how to use the power of the womb. I did not really appreciate it at the time, but looking back, I really have to admire what she accomplished. She knew the power of the womb!

It is not well known that during the Vietnam War, Ho Chi Minh had women put their men out of the bedroom and ordered them to get up and fight in the Army. Many of these women became generals in the Army and helped their men run America out of their country. Once again, this shows the power of the womb and how that divine gift can be effectively used.

In 2006, a sex strike was launched in a Columbian City of Pereira known for its drug trafficking and violent crimes. The sex strikes were done by the wives and girlfriends of gang members to get them to change their lifestyles and hand over their guns. Imagine if we could get our women in the urban communities to do the same thing. I often say it's not the power of the gun; it is changing the mentality of the people using the gun in a destructive manner that is the ultimate solution to dealing with gun violence in America.

CNN News also reported in 2006 the woman of Kenya did the same thing in a similar campaign to protest the divide in Kenya's coalition government. Last but not least, just to prove it still works, a group of woman in a violence-plagued area of the Philippines came up with a sex strike as their own weapon to end fighting! The violence between two warring factions stopped women from delivering the goods they were producing and the women had had enough! By using their feminine wiles, they were able to enforce their will to the benefit of everybody!

It turns out this strategy is at least 2,400 years old. A play called Lysistrata by Aristophanes was performed in Athens, Greece in 411 B.C. It is a comedy about one woman's mission to end the Peloponnesian War. Lysistrata persuades the women of Greece to withhold sexual privileges from their husbands and lovers as a means of forcing the men to negotiate peace. So, it is clear that the power of the womb is not new but it is no less powerful than it was in ancient times.

The most powerful experience we had with this was through the teachings of Rev. James Bevel on how they organized the youth to end segregation. There were times when the brothers from the hood wanted to go outside of their nonviolent teachings when they were attacked by the police and racists who did not want things to change in America. These guys were not cowards and they didn't have a problem with fighting back. If they had retaliated, things might not have gone in a positive direction. We know in hindsight nonviolent protests of segregation led to a victorious Children's March.

Rev. Bevel taught us how they used females to persuade the boys to maintain peace by looking at the big picture and because those boys loved those pretty girls they were willing to work together and even sing together from opposite jail cells as they succeeded in bringing down the walls of segregation. We used this same concept to some degree in which we succeeded in one of the most successful truces known in D.C. In negotiating a truce in the Choppa City and Lynch Mob beef, we got the girls first and then the boys followed right along once they saw how the females from rival gangs benefited from squashing their petty beefs that caused so many to be hurt and put into harm's way.

We also had a program called SOS, Saving Our Sisters, in which we had over thirteen female gangs meeting weekly to broker peace. The majority of these conflicts became violent. The Washington Times did a story entitled "No More Sugar and Spice" around this time about the rise of girl gangs in D.C. and the overall increase in female incarceration.

The District Youth Gang Task Force reported that during that same time period there were 270 female gangs in D.C., but our assessment found that thirteen of these were serious and the others were copycats with what we called a wannabe syndrome. By focusing on the thirteen most serious gangs we were able to change the culture of violence that had seen a 43 percent rise in violent crimes committed by girls. The D.C. courts also did their part with a program called LOTS.

Mediation at a Peaceoholics office with two rival female crews. Officer Sheila of MPD who had a good relationship and trust with some the girls was also there.

One of the welcome consequences of having the girls hanging around the office was that the guys who were causing all the problems throughout the city started coming by to see them. Seeing all these pretty girls being put to work was a turn-on to the guys from all over the city.

These were the very guys we were looking for in many cases, who normally would try to duck us until we caught up with them. Our outreach team members sometimes caught up with them at the wrong time and place. Whali, Al, Aunt Caroline, Isaiah, and Walter often showed up in the middle of gunfire risking their lives and on many occasions while trying to defuse gang beefs throughout the city involving these same guys. We enrolled many of the gang members, both boys and girls, in college.

I credit the power of the womb for helping us influence the few guys we couldn't otherwise reach. We used everything at our disposal including the power of the womb to change as many lives as possible!

Youth from Barry Farms public housing in Peaceoholics' Saving Our Sisters program, join Moten with Hip-Hop star The Brat and Dr. Cornell West at an event with the Washington Mystics of the WNBA.

3

Peaceoholics Part II

Politics Kills the Promise of Peace

I prefer to be true to myself, even at the hazard of incurring the ridicule of others, rather than to be false, and incur my own abhorrence.
—Frederick Douglass, Civil Rights Republican

Eventually we became the victims of our own success. We had no idea that we would be managing so much money so fast. It was my job to focus on the work, but I should have made sure that we brought in some sharp accounting people to dot the i's and cross the t's when millions of dollars started quickly flowing into the organization. Our intention was to never become top heavy like most nonprofit organizations in D. C. where the lion's share of the money goes for administration and fundraising while too little goes to the people.

We changed how the game was played and people copied our style and model, but our enemies used our honest lack of attention to bookkeeping details against me personally. I was the face of the Peaceoholics. I was the one getting all the attention and props in the press and elsewhere even though we were a machine with many parts. I learned the hard way to always pay close attention to the money because things can get messy real fast. We even had a bank steal from us which no one ever anticipates. So, while I never intentionally did anything wrong, I wish we had made some better decisions to better document the fact that we were being totally accountable.

The City Council and community were calling us for everything. We were partially funded by CYITC (Children's Youth Investment Trust Corporation) which was started with good intentions over a decade ago by then Mayor Anthony Williams. Unfortunately, it later turned into a slush fund that was not interested in supporting our work! I will never forget that its best CEO, Greg Roberts was replaced shortly after Councilmember Tommy Wells asked him how much money he made.

The answer was that this black CEO of a $15 million company made more than a part-time City Council member. God forbid that he would make a salary comparable to a private sector CEO! Dirty politricks and institutional racism still exist. Greg Roberts left disrespected, but with his dignity intact. I was happy to see God blessed him with the opportunity to go to Kentucky and run the Muhammad Ali Foundation.

Several directors later, they finally brought in Ellen London and she was the final nail in the coffin that destroyed the agency. She took what was a slush fund and turned it into a super slush fund on steroids for council members! They no longer wanted to mentor nonprofits on the rise as was the initial mission of the agency. When the City Council got mad at us, they tried to kill us by putting it out that we were not managing the money right. Mayor Vince Gray's strategy for killing us off was to end all earmarks from the Trust, which was the only way an organization like ours could get funding in D.C. If that method is not the best, reform the process, but don't use it to punish an effective organization because you don't like Ronald Moten. Ironically, the mayor was still able to get funding to his pet programs like the ones who pledge allegiance to the mayor and his real cronies like Harry Thomas, Jr.

The saying goes, "Success has enemies," and boy, did we have our share of enemies! I remember what we taught about "The First Murder" (see the lesson following this chapter), which has never been dealt with in our society and the seeds of jealousy and envy are evident everywhere causing endless acts of violence and senseless homicides. Mayor Gray and certain council members used the seed of envy against us. You can imagine them laughing as they put birds in a cage.

They starve these birds so that they are ready to turn on each other to fight for the crumbs from the slush fund. Once the birds were all desperate for food (funding), all they had to do was throw a single crumb in the cage and watch. They knew that the bird who had worked hardest to get that one crumb would become enemy number one. That was Peaceoholics and, yes, me! This also put my life in danger because people believed I had a bag full of money like Don King. What we had was a staff of sixty people and many effective initiatives.

Even though Vincent Gray eliminated all the earmarks, which was really a move to starve us out, he still had ways to get money to his favorites. This is wrong because politicians use these little tricks to reward loyalty, not to fund groups who actually do the work and get results. He gave Councilmember Harry Thomas, his pit bull and political assassin of the Fenty administration, a $1.3 million earmark for Ward 5.

This allowed Thomas to keep stealing money meant for the people, especially youth, for his personal use. In the meantime, Gray was lying to more than fifty organizations who testified at a budget hearing in order to keep their funding. He tried to tell us that there was no more money and therefore, they could no longer be funded! It was Thomas who Gray used to help destroy Mayor Adrian Fenty, so he continued to send money his way meant to save our children.

As of this writing, Harry Thomas is in prison for stealing more than $350,000. That, of course, does not account for the $1.3 million he gave to friends who, in return, gave him kickbacks. Some of the money would have gone to crime-ridden communities like the Trinidad neighborhood which had fifteen homicides in one year. This was just an excuse to give Harry Thomas more than a million dollars after earmarks were supposedly eliminated by then City Council Chairman Vincent Gray. We worked hard to help reduce violence and homicides in Ward 5's Trinidad neighborhood.

When we met with Harry Thomas in his office, he told us the money was his and he was going to give it to whomever he wanted. He said that maybe we could train whoever he gave the money to, but it would not be going to Peaceoholics. He then told other organizations who came to him for funding that it was Peaceoholics who messed it up for everybody. Imagine the harm done to us and the silent enemies he created for us.

He also conspired with council members and convinced them to misuse more than one hundred thousand dollars of CYITC funds to host an Obama inauguration celebration at the John Wilson Building! I will never forget seeing Harry Thomas on the stage with my friend Sugar Bear and EU doing Da Butt to the number one hit with other elected officials! I raised hell at hearings and the council members tried to make people think I was crazy. They had to be careful though because they were the ones who were like criminals on the street, but all dressed up like respectable people. Given that some of them were stealing the people blind, how could they confront or report Harry Thomas?

I will never forget the meeting Jauhar and I had with Tommy Wells about CYITC, the agency for which he had oversight. He was another person I respected who could have put a stop to this corruption. We told him that our children were being slaughtered in Ward 5 partly because Harry Thomas took the money meant to save them. Wells told us that we should stick to what we do best because we were like public figures and when we talked, people listened. To his credit, he was right.

This is the same person who stopped us from getting funding from the DYRS even though the agency owed us $272,000 that we were never paid and which threw our books off. We refused to play his games. He was able to deny us the funds because of Vincent Gray's "no earmarks" rule and since we wouldn't do what most people do with the money. We should have received the money as sole source provider of a service that no one else could offer. The end result was that the money stopped, the work stopped, children died, and people were being robbed at an alarming rate. I say shame on all of them.

DYRS is supposed to be responsible for children who are being murdered, committing murder, assaulting police officers, and other destructive behavior. Instead, in too many cases, they were irresponsible and the youth were never given the rehabilitation services necessary to change their behavior. You don't hear that part of the story in the news media. What you heard in the news was that Tommy Wells announce that he stopped Peaceoholics from getting an earmark. Of course, it was no problem that Director Vincent Shiraldi got millions without producing any results and left the agency in a shambles in the name of reform. Wells did nothing about the DYRS or the Harry Thomas scandals, both of which could have been stopped in their tracks.

This is the same Tommy Wells who only began to act like the ethics king when City Council Chairman Brown stripped him off the powerful transportation committee he loved. Wells got that treatment because he had thrown Brown under the bus in the fully-loaded Lincoln truck scandal investigation. Brown thought Wells was trying to position himself to make a power move on the council and Wells went against the code of silence in a one-party city which produces this kind of behavior.

In the streets and in the halls of the John Wilson Building, that's called snitching! I still wonder how Harry Thomas Jr. could steal hundreds of thousands of dollars from the children in a ward that made national news because of all the homicides. So many people, including me, worked particularly hard in the Trinidad community, especially my colleagues, Whali, Aunt Caroline, Black Lump, Smith-El, and Ms. Princess Taylor-Whitaker! There were fifteen homicides in one year. It was so bad that police put up military-style roadblocks and residents had to show identification to enter their own neighborhood. These actions were ruled unconstitutional and resulted in a multi-million-dollar judgment.

Former City Paper writer Mike DeBonis finally listened to me when nobody else would and wrote a story called "If Earmarks Were Prohibited, How did Harry Thomas, Jr. Get Them?" Fellow Republican Tim Day and Paul Carney, former Director of DCGOP (D.C. Republican Party), and I met at the DCGOP office downtown on K Street. Tim, who is an accountant, followed the leads and would eventually bust Harry Thomas' scam wide open and expose something that would stop corrupt D.C. politics as we know it today. This is the hypocritical nonsense that boils my blood! Instead of being a hero, Tim became the villain and received death threats. Nor would his party raise any real money to help him win Harry Thomas' Ward 5 seat! Tim Day's car was keyed over and over and the council members who were crooked hated me even more because I stopped the corruption gravy train. .

The Washington Post ran a picture of me wearing white gloves with red die on the palms while testifying in front of the City Council. My point was that they had blood all over their hands. I told them God was going to deal with their corruption and repay them himself for trying to tear me down when all I did was put out the truth and support Mayor Fenty. In effect they were saying I had to either drop Fenty or they were going to destroy me. What they did not count on was how well I had learned to drink muddy water.

They wanted to destroy the Peaceoholics' image in mainstream media and make it appear that I got rich stealing from the people. In other words, they were accusing me of doing what they themselves were doing. Except that I must not have been very good at it since I was dead broke living paycheck to paycheck. One of the civil rights icons that mentored us had already warned us that this was going to happen if we refused to cash in and sell out the people. He saw the same thing happen forty years ago. This, he told us, was why he and many others stayed in Alabama and Mississippi drinking muddy water. They still had the flame of freedom burning in their souls and their job was to pass that torch on to us!

There is a saying, "Whenever you point your finger at someone, you have three pointing back at you!" Well, I know firsthand four council members that are worse than anyone they are pointing their fingers at. I want to be very clear that there are some good councilmembers in the John Wilson Building. One good thing we did accomplish before the attack on us by certain City Council members and the new mayor and crook, Vincent Gray, is that we planted many seeds that are now blooming flowers! If God does not give us the privilege to deal with them, our seeds will! There are now organizations started by people who worked for us or people who studied us.

We created strategies and initiatives for the D.C. government that helped reduce homicides. Reported shootings were up 10 percent in D.C. and robberies 27 percent. The broader strategy was called "Yes We Can." Under that strategy we drafted a plan for FIA (Focused Improvement Areas) that the Fenty administration enhanced and implemented. We have video footage of events and news reports in which we are praised for our work. The Department of Justice gave us letters of commendation and praise and we also received many honors from groups like Search for Common Ground. None of this made it into our audit, which still concluded that we were guilty of nothing more than not being appropriately diligent about bookkeeping details.

We received prestigious awards whose other recipients have been civil rights icons like John Lewis, Muhammad Ali, the Freedom Riders, and President Jimmy Carter. We advised professors and lectured students at Georgetown University under Dr. Jennifer Woolard and Johns Hopkins University under Professor Webb. I am proud of all of those achievements, but the story of my life is not yet finished. Now it is time for me to go to the next chapter of my life!

The one thing that still bothers me is that Peaceoholics was destroyed because I took a more vocal stand. Those I stood up to then really came after me. I was the face of the organization and they thought I handled the money. They knew that all they had to do was make it appear I was stealing! Little did they know I was a man with my feet dug in the trenches of my community ready for war and ready to "drink muddy water" and lost everything I had fighting for what's right!

No, I was not perfect and neither was Peaceoholics, but I learned from my mistakes. Without trials and tribulations, I would not be prepared for the next stage of my life! We planted a lot of seeds that will bear a great harvest in the next ten to fifteen years. I have often found myself making decisions to help other people succeed while I was struggling for survival. It goes against the laws of self-preservation to love others more then you love yourself, but I think, in the end, it saves your soul. I hope that those I have helped will learn from my example and from my mistakes. Now you have had a glimpse of the success stories and failures of our work.

If this is what they call stealing or mismanagement, I will take what comes and stand by it a thousand percent. I will let God and the U.S.

Attorney's Office deal with Harry Thomas and Vincent Gray; karma is better than revenge. They planted seeds that produce weeds that both then and now that do nothing but strangle the growth of the good things I and others have done. It has been over three years since my departure from Peaceoholics. I gave it all I had in me to do the work and tried to save the baby that Jauhar Abraham and I birthed. My God, how things have changed in the city I love so much since I left Peaceoholics in 2009.

Propaganda

Once the toothpaste is out of the tube, it's impossible to get it back in. A person can work an entire lifetime to build a reputation and it can all go down the drain the minute somebody plots to assassinate your character and reputation. We learned this firsthand and it's something anybody in this line of work or in politics has to prepare for. As I expose the politricks of our town, I want to share some of my experiences with this craft of personal and political destruction that unethical and self-serving people in and out of government use to destroy public servants or those who fight for the best interests of the people.

My phone rang. It was Sinclair Skinner, one of Mayor Fenty's friends, telling me he needed help doing a good deed. This good deed would later get us two black eyes and many headaches. Was it a good deed? I would say being the nonprofit organization that received an almost worthless surplus fire truck so that it could be donated to Sosou, a poor third world city in the Dominican Republic, was a great idea. In addition, children from the Ward 7 Headbangers Boxing Team were invited to return to the Dominican Republic a second time for a boxing exposition. This was the idea of William Williams, a military veteran and great public servant.

By law, they could only do this with a nonprofit. I was told they tried it with Mr. Williams, but had some problems getting him all the required certifications needed to receive and distribute surplus property. So, I agreed to let our organization be a part of this good deed. I consulted Mayor Fenty's ethics lawyer to make sure we were not violating any laws. I was advised it was legit and they outlined the process to complete this good deed. I was very excited. I talked to the President of Sosou and he was so grateful that he made plans to lay it out for our children from the Headbangers Gym. We honestly thought it was a good idea and that it was going to be something great for the citizens of D.C. and the Dominican Republic.

William Walker (l) with Dominican Mayor (c) and the youth
returning to the Dominican Republic for a boxing tournament

What happened next is Propaganda 101. Reporters called from the Washington Examiner and made it look as though we were committing a crime. Then they put it out in an article that Mayor Fenty gave a nonprofit $340,000 worth of fire equipment consisting of a fire truck and an ambulance taken off the streets and put in surplus for public auction. The first article was written by Mike Neibauer. Mayor Fenty unwisely brushed it off. Clearly, he did not understand that perception is reality in politics. The crafty, old school politicians who were attacking him to gain his title understood that concept very well and used it to their advantage.

I talked about it because I had nothing to hide but everybody who got me into this mess was ordered by lawyers to be quiet. They really did not understand the positive and negative power of public perception. This turned a one-day story into a one-year story. It became a two-year investigation after which the Attorney General concluded no laws were broken.

Before the report came out, I was subpoenaed for a deposition. I had no problem with that, but I refused to do it behind closed doors and wanted it open to the public. I retained a bulldog lawyer named Rodney Mitchell who was formerly the director of the Office of Ex-Offender Affairs now the Office of Returned Citizens Affairs.

Before the deposition, I went to both councilmembers because I was innocent in this ordeal. I would find out later that I was just collateral damage and this was about making Mayor Fenty look bad. It was all just part of a plot to remove him from office. The following Washington Post editorial said, "Clearly, there are questions about the gift to the

Dominican Republic but we share Mr. Moten's concerns that the council is more interested in scoring points than finding answers."

Councilmember Mary Cheh attends a celebration for graduates of the Peaceoholics Street Commission Academy. This is the kind of work that Mary Cheh and others praised us for and then turned against us for political reasons.

Ward 3 Councilmember Mary Cheh was very aggressive. Cheh, a professor at George Washington University, charged into the deposition room like a pit bull forcing me to bark back. This was war. She tried to intimidate me with legal antics and treated my attorney, Rodney Mitchell, as if he was nothing. What she didn't understand was I've had to respond to pressure all my life and the scare tactics that normally work for her were a joke to me. She even told my lawyer he could not assist. All this tough talk came from the same person who did not call for an investigation of her thieving colleague Harry Thomas who stole three hundred thousand dollars from the children of the District of Columbia.

I filled the room with my supporters and caring citizens. The whole city was watching. The deposition was recorded and she tried to keep it off TV. The Washington Post wrote that even though the session was open to the public, attended by reporters, and taped by the Office of Cable Television, councilmembers Cheh and Phil Mendelson made the claim that it should be withheld from broadcast until the council completes its investigation.

I had refused the council's request for a closed-door deposition. Perhaps there were reasons for keeping my testimony secret, but if so, the council should have figured out lawful ways of keeping the questioning confidential. They cannot retroactively take something off the public record. With the council's recent decision to take control of the local channel devoted to council proceedings, we can only imagine what else will be deemed unsuitable for the voting public, maybe a misstatement or an embarrassing moment by a council member.

Ultimately, Mayor Fenty and Attorney General Peter Nichols enforced D.C. law requiring DCTV to broadcast the deposition. I was getting calls from everywhere. People were hitting the pause button so they could get popcorn to watch what seemed to be reality TV. I gave her what she asked for because I knew she was wrong and God would be with me. She slammed her gavel down telling the audience to stop applauding. It was a sight to behold. Little 'ole me' talking truth to power, to a politician who had been corrupted by old school poverty pimps like Vincent Gray.

It was revealed later by NBC News Channel 4 that the fire truck and ambulance sold for $10,000 not $340,000! In fact, these trucks normally sell for $4,500 but everything about this deal was totally sensationalized for political reasons.

The Washington Post reported:

> Attorney General Peter Nickles noted that the donation involved outdated equipment originally purchased for $316,027, and he described the market value as "minimal." He also said the city has donated surplus property to nonprofit groups and foreign countries before....Nickles said in a report Friday that he found no wrongdoing.

Later, when I saw Mike Neibauer at the Wilson Building, I asked him why he would print something as fictitious as this. He told me that this was what they told him it was worth. How about checking your sources, Mike? Nice investigative reporting. That is yellow journalism, at its best, if you ask me. I have never received an apology from him. I'm still waiting! I also found out later from Denise Rolark, editor of the Washington Informer, that her father, legendary philanthropist Calvin Rolark, often donated similar surplus property. It was donated to third world countries that were in desperate need of vehicles we no longer needed and were headed to the scrap yard.

Former D.C. Mayor and Ward 8 Councilmember Marion Barry also had to know about this. As much as he said he loved us, he let this happen all in the name of politics. If I could do it all over again, would I have touched the fire truck that made it to the ports of Florida and returned to D.C. before it was loaded on a boat headed to the Dominican Republic? Hell no! I would not have let myself become collateral damage just for trying to do a good deed. Lesson learned!

After all of this drama about a fire truck, I come to learn that Councilmember Cheh's former campaign manager, Clair Blotch, became a partner on the $69 million Parcel 69 deal. Just like Omar Karim, Ms. Blotch is a good person, but if the Omar Karim deal was a conflict of interest then this deal was also. The irony of it all is that this deal included, of all things, building a fire station! The Washington Business Journal printed a story on this deal and Mary Cheh attacked the reporter as if it wasn't his job to expose her mess. She was always quick to jump on other people when they were accused of doing the same thing as she. I have no idea why the media had no interest in this story other than we seem to have two standards in our city, one for regular folk and another for the high-and-mighty.

Councilmember Cheh held hearings and voted on it. Yet, a leader of the pack in dozens of so-called crony investigations against Mayor Fenty, she never recused herself. These are the things that I wish the media would have looked into and made available to the public. For some odd reason, she and others got a pass! Now, many media outlets have egg on their faces as one after another of these phonies are indicted or shown to have been far less than what they portrayed themselves to be.

Then there was Sandra Seegars, the ANC (Advisory Neighborhood Commission) commissioner who was cool with Vince Gray. Ms. Seegars is always ready to help self-serving politicians and developers advance their agenda for some reason. I don't know what she was thinking or if she was thinking at all, but she sent baseless complaints to the FBI, list serves, etc., telling lies about Peaceoholics to anyone who would listen.

She attacks young black leaders who are on the rise. She finally crossed the line and accused a member of Peaceoholics of pushing one of her constituents at an ANC meeting. The City Paper printed her accusation and let it hang out there like it was the truth. Because we are not in the streets anymore, we did not do what most expected us to do to this activist who I respect, but who also has some serious issues. Instead, we decided to file a lawsuit against her for libel and slander.

Did the paper ever correct the mess they printed because she was a story? Yes, the Washington Post did a story asking whatever happened to the lady Peaceoholics sued. The following email is part of the settlement of the suit. It was sent to our attorney by Sandra Seegers' legal representation which was the District of Columbia Attorney General's Office.

The email read as follows:

From: Knapp, Sarah (OAG) sarah.knapp@xx.xxx
Date: Apr 7, 2011
Subject: Peaceoholics v. Seegers
To: rmitchell@xxxxxxxxxxxxxxxxxx.com

Mr. Mitchell –

As we discussed, the text of the email that Ms. Seegers will be sending to resolve this action follows. Please let me know if your client has any concerns. If I do not hear from you, I will instruct Ms. Seegers to send the email tomorrow morning.

Subject: Clarification of email regarding April 2010 ANC 8E Meeting

On April 22, 2010 I forwarded an email from one of my constituents stating that someone was pushed by a member of the Peaceoholics at this meeting. I have since learned that the alleged "pusher" was not a member of the Peaceoholics. I appreciate the efforts made by the Peaceoholics in resolving this issue. In addition, I appreciate the good works done by the Peaceoholics organization.

Regards -

Sarah L. Knapp
Assistant Attorney General
Office of the Attorney General for the District of Columbia
441 4th, NW, Suite 600 South
Washington, DC 20001

Office (202) 724-xxxx

The email discloses that Ms. Seegars wrongly accused a member of Peaceoholics of pushing one of her ANC constituents. Ms. Seegars never actually apologized but she did retract her statement and attested to the good work we were doing, thereby joining a long line of D.C. politicians who are on record praising the efforts of Peaceoholics.

Still, the damage was done and many people will never know what she did to us. She also stopped us from realizing our dream after we completed an affordable housing development project to create housing for at-risk youth allowing them the opportunity to own their co-operative units. Seegars took pride in blocking this initiative and throwing things off track. I didn't deal with the behind-the-scenes stuff of the housing deal. We were supposed to be mentored through its completion. This was a great idea but Vince Gray made sure the project was dead-on-arrival once he won the 2010 mayoral election.

Sharece Crawford at Peaceoholics' NYC
protest against *Bully* violent video game

The council called for another investigation about this project led by our so-called ally, Jim Graham. I later learned that when you are involved with a deal of this magnitude, you don't trust anybody and you watch everything. A good thing can go bad because your enemies are looking for ammunition to seek and destroy your dreams.

After everything we did for Jim Graham in Ward 1, he had the nerve to tell us, behind the scenes, in the News Channel 8 studio to "chill out" for four years because Mayor Gray is in office and he doesn't like Peaceoholics. He said he wouldn't be able to fight for us and would even call for a hearing on the housing property we acquired. How does two-faced, ungrateful, political coward sound? To this day, he tries to find a way to destroy people like us in order to deflect the spotlight from his own gold-plated mess!

Things never seem to change with Ms. Seegars. For instance, the City Paper reported that she allegedly took money from her ANC to buy a new car. Whether she is proven guilty or not, there are emails and voice mails as evidence that something might not be kosher. There always seems to be something shady going on with her and D.C. politics does not need any more scandal or drama.

I would like things to be cool between us, but her attacks have continued on the next generation of young black leaders. One of those was one of our mentees Sharece Crawford who made it out of the dangerous community of Congress Park. She graduated with honors from Shaw University, returned home to D.C. to assist her community, and won election as Advisory Neighborhood Commissioner. Ms. Seegars challenged Ms. Crawford's residency with the Board of Elections. Not a very classy move.

The Wrath of Alexander and Company

The cell phone rang and I said hello to Amin Muslim, director of constituent services for Councilmember Yvette Alexander. "Hey, Bro Moten, my brother is coming to see you tomorrow for an interview. As you know, he is in the Project Empowerment program and he had a petty drug charge and a twenty-year-old robbery charge." He asked me to look out for his brother, Barry Harrison. I agreed and learned a hard lesson "what you don't know *can* hurt you."

Project Empowerment is a great job training program that pays participants a salary for six months after their initial training. We would give them on-the-job training and a skill set that was perfect for most returned citizens. Up to this point, we had trained close to 200 returned citizens and employed more than 230. Most of these were D.C. citizens. That means we employed more District residents with our relatively small budget than the three-billion-dollar Homeland Security stimulus project that President Obama located Ward 8, which has a 25 percent unemployment rate!

Peaceoholics had a partnership with DOES to train people like Barry. If the training worked out, we hired them as part of a workforce development program, which helped us provide jobs for more people. I really did not know who Barry Harrison was. Because he had been incarcerated for twenty years and of course, Amin neglected to inform me his brother had a murder charge. We had not conducted our normal Street Background Check (SBC) and the MPD background check did not flag it as well.

The hammer fell when we received a call from a detective who informed us that Barry was questioned for allegedly trying to kiss a gay female at Spingarn Senior High School. Before this Amin and I were cool, but that's how it is think when dealing with a friendnemy. I didn't know it then, but this one phone call could have adversely affected the lives of 60,000 returned citizens employed in the District of Columbia.

Because of Barry's alleged criminal behavior, I came under a lot of scrutiny as people wondered why I would hire a convicted murderer and assign him to work in a school. It tells you what kind of person we have serving the people of Ward 7. Councilmember Alexander and Barry's brother, Amin Muslim, stayed far away from this one. Nobody stepped up to say, "I'm sorry for not letting you know about this."

Barry was found guilty, but I do have some unanswered questions because some other girls from the school called us and said he was set up. Barry also told me that he and his brother did not get along and Barry thinks his brother set him up! If he was set up, I was also set up. No one will ever really know except Barry and the female student. I will accept the court's decision. What I have to live with is the fact that a selfish councilmember and staffer hung me out to dry.

It is possible that I would have hired Barry anyway even if I had known about his murder conviction, but I would not have assigned him to work in a school. I believe in second chances for everyone including returned citizens. I have always been struck by the fact that both Moses and King David were forgiven and used in mighty ways by the Lord after they had committed murder. And before St. Paul became a Christian, he stood by and did nothing while the religious leaders stoned St. Steven for his faith in Christ. All three of these great men of the faith were blessed with second chances from God.

The temporary damage of this incident was that DCPS banned everyone associated with Peaceoholics from all schools, even those we had contracted with to implement our Rebuild the Village Model. This might have been avoided if Councilmember Alexander's office had made known the part it played Peaceoholics hiring Barry Harrison. Banning

Peaceoholics hurt the children in our schools and caused many good people to lose their jobs.

My next encounter with Councilmember Alexander was during the heated 2010 mayoral race. She was Vince Gray's puppet and requested an audit of our organization to put out the perception that we stole money from the people and to link that to Mayor Adrian Fenty's support for Peaceoholics. She acted like she did not know we had received the funding and was undeterred by the fact that she voted for nearly every dollar we received from the D.C. government. Grays' people and the corrupt seven considered us Fenty loyalists who were a threat to their hopes of stealing the election for Vincent Gray. Following is the request by Councilmember Alexander for an audit of Peaceoholics.

August 19, 2010

Ms. Deborah Nichols
District of Columbia Auditor
717 14th Street, NW
Washington, DC 20005

Re: Request for Audit of the Peaceoholics, Inc.

Dear Ms. Nichols:
    I am formally requesting an audit of the nonprofit organization, Peaceoholics, Inc. It has come to my attention that there are some irregularities in the structure of the organization, a claim that they have failed to comply with District and federal tax laws, and claims that the organization is involved in political activities.
    I am particularly interested in determining the following issues: (1) Whether or not Mr. Ron Moten is in a leadership position or is an employee of the organization; (2) Whether the Peaceoholics is current on their local and federal tax obligations and annual financial disclosure reporting requirements; (3) What role the Peaceoholics violates federal prohibitions on nonprofit engagement in political activities; (5) Whether the Peaceoholics has submitted its quarterly financial reports; and (6) Whether government funds granted to the Peaceoholics have been properly used for its intended purposes.
    I look forward to the results of this audit and ask that you please submit your preliminary findings to me by September 3, 2010.

Sincerely,

Yvette Alexander
Councilmember Ward 7

After the audit was ordered in August of 2009, it took almost six months to even start. In November, while waiting for the audit to begin, our offices and many others in the neighborhood were burglarized. In addition to the Peaceoholics offices, they broke into Imagine Charter School, Washington Informer, the barbershop, City Beats shoe store, and robbed and killed a gas station attendant. The offices were ransacked and many of our files were destroyed and our computers were stolen. This made documentation for the audit extremely difficult.

Then Councilmember Alexander and others who wanted to kill Peaceoholics used their power to prolong the release of the audit. What should have taken three months was stretched out to a year-and-a-half. From the day when the audit was ordered we were prevented from receiving additional funding and just the fact that we were being audited was used to paint our association with Adrian Fenty in a negative light.

Ms. Alexander and her fellow members of the corrupt seven apparently did not care that the work of Peaceoholics was severely limited by being denied funding for almost two years. On top of that, people who owed us fee for services were told not to pay us. This was also done to make us look bad in order to tarnish our reputation and reduce our influence and the trust we had in communities across the city. As a result, our work all across the city was negatively affected. This was a death sentence not just for Peaceoholics, but for the children and families and schools in the communities we were helping.

The same week our funding was cut off, there were three fights in Southeast, D.C. The local CBS affiliate, 9NEWS NOW wrote the following story:

WASHINGTON, DC (WUSA) - Just as a Southeast Washington community starts to recover from last week's bloodshed, 9NEWS NOW has learned that one of the only organizations in the neighborhood that helps troubled youth is forced to close its doors.

Peaceoholics has been widely praised in the past for making peace between rival crews, but tonight, its days are numbered--a casualty of DC budget cuts.

Six days after the shooting rampage, the community is still seething. Three fights erupted in Southeast in three hours. A dozen police cruisers responded in less than a minute. Residents have had enough.

"We need more help," says Martha Smith, a resident of Southeast.

"They need more jobs out here, activities to stop this violence. It's ridiculous. It's terrible. It's pathetic. I'm tired of it."

Adds Southeast resident Mike Washington, "I'm fed up. I'm fed up. I'm fed up. I'm not gonna talk to nobody or tell anybody no more. I'm just not gonna do it because I value my life."

In the midst of all the recent bloodshed, the group Peaceoholics says it has lost more than two million dollars in funding. It is closing its doors this week, losing its location in neutral territory between rivals.

"We can't count the amount of retaliations, shootings, stabbings that we prevented just by bringing people to this mediation center and helping them work through their differences," says Peaceoholics' Jauhar Abraham.

In just the last three years, the group has helped more than 100 troubled boys and girls sent by the city.

"None of our children have been involved in a murder. Have been murdered or charged with being involved with a murder," adds Abraham. "How do you not make sure that's part of the budget with the crisis that we have?"

"I was shot at the age of 12," Anwan Glover tells 9NEWS NOW. "All of my siblings are dead."

His three brothers, gunned down. But Glover transformed a bleak future into a successful acting career, including a lead role in HBO's "The Wire." He's also a legendary Go-Go musician, known as Big G. And now, he's a regular Peaceoholics volunteer, working with at-risk youth.

"You have to work with them year-round to really find out what's going on, because he might have a broken home. And you just can't turn your back on him," says Glover.
But the walls are now bare at the Peaceoholics office. Their accolades taken down. The memories packed up.

"These are like bricks of a Greek foundation," says Abraham. "So we have to fight to keep this alive. We have to live, so we can fight another day. We will. We will."

DC Councilmember Tommy Wells, whose committee decided against funding the Peaceoholics, told 9NEWS NOW in an email that he did not support the mayor's earmark for them in this year's budget.

Wrote Wells, 'I did not support just writing them a check with no competitive process.'

Who did win that bid? DC officials won't say.

Written by Andrea McCarren
9NEWS NOW & wusa9.com

Isn't this ironic? Wells allowed his fellow council member Harry Thomas to steal money after we had warned him about it. But in a one-party system, most people are hesitant to bring accusations of wrongdoing against colleagues in their own party. The code is for everyone to just go along to get along. It did not matter that we were not stealing and, on top of that, being we were being highly effective.

After the damage was already done to Peaceoholics and the audit was finally released, the Office of the District of Columbia Auditor concluded the following:

Peaceoholics is a nonprofit organization that fulfilled a unique role in the District by quickly defusing volatile situations by connecting agencies with communities that needed immediate assistance.

Despite the significant contribution that the Peaceoholics made to the District of Columbia, we found that grant funding entities did not provide Peaceoholics with the necessary monitoring and support the organization needed. Additionally, funding agreements did not consistently include program objectives that required Peaceoholics to provide written reports documenting fund allocations. As a result, Peaceoholics did not develop the appropriate internal controls or written program objectives to verify that all District funds were consistently used for the intended purpose.

To ensure that organization, like Peaceoholics, continue to effectively work to improve the lives of District residents, the Council of the District of Columbia should amend 1 DCMR Section 50 to establish standard, uniform grant and sub-grant agreements for District government agencies and the Children's and Youth Investment Trust Corporation.

Does this sound like thieves at work? Our effectiveness was never in question. Our work was brought down by the same politicians who previously had publicly praised Peaceoholics. We recognized then and reaffirm now that we should have been as detailed and diligent on the administrative side of things as we were on the programmatic side. That said, what was done to us had nothing to do with either of those issues, it was motivated purely by the politricks of corrupt politicians worried that the outstanding work of Peaceoholics would be associated with Mayor Fenty and harm the mayoral hopes of Vincent Gray.

As you can guess, the conclusions of the audit never made it on any television news programs. However, I am grateful to the print media who did report on the findings. The Washington Times had an article entitled, "Audit Clears Peaceoholics, Calls for Changes in Grants Program." The Washington Post and other papers followed suit saying the same thing about use being cleared and the need for changes in the process.

I know we should have paid more attention to administrative issues, but when your heart is in this stuff and you are about the people, it's hard to say no. Sometimes you don't have time to dot all the i's and cross all your t's. That not good, but you can recover from it if you don't have enemies who want to bring you down. Unfortunately, we did.

Do I regret being totally committed to doing good things for others that I was not being paid to do? No! I am incapable of turning my back on my people or my city even when I am flat broke or being falsely accused of wrongdoing. I do, however, regret that when I was with Peaceoholics I was not a better businessman. I should not have let us become so dependent on government funding. Organizations like YAP have avoided that trap. They have sufficient non-government revenues to survive a season when government funding dries up.

If I had paid more attention to documenting the financial details it would have saved people jumping to the conclusion that we must have misspent the money. The fact that I had done the same work for nine years without receiving a dime did not mean anything to those who wanted to punish me for supporting Adrian Fenty in his run for mayor.

Most people don't know we had an average of more than sixty people on our payroll. Anyone who has run a business knows payroll, insurance and other benefits are big expenses. Then add to that the youth we got into college. We gave them a lot of financial support. These were almost all kids who were the first in their families to go to college. There are also costs associated with GED and GED preparation programs. Less glamorous, but still important, are monthly utilities, office rental, legal fees, and administrative costs.

Beyond these standard expenses, we spent money on Civil Rights Tours, the New York City *Bully* protests, and college visits. We also provided food and clothing assistance, entrepreneurship and citizenship training. We held empowerment retreats, conferences and community events for the people of our neighborhoods and city. We also put financial resources into putting our strategies on paper so that the government of D.C. and other cities could implement them.

I am proud that I was part of negotiating forty truces, helping over 160 children get into college, and assisting more than 360 people find employment. We got youth hooked on peace and we honored and recognized their successful transformation into productive citizens. I have been committed to building up the community that I helped tear down before I came home as a returned citizen. And whether flush or broke, I have never lied, stolen, nor have I done anything unethical to achieve these results. I know Vincent Gray and Harry Thomas can't say that with a straight face. Outside of seeing my own children succeed, seeing the thousands that we have worked with for nearly two decades do well is the true joy of my life.

I learned valuable lessons from this. I recognize we made some mistakes. I can't save the world and that running a nonprofit organization that depends on government funding makes it dangerous to truly speak truth to power. Peaceoholics, and I as its public face, was targeted for destruction, for daring to tell the truth while receiving city funding.

Unfortunately, the attacks against me did not stop with the audit. As you know by now, I was seen as a major threat to candidate Vincent Gray's challenge to the incumbent, Adrian Fenty in the 2010 mayoral election. The Gray campaign spent big money on a commercial calling me a $10 million crony. The implication of this was very damaging. For example, Natalie Hopkinson who wrote a great book called *Go-Go Live*, read about Gray's "ten-million-dollar crony" accusation in the City Paper. Assuming it was true, she referenced the article saying that Peaceoholics had received "ten million dollars' worth of earmarks."

That is how unscrupulous politicians use toxic misinformation as propaganda to destroy people. By the time the truth came out in the audit only some of the money came from earmarks, most of the PR damage was already done. First, let's be real, officially or unofficially, most D.C. government money is an "earmark." Second, we were called upon to perform emergency services like snow removal or gang intervention for which we later received earmark funding. We also received funding which was, in effect, for sole source services that only Peaceoholics was prepared and qualified to provide.

I should mention here that my friend Marion Barry tried to convince Gray to not run that commercial, but Gray would not listen. Barry and I might not always see eye to eye, but I know that he would not do anything to tear down a young man or woman who has done so much for his community even when they are political adversaries.

Our political enemies tried to make it seem as if we were just given money and without giving the city any bang for its buck. The truth is that the real thieves are some of those sitting on the City Council and former City Council Chairman Vincent Gray. The City Council knew that they had approved almost every dime we received, but they also knew that the people were unaware of that fact. As you read in the last chapter, "Keeping My Promise," just at Ballou Senior High School alone was miraculous and far beyond what any government agency has every achieved in a similar situation.

We stabilized the environment at Ballou by reducing violence, ran college tours, helped students get into college, as well as supported the students while they were there. Then there were all of the beefs we squashed in the school. The fact that my own son graduated from Ballou is evidence that I always put my money where my mouth is and simply just wanted the haters to leave us alone so we could keep helping people.

I understand the need for fiscal responsibility and had no problem being accountable for the funds we received, but that was not enough for them. They had to destroy us because the unprecedented success of our work was being associated with the Fenty administration. In the eyes of Vincent Gray, that could not be tolerated. It did not matter that we began our work in the city long before Adrian Fenty became mayor.

So, in our own small way, we had to drink a lot of muddy water like our heroes in the Civil Rights Movement. Thank God the truth is finally coming out. The wheels of justice move slowly, but eventually what we do in darkness is brought out into the light of day. It seems now that not a week goes by without new and disturbing revelations of corruption in the Wilson Building and the mayor's office.

Some are already in prison, others are awaiting trial. Unfortunately, it seems like almost every week people who were close to Vince Gray is being indicted. The Council Chairman Kwame Brown got thrown under the bus by his peers on the council and has resigned in disgrace as part of a plea bargain. Harry Thomas has been indicted and sentenced to three years in prison, Jim Graham's name is ringing like a bell with all kinds of allegations, and former Councilmember Michael Brown is cooperating with the feds against Vincent Gray and is on his way to prison. The dominoes continue to fall and one by one the accusations about me and Peaceoholics are being proven false.

In fact, the lies they told about me were the truth about my accusers. Folks down South call the tongue the "pink tornado" for the damage it can do. My opponents unleashed their "pink tornados" to temporarily damage my reputation, but the real damage was done to the children of our community by shutting down Peaceoholics. They also damaged the reputation of the D.C. government and all Democratic run cities across the country where they rule without significant Republican opposition.

The Attacks Continue

It has now been four years since I left Peaceoholics and was cleared of any wrongdoing by the Office of the D.C. Auditor even after they were pressured over and over by elected officials to screw us. So, I was surprised but not shocked when some of my confidential sources in the news media informed me that Vince Gray is still going after me behind closed doors. On June 21, 2013, I was officially notified that Gray's Attorney General Irv Nathan is investigating whether I intentionally gave the CYITC misinformation in order to obtain funding. This is all just meant to be a ploy to take the attention away from the investigation of the Gray campaign and administration.

In spite of the fact that we were cleared by the previously mentioned audit we came up short on the administrative side in some instances while excelling on the program side. The audit clearly shows that we did not use the funding to enrich ourselves. As documented in these pages, the District of Columbia government and CYITC continually asked us to come to their rescue and would provide services before we officially awarded a contract on numerous occasions.

Because of our commitment to the citizens of the District of Columbia, we responded positively and effectively to these requests whether from the mayor's office, the City Council, or agencies. In order to accommodate these requests without funding contracts in place, Peaceoholics as an organization and Jauhar Abraham and I as individuals often used our own money hoping that we could be reimbursed when funds were available. It was too hard to say no to our community as we had to absorb stress and grief on a daily basis.

Knowing what we know now, maybe we should have said no when asked to do snow removal after massive storms paralyzed the city, kept children out of school, trapped seniors in their homes, and prevented emergency services including food delivery and EMS from getting to those in need. We also could have refused to respond to Benning Terrace when Lil Cindy was gunned down. We took an entire community in grief on a retreat to empower them to retake their community.

Now we are being sued for doing exactly what were asked to do out of the goodness of our hearts. With the best of intentions, we spent our own money to assist the government in helping the people we love so much because we foolishly trusted that the city would help us build our financial capacity to handle all the demands put on us.

That trust is now being betrayed. Vince Gray is even filing a civil suit against me saying I should pay back some of the very money that we used to do things for which he himself praised us. He told WUSA 9 reporter Bruce Johnson that we were not funded because he did not know of any work we provided. Read the book Vince or watch the video of you on my website praising our work.

It isn't enough that self-serving politicians defunded and effectively killed Peaceoholics; they are ignoring the findings of the very audit that Councilmember Yvette Alexander called for and that exonerated us in 2011. As the audit concluded from looking at the results of our work, Peaceoholics provided a valuable and much needed service to our community. While it is frustrating to have to fight this same battle all over again, I look forward to the opportunity to finally have my day in court. The truth will be brought out and I will be able to put all this behind me as we now have a chance to expose these wicked liars.

What should really happen is the people of the District of Columbia should sue Vince Gray for repayment of his salary as the illegitimate mayor. Vince stole the election with an illegal shadow campaign, so I'm sure he can set up a shadow organization to blackmail all the people he could implicate if they do not contribute to his defense fund.

Not only did I earn every dime I received, I never turned my back on the people and to a lot of time away from my family. The truth is, and Gray knows it is true, that the people know exactly what is going on as evidenced by the merciless boos he got on Saturday, June 15, 2013 when he was at the Washington Convention Center for the Ty Barnett fight.

Vince Gray is not a man of the people as much as he wants everyone to believe otherwise. In fact, he seeks revenge on those who are exposing his corruption. He tries to take the spotlight off himself with false accusations about me and others who stand up to him. It does not help him that we won our first case against the same office when we sued ANC commissioner Sandra Seegars for slander. We will be filing a counter suit and will fight this to the very end. Keep us in your prayers!

He has now used his handpicked Attorney General Irv Nathan, a former white collar criminal defense attorney for a major law firm, to file a suit against us saying we committed fraud by not reporting our true salaries. Additionally, they are charging that Jauhar Abraham, the co-founder of Peaceoholics, enriched himself by buying two uniform SUV's and paying for it with Peaceoholics money.

The reality is that we were a new nonprofit organization with no credit and Jauhar was willing to risk his own credit by making the purchases for the company all which was shown on our audit and 990 which was proof it was legitimate. This saved Peaceoholics vehicle rental expenses for our civil rights trips and for transporting our many college students to and from college and daily city activities. If you have read about this elsewhere, you got the sensationalized version which left out the fact that the vehicles were four years old when purchased.

The Propaganda of Politricks

The fire truck flap is the perfect example of how the propaganda of politricks works. Those who wanted to smear us put the lie out to the media that the truck cost $340,000 when its actual value was less than $10,000 and was ultimately sold for scrap metal. Then you repeat the lie as often as possible.

This is the formula for destroying a person's reputation, power, and influence over the people. First, put out the lie to the masses through the media. Second, repeat the lie as often as possible so that people hear it so much that they get hooked on the untrue version of the story. It then becomes like a song you aren't sure you liked, but after hearing it over and over again, the beat and the hook win you over. Pretty soon the lie is in the public consciousness no simple denial can change anyone's mind.

Then, when you are vindicated, the truth only comes out in a whisper. It is not broadcast to the masses over and over again like the lie that the media was all too happy to spread. In the people's minds the politicians have won because perception is reality. Their minds are still stuck on the lie that they have been programed to believe.

To my political opponents, I have always been a bull in the china closet. They continue to do everything they can to castrate the bull that brings public attention to all their corrupt schemes. They succeeded in temporarily killing the promise of peace in our great city by bringing down Peaceoholics, but they could not, and will not, kill me or my passion for the people. I am still as determined as ever to fight for the people of D.C. as a Civil Rights Republican and I plan to fight until I take my last breath.

Vincent Gray's Attorney General Irv Nathan
and me after a forum at the University of the
District of Columbia.

The photo above is of me having a respectful conversation with Vincent Gray's Attorney General Irv Nathan after a June 25, 2013 public forum on the Attorney General being an elected office. When I asked him why he did not give me any time to respond to the false accusations, he said that he gave me two weeks. I thought he was joking. His office and colleagues gave Harry Thomas, Jr., his corrupt colleague and proven liar, a year to respond to the charges against him.

I had intended to write this book as a way to share my early life, the mistakes I made that landed me in prison, my work with Peaceoholics, the political corruption that killed Peaceoholics, and to look ahead to my dreams for the future as a Civil Rights Republican. When I began writing the book in November 2011, I had no idea that Vincent Gray's hate for me would result in his Attorney General renewing the attacks by dredging up allegations for which I have been cleared by a government audit. Bring it on Mr. Mayor; I know how to drink muddy water and I'm ready to do it again with the help of God and the people.

Speaking at press conference joined by Marion Barry and Mayor Fenty who often called on Peaceoholics to address various issues in the city, especially violence. In this case, several people had been murdered the night before.

With Whali, Lump, Jauhar and Street Commission members receiving awards from Peaceoholics' Brothers Helping Brothers program.

My mentor Richard Norman and former CIA Director Admiral Stanfield. I spoke before Stanfield during a lecture at The Carnegie Endowment for International Peace. My lecture was titled: "Pray for Peace and RECONCILIATION."

Peaceoholics receives an award from Mayor Anthony Williams at Youth Truce Day. Youth Truce Day was created by Mayor Williams and Peaceoholics.

Lesson Three

The First Murder

Why can't we stop violence and murder in our communities? One of the reasons is we haven't examined and resolved the first homicide known to mankind when Cain killed his younger brother, Abel. On October 13, 2007, we conducted a mock trial. Judge Zoe Bush from D.C. Superior Court and Judge William Jarvis, then a prosecutor from the Commonwealth of Virginia, partnered with us to examine the causes, solutions, and blame for the first homicide. Evidence was presented to determine whether to indict Cain for killing Abel or to accept an insanity plea based on poor parenting.

The Old Testament book of Genesis attributes the first homicide to Adam and Eve's oldest son, Cain. The motive was jealousy and envy but there was more to it than that. There was also Cain's anger at his parents, which the defense claimed drove him temporarily insane. I portrayed Adam, Cain's father, and the prosecution grilled me on the witness stand. "You indicated that you blamed yourself, but what responsibility does Cain have?" the prosecutor asked me. "I believe that no murder should be excused," I replied, "I just believe that I played a part in it."

What caused Cain's anger to drive him to kill his brother? When it became time to sacrifice to the Lord, Adam failed to teach his children how to make a proper offering that would please God. So, Cain, being a farmer, brought the best of his crops to the altar as an offering. Abel, a sheep herder, sacrificed a lamb to God. God was displeased with Cain's sacrifice because the shedding of blood is part of a proper offering.

God gave Cain a second chance to make a pleasing offering, but Cain's jealousy and envy of his brother became rage when Abel's sacrifice was acceptable to God and Cain's was not. There was no way Cain was going to humiliate himself by asking his younger brother to trade him a lamb for some of his crops. Cain did not think rationally; he reacted emotionally and basically said to God, "You want blood? I'll give you blood!"

Then he lured his brother out into one of his fields where there were no witnesses, slew him, and buried him. Someone once told me "anger makes us stupid." He wasn't just saying that it makes us do stupid things, which it does. He was stating a scientific fact that a person's IQ drops twenty points when angry and, literally, makes us stupid. Well, it made Cain stupid enough to commit murder and think he would get away with it. That was before he realized God witnessed his crime and asked him, "Where is your brother, Abel?" To which Cain gave the infamous reply, "Am I my brother's keeper?"

The courtroom was filled with young parents with small children from all eight wards of the city, but they were mostly from the most impoverished neighborhoods where the majority of our single parent and dysfunctional households can be found. The data show that in these communities 70 percent of children are born to single-parent homes. This is the reverse percentage of what it was when I was growing up.

During the break, Judge Zoe Bush stated to Washington Post reporter, Hamil Harris, "I hope this exercise will be productive so that people can think not just reactively to murder and emotionally to murder, but what gives rise to it." She also said we need to find out what you can do "ahead of time to put services and interventions in place, so that people have alternatives to just acting without thinking."

Judge Bush has presided on the bench for thirteen years in juvenile court. She revealed for every child that commits a crime, there are several factors that contributed to its commission. "Children," she told the reporter, "are not just acting out because they are bad; they are acting out because they are not getting proper direction. A lot of our children are traumatized [from growing up] in violent settings and they react to being under constant stress."

The Washington Post story quoted me as saying, "It is very important that we go back and take a look at the root causes of homicide, so that we can solve the problems of homicides today." We often deal with the "who did it?" but not the "why."

Following the proceedings, the grand jury voted 11 to 1 to indict Cain. My biological father, Ronald Starks-El, was the one jurist who voted against indicting Cain. He said, "The parents were at fault for neglect and for treating one child better than the other," which cultivated the fertile ground to produce the first homicide known to mankind. I believe this particular juror had a valid point. If Cain was supposed to be his brother's keeper, then Adam was also responsible for not giving his son, Cain, guidance on pleasing sacrifices to God. We see most homicides today also come from different forms of jealousy, envy, self-hatred, and poor parenting. What would it take to fix this problem?

If two parents had a problem which produced the first homicide, it only makes sense that violence and homicides are more prevalent in single-parent households. In the communities that I serve, one-parent homes are as high as 80 percent. For African Americans, this would be a perfect place to start. We also know that if we treat one child or community differently than another, one school differently than another (not based on merit, principle, forgiveness, and love), we will continue to perpetuate the violence, homicides, and disparities that lead to a divided, city, nation, and world. It is time to balance the eagle.

Civil Rights icon Rev. James Bevel gives his opening statement as defense attorney in a mock trial of the "First Murder." The prosecutor is at the table.

Me on the witness stand with Judge Zoe Bush in Washington Informer newspaper article on our mock "First Murder" trial.

4

Politricks

Deceiving the People

Politricks is today's number one enabler of the African-American community as it has surpassed the harm of any Jim Crow law, which for some time kept us in mental and physical bondage.
—Ron Moten, Civil Rights Republican.

Today's politicians use what I call politricks to mislead and control ordinary people who have entrusted them with power. Many politicians in my community are put into office through the votes of the people and that right to vote was paid for by the sacrifices, even the deaths, of our courageous ancestors. I think Boynton and Dr. King would have expected more of them once they were elected to serve WE THE PEOPLE. These politicians abuse their power in ways one can hardly imagine. I found out the hard way what the rules are to the game of politricks.

If you think the streets of Washington, D.C. during the crack epidemic in the late 80's early 90's were bad, I have another story to tell you. I can tell you how with the stroke of a pen more lives can be wiped out than ten A-K 47's combined and you won't even see or hear it coming. You must understand how many politicians in the Nation's Capital and throughout urban America use perception to distort truth and destroy those who fight to help empower those who are voiceless. They fear someone will help them wake up and find their voices. You must see how often they use the race card when they get in trouble instead of dealing with the facts. I learned, too, the hard way in the game of politricks, that you have no permanent enemies or permanent allies.

I hope the politicians who read this book understand their tricks must stop because most of them have forsaken everything they promised the people. Once they take their hand off the Bible, they immediately abuse their power and become self-serving pigs at the public trough.

Most importantly, WE THE PEOPLE must understand you have to read between the lines and go beneath the surface before you believe what a politician, any politician, is saying. They put big lies out into the universe to mislead you so that they and their cronies can capitalize off our ignorance. WE THE PEOPLE must stand up as citizens and force the people who you entrusted with your vote to do what's in the best interest of the people. We are the people and the government works for us! For some reason, they think we will all remain ignorant of the facts and bamboozled by their politricks. Now, let's take a look at this in the Washington, D.C. where I reside.

First, I would like to give the very politicians who don't know a damn thing about Martin Luther King, Jr. and yet praise his teachings and words, a reality check. I did some of my writing for this book at his memorial and I hope what you read here will reflect the wisdom he has passed on to us. For some reason, D.C.'s elected officials including Vince Gray and Harry Thomas grasped that Dr. King did not die and Amelia Boynton Robinson did not take a brutal beating on the Edmond Pettus Bridge so crooked politicians could prosper from their political offices. They need to know Dr. King's view of power is its political use must be used for a good purpose because it is a divinely given gift.

In one of Martin Luther King, Jr.'s last speeches he stated, "There is nothing wrong with power if used correctly. One of the great problems of history is that the concepts of love and power have usually been contrasted as opposites so that love is identified with a resignation of power, and power with denials of love."

He goes on to say, "Now power properly understood is nothing but the ability to achieve purpose. It is the strength required to bring about social, political, and economic change. What is needed is the realization that power without love is reckless and abusive. Also, love without power is sentiment and anemic power at best, love implementing the demand of justice, and justice, at its best, is power correcting everything that stands against love."

I remember 2006 like it was yesterday as politician after politician jockeyed for a position to talk about the great works of Ronald Moten and Jauhar Abraham. Everyone loved and praised our grassroots organization. Peaceoholics was honored and our work acclaimed by Councilmembers Vincent Gray, Linda Cropp, Jim Graham, Jack Evans, Kwame Brown, Adrian Fenty, and Marion Barry. We were acknowledged by then Mayor Anthony Williams at his State of the District Address. We were the cover and face of youth work in the Washington Metropolitan

Area and we received all types of awards and proclamations from this council and two mayors.

The Justice Department recognized us as the face of D.C.'s crime prevention and community organizing as well as spokespersons for the voiceless. One of our most cherished awards was presented at the Canadian Embassy by the Search of Common Ground Foundation. In the past, they honored people like Muhammad Ali, Congressman and civil rights icon John Lewis, The Freedom Riders, President Jimmy Carter and they all came to D.C. to receive this prestigious award.

I was happy with our City Council for the most part because I felt they were listening to the people's testimonies. This was when the council still loved my passion for the communities I worked with as well as my commitment to pushing them and holding our communities and my fellow activists accountable. We later learned these hearings were mere formalities. Most of the issues were brought up year after year with some small victories but nothing that really fixed the problems. It was all just dog and pony show stuff. They just invited me in and pretended to listen. Now I know they do this with the average constituent who is coming to them in tears, crying and fighting for help.

It hurt my heart when I got a call from my seventy-four year-old grandmother saying Vince Gray just aired a commercial showing my picture and calling me a $100 million crony. Before the commercial people were focusing more on the work I was doing and not on the money I was perceived to be getting. I put out one cartoon before that commercial was released and the commercial gave me the opportunity to put out two more cartoons, one each about Gray and Harry Thomas.

These cartoons proved to be true. I really did not want to go so hard on the people involved, but I was finding it hard to get the truth out any other way. It is nice to have the luxury to always take the high road, but when the other side is putting out lies, there is no choice but to play hardball. The cartoons are reproduced on the following pages.

The information in these cartoons led Mike DeBonis, then with the City Paper, to write an article on March 19, 2010 entitled, "If Earmarks Were Eliminated, How Did Harry Thomas Get Them?" The answer is right there in the cartoon, his name is Vincent Gray!

A cartoon I drew and published in my online magazine. It is about the Vince Gray and Harry Thomas scandals before they became public knowledge.

Harry Thomas hated me for this but I loved my people and city too much to engage in hush-to-play politricks.

Naturally, as fighters who didn't believe in lying and misleading the people, we started to turn it up a notch even though our funding increased annually. Most nonprofits that get increased funding do not make waves. They may not be part of the corruption but they close their eyes to it because they are getting more and more money each year. Other's simply try to hold on while barely keep their doors open. It is a known no-no in the nonprofit world to stand up to corrupt politicians. We did and we paid dearly for it.

Just because a nonprofit is successful at receiving government grants does not mean they "pay to play." Some do pay to play and some engage in "hush to play." Hush to play is when you look the other way. The truth is coming out now about me and Peaceoholics. We refused to either hush to play or pay to play. We knew calling attention to the corrupt politics of Gray, Thomas and others would jeopardize our funding, but right is right. We were funded because we got results. We were defunded because we told the truth about D.C. politics and politicians at a time when it could not be tolerated because some were on a mission to take control of the city government.

We did not cooperate with their little game because we were not conformers. I would go crazy if I didn't speak up on the injustices these people were committing against the very people they took an oath and swore they would serve. I was amazed to see these crafty politicians would even use the anxiety, grief, and passion I had in my heart against me. As I witnessed the injustices done to the people, I came to the conclusion I and Peaceoholics and, worst of all, the communities we helped would soon pay a price for my passion to do what was right.

Many misled blacks in particular were being used and abused and would soon pay a price for their naïve ignorance of the facts that most politicians hide from them. Words are powerful and in politricks, they are used to giving people the perception politicians are acting in their best interest. Ignorance of the issues keeps people flocking to the voting booth to vote for the same people who are destroying our communities.

The gentrification caused by the HOPE-6 program described earlier is one good example. It happens gradually but it is, without question, planned. What happened with Kimi Gray and Kenilworth is a typical of this displacement by bulldozer policy. When the new housing is ready, it is rented and not sold to the original residents like Civil Rights Republican Jack Kemp envisioned it. What if Republicans were doing right by us and Democrats were screwing us? Would you refuse to vote Republican because black folk are "supposed" to vote Democrat? You are a fool if you don't use your vote to let Democrat politicians know they don't own you or your vote.

Most people who hate the Republican Party would acknowledge that if most urban cities such as D.C. had a balance of Democrats and Republicans, we would not see the corruption we see today. I believe if D.C. was dominantly Republicans, the same balance would have to be instituted at some point because our country was built on a two-party system.

Nannie Helen Burroughs once said, "The only thing more expensive than education is ignorance. We have lost so much ground in America because we don't take the time to study the issues and we are too fast to get frustrated with ones faults instead of evaluating the good." This is the mentality that put the corrupt Vince "Speed Camera" Gray in office!

Developers who donated to his campaign were sold city property well below its market value. A WMAU investigation found that 110 developers received $1.7 billion in subsidies. Less than 5 percent approved were for the city's poorest areas. A third did not fulfill the requirements to hire local businesses or the city did not have the paper work for them. Another 15 percent downsized or delayed benefits costing the city millions in lost revenue and others did not need the subsidy in the first place. This cost the city at least $100 million in revenue that he and the City Council decided could be made up for with fines from traffic cameras. I guess this is a way to tax the people without saying you are taxing them.

Thomas Jefferson said, "I predict the future happiness for Americans is if they can prevent the government from wasting the labors of the people under the pretense of helping them." This is exactly what we are dealing with today. Once we saw this happening, it was in our nature to address it and not care about our own self-preservation. The politicians had a problem with this as we testified about our dysfunctional juvenile justice system, which produced more murders than the KKK (Ku Klux Klan) could commit in their wildest dreams and all in the name of reform. I remember DYRS representatives testifying in front of Rep. Tom Davis and he asked them why they didn't listen to us.

In one case, the Washington Post reported Marcel was responsible for six murders. This all came out after Marcel and a close friend themselves were murdered. Their bodies were thrown on the Suitland Parkway which is often used by our presidents going to and from Andrews Air Force Base. In addition, we raised the issue of how returned citizens, fighting for funding for grassroots organizations that actually produce results and not just pretty paperwork lose out to no-account wannabe groups that get funded based on lies and counterfeit data! We also brought attention to the D.C. councilmember who chaired public safety and passed laws that affect communities that he never bothered to visit to see what is really going on. To his credit, he now comes out, but I ask whether it is because he knew he was running for the soon-to-be vacant chairman's seat. Only he and God know.

Pointing out corruption makes enemies and is bad for funding, but we never hesitated to speak out for the people. But it isn't just outright corruption; it is also the pervasive dependency policies of some liberal Democrats that resulted in high unemployment and, no job creation, and no training pipeline to take people from being unemployed on street corners to new jobs. All we get are more and more prison beds. The lack of small businesses or the creation of micro enterprises to move poor people off welfare is a deliberate trick most can't see or don't want to acknowledge.

Key liberals see the role of government as the rightful regulators of every area of the citizen's life. Well-meaning Democrats look at regulations as protections for the people in regard to work place safety, the environment, building codes, and food just to name a few. Reasonable regulations are necessary, but burdensome and unreasonable regulations discourage businesses from moving to D.C. and deter entrepreneurs from starting new business ventures.

This anti-business mentality pervades many other major cities also run by black Democrat politicians. The big lie is that over-regulation is needed to make the big bad corporations pay more fees and punish them for their success. The reality is, it is the little guy who seeks a vendor's license who is hurt most by over-regulation and fees. Only a liberal Democrat-run city would impose a moratorium on vendor's licenses as we now have in D.C. That is just another reason why our politicians have a strangle hold on us. As a one-party town we have to swallow the good and the bad of what it means to be a Democrat. I am proposing we become a two-party town and get the best of both parties and have options to get rid of the bad policies of both parties.

The whole premise behind this kind of over-regulation is wrong. First, these so-called "evil" corporations provide jobs and the more people they employ, the more tax revenue for the city goes up. The more a small or large business has to pay in taxes and regulatory fees, the fewer jobs they provide for our people.

The second problem is the misconception that the Republican Party is anti-government and wants no regulations. The truth is, for sake of freedom and to maximize economic opportunity, Republicans want limited government and limited regulations. Both good government and reasonable regulations are necessary to provide a safe and orderly society. However, it is foolish to think that if ten regulations are good, then a hundred regulations are better.

Our local politicians don't enforce the first source laws on the books that would guarantee many jobs. Of course, you aren't going to enforce such a law when you are getting what appear to be political or financial favors as Jeffery Anderson of the Washington Times newspaper reported about mega developer, W. C. Smith. He was affiliated with major work being done in D.C. including a jumbo fence around the home of City Council Chair Vince Gray. Amazingly, W. C. Smith has received over $500 million in city contracts.

The second problem with anti-business, "nanny government" Democrat Party policies is that these burdensome regulations make it easier to sell illegal drugs on the corner than to sell bottled water or t-shirts. When we only vote for Democrats, that's what we get because more regulations means more fees to feed the endless need of government for more and more taxpayer money.

The money that corrupt politicians use to line the pockets of their big supporters with government contracts come out of your pocket! It is not an accident getting a business license in D.C. is an expensive and long, drawn out nightmare. It is designed to take away our freedom to pursue happiness and make us more dependent on government handouts. We need a better balance of African Americans in the two major political parties.

During the 2010 mayoral campaign and election, Vince Gray stole like a thief in the night while promising everybody everything. He went as far away as China to find investors to buy up the parts of D.C. that he and other politicians had not already given away to his developer friends. Promises to investors and developers were always kept; unfortunately, the same is not true for the promises to the people in our communities.

I hope the Chinese investors he brought in have the same level of integrity as Mr. Park who owns businesses in the Petworth community where I grew up. His children even have a nonprofit organization to help children called Little Lights. This is another example that it isn't always about race or political beliefs but your commitment to people.

Popular Asian merchant and philanthropist Mr. and Mrs.
Park with Mayor Marion Barry, me, and Cease Fire
member Eric Tapp and founder Al Malik in 1995

We were different. We were active in our communities so the politicians had to deal with us. When I was COO of Peaceoholics, we were not sheep or slaves to the government. Government works for us. We conducted marches that brought out over 2,000 people, mostly disenfranchised youth and young adults. This was all a part of our model and part of what made us so powerful and feared. We produced results in some of our toughest hoods and schools. Places nobody else wanted to go. What was different about us was we were spiritually empowered because we held people from the streets accountable.

I've never had that whiney liberal "poor little black folk" attitude. If we are going to hold public officials accountable, we need to hold the people accountable, too. Our marches were peaceful and legal. We called on God in peace rallies with prayer and singing as our mentors did during the Civil Rights Movement. We did not tolerate criminal behavior of any kind but we understood it, so we methodically moved people forward when necessary. I used to be one of those people who helped tear down my community not build it up. I was a curse and not a blessing to D.C. until I served my time and came out a returned citizen eager to redeem my former self.

So, even though we were socializing with some of the same kind of people who were like we once were, a curse rather than a blessing, we held them responsible for their behavior. We didn't let the gangs and crew members get away with anything. If they want to work for us and with us, then they had to do the right thing. We understood why young people join gangs and crews and why they are carrying so much anger and hurt but understanding doesn't mean we excuse it.

As the years went by, we became better at our work. Our work model was constructed and strengthened by the mistakes we made as well as the successes we achieved. It was so easy and natural for me to work with the people from the community because *I am* from the community. Some people learn how to work from studying books and others learn from their life experiences. Both are good, but people who learn from the book have a steeper learning curve. They can have as much heart and good intentions as the Peaceoholics, but nothing replaces real life experience.

That's why we also were dedicated to training those without our vast experience. The antidote for a snake bite comes from the snake. I had been one of the snakes that bit the community and poisoned it, now we were back as the antidote. We weren't just back with the antidote; we were back as the antidote. In 2006, we began to receive national attention for our work on shows like NBC's Nightline speaking about the problem of bullying. Most people had not yet made a connection between violent video games and the effect they had on our children.

As we demonstrated in the Lesson Three, "The First Murder," the root of the first homicide was jealousy and envy. Some politicians and people who did not want to see things change for the better in our city were clearly envious of the attention and credit we were receiving. Once again, forcing effective nonprofits to compete for crumbs from the City Council's funding table was the best way to divide us. Our sacrifices, labor, and obvious successes resulted in a stream of funding. This stream allowed us to train and hire many people who might have never received a job in the District of Columbia if not for the efforts of the Peaceoholics. Mayor Anthony Williams and a white councilmember, Jack Evans, from Ward 2 gave us our first four-hundred-thousand-dollar earmark.

Mayor Anthony Williams soon became a supporter of ours also after seeing our effectiveness perform through grants administered under the leadership of Deputy Mayor Brenda Donald Walker. Ms. Walker proved to be a wise and crafty leader in the youth engagement and social service field who later worked for the Annie Casey Foundation. However, I was not a big fan of Mayor Williams until I got to know him personally. I found him to be honest and discovered we had a lot in common.

From our inception, things moved fast. We went from a $50,000 annual budget to an average of $3 million in two years. We worked hard, got results, and were the rising stars in the D.C. nonprofit community. Mayor Williams even mentioned us in his final State of the Union Address during the year that we were granted 2.3 million dollars. We had sixty people on the payroll and we never received any money from the people who you would have expected to support us.

This reminds me of an incident at Gallaudet University where I was speaking. I had challenged local government to do more to uplift the citizens in impoverished areas of D.C. Dan Tangherlini, then City Administrator and recently appointed to head the GSA (General Services Administration) by President Obama, was in the audience. Dan took my comments as a criticism of the Fenty administration and went to the mayor to tell him that he had a problem with what I had said. To his credit, Mayor Fenty told Dan to talk to me directly about it. That is how honest politics should be done. Dan and I came to a personal understanding through that incident and have not had a problem since.

Adrian Fenty, the Ward 4 councilmember, saw the results we were getting in his ward but could not help fund us because he was the low man on the totem pole and his fellow council members often disrespected his ideas and straight forwardness. Although he wasn't getting any love from his colleagues on the City Council, Fenty was loved by the entire city because of his responsiveness to Ward 4 and beyond. January 9, 2007, Adrian Fenty became mayor and we helped him with strategies to reduce homicides, engage children, families, and much more. We never disappointed him and, while we produced results, we had no problem challenging him when we disagreed with his policies. We both could live with that as long as we were up front about our disagreements.

It was frustrating that results never seemed to matter when evaluating the work of Peaceoholics. No one seemed to notice that an organization that received $15 million annually boasted about all the youth they were working with. The fact is that they could not get twenty youth to turn out for the Ward 4 jobs fair where Mayor Fenty was trying to deal with root causes of shootings involving rival gangs. He rescheduled the event due to the low turnout. For that event

Peaceoholics turned out over seventy youth, many involved in the violence plaguing the Petworth community.

To this day, no one questioned why a group with $15 million in funding couldn't turn out twenty youth for a job fair. That's because this city is too much about "you scratch my back and I will scratch yours" rather than producing results. This group knew how to keep the focus off the fact they have not facilitated one truce in either Ward 1 or Ward 4. Fenty, proudly and often spoke highly of our work just as Gray had done before we told him we would not be part of his mess. This same group also worked behind the scenes to destroy us and worked with people like Vince Gray to bring down Mayor Fenty. Now that Vince Gray is the mayor, he has made certain this group received Wal-Mart dollars given to the community.

Unfortunately, with Fenty putting the spotlight on us, envy began to consume people who did not receive funding like we did. The council made sure "the little people" were fighting over crumbs instead of empowering us to sustain ourselves with business models that could help us take care of our families and the people we serve. This was one of the tools they used to destroy us. As Vince Gray said to his friend Harry Thomas during his 2010 campaign, "I'm going to stop the Peaceoholics gravy train," while at the same time, sliding Thomas $1.3 million and telling groups like Peaceoholics there was no funding available.

One summer day, Fenty and I were doing a walk-through at the Ferebee-Hope Recreation Center in Southeast where he promised the community he would clean up. As usual, he came through for the people. Unfortunately, no one knew the good he accomplished; they only wanted to see or were only told about our challenges. The perception of us put out to the media by crafty, disingenuous veteran politicians was beginning to have an effect.

We were inside and everybody was happy. The mayor beat one of the youth on the recreation center's new bumper pool table. I hit a half-court jump shot in the newly-remodeled gym and everybody went crazy. Nikita Stewart, a writer for the Washington Post was taking notes and I thought to myself, "This is finally a good day of news in the poverty entrenched Washington Highlands part of D.C. East of the River." This neighborhood had the highest unemployment rate in the country. Things like this don't often make the local news.

Mayor Fenty made one of his biggest mistakes, showing his honesty and political naiveté! As we walked to the car, he told Nikita Stewart,

"Moe and me are friends and we go way back to Alice Deal Middle School," which was true and yet not true! One thing I would soon find out was that Fenty was not a great politician, just a great doer. The mayor needed to learn the old saying politicians have to be honest, but politically honest! He should have known better but he honestly didn't. Ms. Stewart made that comment a highlight of her story and we became a fly under the microscope like he and I were bosom buddies!

The truth is Mayor Fenty and I went to school together, but never talked on the phone and never ate lunch together. We might have waved at each other and everybody shopped at his parents' shoe store, Fleet Feet. Still, he only knew of me because on any given day he might hear Mr. Reginald Moss, the best principal D.C. has ever had, call me and my best friend, Roosevelt Jackson, to the office where he told us we had twenty-five words or less to explain why he should not suspend us for one reason or another!

The great work of the Peaceoholics continued and now we were the center of attention. We were in the same boat as the mayor's fraternity brother, Sinclair Skinner. Mr. Skinner was being scrutinized for receiving part of $80 million worth of deals to build recreation centers and libraries and was under attack by Harry Thomas among others. Fenty's haters used their power to hurt anyone who had a relationship with the mayor in order to turn residents against him. Going after Skinner personally helped their cause as did going after me for my passion for the people. Everyone seemed to be blind to what was happening. It was as if the corruption was so rampant that it became the new norm and was invisible to people.

In my view, Mayor Fenty was focused on being a doer and had tunnel vision, which is not always a good trait for a politician. As far as I could tell, he had very good motives for the most part. When he was on the City Council, he saw how the bureaucratic mess stopped things from getting fixed in the schools. For example, text books sat in warehouses for years while children went without them. He saw how corrupt politicians just let the city's poorest residents go down the drain. He had the heart to bring about change and get results but D.C. residents would never know half the things that he did for them.

He was under the politically innocent idea that results were the answer. He honestly did not want to fall into the category of someone who just said things to make people feel good. He would eventually pay for his decency by getting a good old fashioned political ass whoopin' and lose his job to a corrupt politician, Vincent Gray who deceived the people by taking advantage of this. Fenty was not as savvy dealing with D.C.'s old school career politicians like Vince Gray as Mayor Corey Booker was in dealing with the same kind of corruption in Newark, N.J.

Shareholders of a corporation don't care if the CEO loves each and every one of them. He or she is judged by how his policies affect the company's bottom line. That's fine in business, but most blacks are emotional people. You can drive some of us to Hell and back and blow smoke about what you will do for us and as long as you can make us feel good while doing absolutely nothing, we will still vote for you.

Look at how our "Mayor for Life" Marion Barry hurt the national reputation of our great city after he reached his peak and lost his way. As I have said before, he has done so much for the District and even our country as it relates to civil rights. But now he has become ineffective in helping the people. He just lives off the countless great deeds he did in the past, not just for African Americans, but for every citizen of our great city. In my eyes, he only stays in office because he always helped the people and the people are fiercely loyal to him.

Mr. Barry's addiction to politics is just like his addiction to drugs. It's a tough habit to break. So, with an 81 percent approval rate among blacks, all he has to do these days is give away two-thousand turkeys on Thanksgiving and a backpack the week before school and he is a shoe-in. In the old days, the Marion Barry who was my civil rights mentor would have made sure a textbook was in each backpack.

That's a great contrast to Vince Gray who has left a trail of people who he did not help because they would not help him. I know Vince Gray sure wishes he helped more people in the past, but too late Vince! And now, some of the people who did help Gray are running to the U.S. Attorney's office to let them know how dirty this guy is.

Smoke Screens

During the Fenty versus Gray campaign battle, the Gray campaign exploited a child saying he was promised a job if he voted for Fenty. Gray had a press conference asking the FBI to investigate days before the election. This was big news right before judgment day and I knew this would be another dagger in Fenty's back. This young man said he had never worked on a campaign before but we later received literature with a picture of him on it passing out Brian Weaver campaign literature.

Once again, the media did not cover this story. Gray asked the FBI to look at this while the whole time he was cheating with his shadow campaign. I wouldn't be surprised if they paid this young man to do this just like they paid Sulaimon Brown who will go down in local history as the one responsible for changing D.C. politics as we once knew it. These guys were wicked and determined to win by any means necessary.

I knew the chickens would come home to roost and now the smoke is clearing and all of this corruption is coming out. Some people say Fenty would have lost regardless and I say not so fast! First, when somebody cheats in the Olympics, people don't ask if the steroids helped him enough to win. They say he cheated and they take the gold medal. Is there an exception for Vince Gray, the misleading leader? Second, there is no way Gray won that election straight up. Why do I say this?

First, it is just my gut feeling from many years involved in D.C. politics, especially in Ward 8. It just did not make sense given the response I was seeing in certain neighborhoods. We did a great job getting Fenty's message out with Go-Go music and its icons in areas where politricks were used to make him out to be the villain.

Second is turnout. Around 2 PM on Election Day, I stood on the corner of Martin Luther King, Jr. Avenue and W Street, Southeast with Jauhar, Rock Newman, who I love, and others who were on opposing sides. We all discussed that there was a low turnout. Our team canvassed a majority of the polls in Ward 8, which is our poorest ward with a historically low voter turnout. Amazingly, it came out later that more people voted during this election than the 2008 Obama election! Now, anyone in his right mind knows in an off-year election, there is no way voter turnout was the same as when Barack Obama was running to be the first black president!

Third, the Gray campaign bought votes. I helped Josh Lopez and others on our team conduct a sting catching Vince Gray's staff paying people with gift cards from the Giant grocery store. It played all over the news but nothing ever happened even though we had video showing people from Vince Gray's campaign driving people to the polls and then returning them to receive their ten-dollar gift card.

My family was personally impacted by this gift card scheme. My son was jumped and beaten outside a church in Southeast D.C. because he saw campaign workers giving out gift cards to people for voting for Vince Gray. Fortunately, he handled himself well and came out with only a few scratches. He wasn't the only person who saw what was going on, but he was Ron Moten's son, so he was a threat. This was the Gray campaign buying votes in plain view without any scrutiny or boundaries.

Fourth is that the Washington Post reported that a DCHA (District of Columbia Housing Authority) database was illegally acquired by the Gray campaign. There are two other interesting points. First, Vincent Gray's son worked for DCHA. Second, Mayor Fenty had used DCHA to legally get around the red tape in order to expedite the renovation and building of neighborhood schools and recreation centers.

Fifth, seals were broken on bags containing ballots and cartridges were missing during the voting count! Sixth, Sulaimon Brown was paid by the Gray shadow campaign to stay in the race just to attack Mayor Adrian Fenty. His job was to antagonize Fenty and to hype the crowds for Gray at the mayoral debates and straw polls. Brown's job was made easier by the fact that there were Gray supporters planted in the crowd and ready to boo on cue.

The Shadow Campaign

Of course, there was the shadow campaign itself. What has now come out into the light of day is that Gray was running two campaigns, one public and the other a shadow campaign. So, it might be technically true that it was not what he calls "his campaign" that was handing out gift cards all over the city, but the shadow campaign certainly was!

A disgruntled, campaign worker named Sulaimon Brown exposed Gray as a liar who knew all the time there was a "shadow campaign" and that he knew what it was doing. The Sulaimon Brown investigation has resulted in several campaign members being indicted and agreeing to wear wires for federal investigators and making plea bargains. Vince Gray says he knows nothing about any of the seven deadly sins of that election. His claim that all the illegal and unethical tactics were not part of his campaign was what I call a true lie.

It was like a business that has two sets of books, the "legit books" they show the IRS auditor and the "shadow books" where the "creative accounting" is done. Gray was doing some very creative "shadow campaigning" and now he is trying to legally distance himself from it. Who on earth believes Gray did not know about people who wanted him elected so badly they were willing to commit election fraud and other crimes to see it happen? And who believes no one in the official Gray campaign did not coordinate and advise the shadow campaign?

At this juncture, I need to introduce two new, but very important names: Jeanne Clarke Harris, owner of Belle International consulting company, and Jeffrey Thompson, whose company held a $320 million health care contract with the District of Columbia. On July13, 2012 the Washington Examiner reported the following in an article by Liz Farmer and Alan Blinder:

> Jeanne Clarke Harris told federal investigators she had help creating the unreported [shadow] campaign that helped elect D.C. Mayor Vincent Gray and that the effort had started two months before the mayoral primary — when she was told his campaign needed "financial assistance."
>
> Harris said her company, Belle International, received at least $653,800 to pay for the shadow campaign's expenses from a single, unnamed co-conspirator, who is believed to be prominent D.C. contractor Jeffrey Thompson whose company holds a $320 million health care contract with the city.

This was done so that no one would know the source of the unreported money used to defeat Mayor Adrian Fenty and to attack me for supporting him. The article concluded with the following timeline of shadow campaign events as revealed in court documents:

- **August 2010 –** The secret campaign buys 4,250 yard signs, 5,000 T-shirts and 200 umbrellas for $41,971.26.

- **August/September 2010 –** Radios, a loudspeaker system, laptops, food, parking for canvassers: $57,992.

- **September 2010 –** Magnetic vehicle signs, 120,000 door knockers, 1,500 T-shirts, 6,000 posters, 10,000 lapel stickers, 4,200 signs, handouts, a banner installation: $67,160.42.

  Worker payroll expenses: $203,084.33

  Sept. 14: Gray wins the primary by 10 percentage points.

- **June 2011 –** Harris finds out the D.C. U.S. attorney and the FBI are investigating Gray's campaign and discusses the probe with the co-conspirator. They agree to cover up the shadow campaign.

- **June to December 2011 –** Harris directs the shredding of documents and electronic data related to the secret campaign.

- **August 2011 –** Co-conspirator offers to pay Harris to leave the country for five years to avoid investigators, Harris refuses.

- **December 2011** – At the direction of the co-conspirator, Harris amends her 2010 tax returns to include a payment of $566,000 from the co-conspirator's company for phony business/marketing services.

  Dec. 31: Harris gets a check for $163, 569 from the co-conspirator to help pay her taxes.

- **January 2012** – Jan. 10: Harris reportedly meets with Gray and tells him about some unreported expenditures. Gray reportedly tells Harris to assist in amending her campaign finance reports.

- **March 2012** – Federal agents raid the homes and offices of Harris and Thompson.

- **July 2012** – Harris pleads guilty to conspiracy and fraud charges.

Sulaimon Brown

Just like the Watergate scandal was not uncovered until after Nixon was elected to his second term, the Gray campaign corruption was exposed after Gray became mayor and failed to reward Sulaimon Brown. It is clear that Sulaimon Brown felt burned after he helped Adrian Fenty get elected in 2006 and was not rewarded with a job. So, when he went over to the other side to help Vincent Gray and to exact revenge on Fenty, he made sure that he had the Gray campaign over a barrel just in case they also decided to stiff him. Well, they did, and he exposed them.

I guess the new mayor forgot the rules of the game he was playing. It seems Vince was not aware of lot of things happening right in front of his eyes. He claimed to not know that the company building the fence around his house was connected to a developer who just so happened to get hundreds of millions of dollars from the Gray administration. He said he did not know about the illegal hiring of campaign staff members' families. He conveniently forgot that he gave Harry Thomas $1.3 million so he could get kickbacks and, unfortunately, he forgot he told Sulaimon Brown that he would get him a job. I'm no doctor, but sure sounds like a bad case of dementia to me.

As soon as Sulaimon Brown became a threat, Gray's people used the media to assassinate his character. They even put out that he stalked a young girl. I know how Brown must have felt with everyone buying into what Mayor Gray or his people said in the media. The mayor is seen as a higher and more credible authority. If he says you are crazy, people tend to discredit anything you say. Sulaimon had a great line, he told Marion

Barry during his hearing before the City Council, "The same people who locked you up, I'm talking to!"

We recorded almost every debate and you can hear my video guy in the background asking Sulaimon, "How much are they paying you?" At the debate on the St. Elizabeth's campus Sulaimon talked about Adrian's mother. That made the guys we mentored from Southeast want to attack him. They knew how much Fenty had done for them. It got very intense and we told them to cool down and lead by example. It was hard because this beat down was hard to put into words.

So much for leadership, character, and integrity, the slogan of the Gray campaign. Those words don't belong in the same sentence with his name. The real Vince Gray campaign was the illegal shadow campaign the feds are investigating now! It's kind of funny how so many people who were part of smearing my name and getting Peaceoholics defunded, now have the FBI all over them.

This was a stolen election! If people can believe that the 2000 presidential election was stolen in Florida, why can't people see this 2010 mayoral election was definitely stolen? People should have known something was wrong; as soon as Mayor Vincent Gray won the election, he arranged to have a security detail including security at his door in the Wilson Building. The Washington Examiner reported that Gray spent a million dollars on his security detail. When Adrian Fenty was mayor, he drove himself in a small, eco-friendly car.

Lottery Contract Corruption

There is really no end to the corruption. Take the lottery contract for instance. That was a ten-year contract that friends of Gray, had for twenty-seven years. It had a lot of problems including security issues for which they were fined $2.1 million exposing $80,000 of fake lottery ticket winnings.

In the District of Columbia, any contract over one million dollars must get council approval and has to be put on the agenda for the council to vote on as a whole. Warren Williams and the Greek company Intralot won the new contract fair and square, but Vince Gray refused to put it on the agenda and withdrew it four times because his people were not added as partners on the contract.

Emmanuel Bailey and Kevin Chavous, a lobbyist and former Ward 7 councilman, who initially worked for Intralot Williams' team, met with Vince Gray and Bailey in private. Bailey's mom worked for Gray back when Gray was destroying the Department of Human Services. Bailey was also friends with At-large Councilmember Michael Brown. Before Bailey was put on the deal, he sent emails to Warren Williams saying, "I can get the old man." The message was, if they put Bailey on the deal, he could get Vince Gray to see that it passes. Warren Williams of W2Tech, in his own way, said, "No thanks!"

The lottery contract lasts for a decade and in the past has been used by the council to take care of each other so this was a case of "I Declare War!" Warren Williams and his wife won the new contract worth more than thirty-eight million over ten years. Gray later did something never done before in the District of Columbia. After the Williams Company, W2Tech, and Intralot won the lottery contract through a fair bidding process, which would have made the city more money, Vince Gray caused so much confusion he was able to get the contract illegally rebid. This was at a time when the city was financially strapped. To no one's surprise, when the contract was rebid, Intralot was the sole winner.

The Washington Times and the Washington Post editorial boards shed some light on the Bailey story. Bailey joined the Intralot team and became the majority partner after they won the rebid contract. Intralot was initially a partner with Warren Williams who won the contract fair and square before Gray got it rebid. Lorraine Greene, Vince Gray's longtime partner in crime or should I say "good in the hood," was on the other new team. She was the behind-the-scenes diva of local politics.

I brought this up later in the council hearings in which Chairman Gray initially decided not to participate. Gray came out red-faced with his hair standing on top of his head as if he had on a toupee. He came storming out because I said something about his friend Lorraine Greene and the lottery deal. Then he asked me to go under oath. I said, "Sure, I'll go under oath if you go under oath, too, because I have some questions to ask you as well." He then said, "If you want to ask me questions, run for office." He then asked to have me removed if I wouldn't go under oath. I asked him, "Who is going to move me, you?"

It was reported by the Washington Times that Emmanuel Bailey listed fake credentials and fake contracts with Walter Reed Army Hospital, ripped off business partners, and was never vetted. Vince Gray later praised Mr. Bailey as a "great company" to fill this void. This was more gangster than anything I've ever seen on the streets and is the main reason I tell people that what our youth are doing in the streets is small time compared to the gangsters in suits, as Jay-Z would say!

Once again, people all over the city were saying that they got popcorn and soda to watch the hearing. It was like a reality show. This turned out to be one of many battles we have with some of the crooked City Council members inside the chambers of the D.C. City Council. We had to stand up for the people because we knew crooks like Harry Thomas were stealing from our communities and literally costing us the lives of our youth. Thomas pled guilty to stealing $350,000, which is an understatement, but that's where the plea bargain stopped.

These public confrontations also proved that I was now in a much more wicked game than any street battle with guns I had ever witnessed. During the time of the lottery debacle, the council members were followed, investigated, and forensically audited. It was exposed that one council member owned a boat called 'Bullet Proof.' It has also come out a married newspaperman who was working on exposing the lottery deal while drunk was photographed with another woman in the Marriot Hotel directly across the street from the Wilson Building. A council member was also allegedly photographed buying a female a ten-thousand-dollar mink coat.

A Hollow Victory for Old School Politricks

This is the world no one sees in local politics in places such as the District of Columbia. I knew who was doing these things and I told them that we didn't want to have any part of it. That isn't how we do business. That kind of surveillance started with J. Edgar Hoover who used it to try to discredit Dr. King and the Civil Rights Movement. What we wanted was a guarantee whoever got the lottery deal would provide a community benefits package. In hindsight, knowing what type of elected officials they are, we should have busted that whole situation wide open. This lottery deal is going to cost the city a lot of money.

Many lives were ruined in the process. Mayor Gray, Natwar Gandhi, and Jim Graham lost their fight against being deposed in a lawsuit brought against the city by Eric Payne who worked for Gandhi in the OCFO (Office of Chief Financial Officer)! Mr. Payne was a whistle blower fired because he would not illegally remove W2 Tech and Intralot from the D.C. Lottery contract. Gray and Jim sent an email to Williams saying they could get the lottery deal if the IG (Inspector General) would investigate.

Unfortunately, it will be just like the Yvette Alexander constituent service scandal and the IG will give these crooks a slap on the wrist. The IG's budget comes from the same people being investigated and when you have a one-party system like D.C., this behavior is tolerated. Vince Gray reminds me of Boss Hog from the "Dukes of Hazard," he either got a cut on everything moving or he would cut it out. Like Frank White said, "If a nickle bag was sold in his city, he wanted his piece." It was never about the people, it was about money and power.

I knew Vince Gray would drag our city government down and that things would be bad for those who supported him. I even produced a YouTube video called the "Misleading Leader" exposing his deceit. It exposed that Gray was about to give Harry Thomas the $1.3 million. I was supporting Adrian Fenty then so no one listened to me.

Gray, Thomas, and others had done a pretty good job of ruining my reputation, now that the FBI is after them and not me, I feel vindicated, but not victorious because four years after I was cleared by a public audit, the harassment continues. Mayor Gray is now using the power of his Attorney General to bring up the same old issues as before just to create political diversions and distract from his own problems.

The reality remains that Vince Gray is the mayor and Peaceoholics was killed by his politricks and all the good work we were doing in the community was stopped. All anyone ever came up with on me and Peaceoholics was that we didn't do a very good job of bookkeeping. We didn't do anything illegal but that was all my enemies needed to bring us down. I regret the fact all my attention was on helping people and I did not make sure we were more meticulous about the administrative side of things. I know I am still a target of the Gray administration. After many years on the streets and all I have been through with Peaceoholics, I am used to being a target.

To be frank, I do not believe that Vincent Gray ever cared about helping the people. All he wanted was to control the money. Big Wax said in his song that no one man should have all that power, he was right. Gray gave jobs to people who sacrificed nothing and left those who worked hardest for him, like Stanley Richardson, swinging in the wind. Richardson was so committed that he buried his mother during the campaign and came back again to do what he could to help. After Gray won, all the old school crooks were back in power.

The Gray administration is the NAACP of politricks: the National Association for the Advancement of Certain People. When Vince Gray was first asked if he was involved in all the alleged scandals, he said, "No way." Now as the allegations pile up from the campaign investigation to the lottery, his response to questions is "No comment."

Speaking at a
candlelight vigil with
Vince Gray and
Kwame Brown in the
background

Jauhar Abraham and I flank Councilmember Jim Graham
joined by then councilmembers Vince Gray, Jim Gray, and
Kwame Brown at Friends of Peaceoholics event in Adams
Morgan where our work was praised.

Gift cards that were confiscated by Team Fenty sting which videoed Vincent Gray campaign workers and what is believed to be his shadow campaign buying people's for votes.

Councilmembers Kwame Brown, Yvette Alexander, and Harry Thomas at fundraiser where they praised the work of Peaceoholics and asked people to give generously before they turned on us for political reasons.

With Marion Barry whose work in his first two terms as the Mayor of the District of Columbia I greatly admire as second to none. Here they are at a press conference outside the 7th District police precinct.

Chuck Brown after performing at Mayor Adrian Fenty's inauguration celebration. Mayor Fenty supported Chuck Brown before it become politically expedient.

Lesson Four

Taking the Bait
Breakfast with Don King

While I was in New York City for Joppy's fight against boxing icon Felix Trinidad, I got a call from John Day. John said, "Moe, get dressed, we're going to have breakfast with Don King and Hasim Rahman." King wanted to make an offer to Rahman who, as a 20-1 underdog, had just knocked out Lennox Lewis! We met at Justin's, which is a famous breakfast spot in New York City.

As we ate, Don King made his pitch. He wanted to hook Rahman into a deal and the bait was a bag of money. The bait was used to hook Hasim into signing a deal that was good for Don King and not so good for Rahman. The shiny bait covering a hook keeps the fish from looking at the big picture. That bag of money on the table distorted Rahman's judgment, which is exactly what King wanted.

Don King pointed at the bag of money on the table and said he would give it to Hasim. He was offering a total of $5 million to snatch him away from promoter Cederic Kushner who had offered Rahman a $17 million deal. But King's offer meant instant cash. Everyone knows that $17 million is better than $5 million including Hasim Rahman, but he was blinded by the lore of immediate cash, immediate gratification.

Rahman took the bait and after a lot of court battles and chaos, Lennox Lewis got a rematch and punished Rahman! That ended it for Hasim. If he had exercised a little patience and stayed with the man who got him there he would have made more money from the four-fight $17 million that he walked away from for the $5 million he made for the rematch he lost to Lennox Lewis!

Hasim got screwed like many of us do in the game of life because we often have no loyalty to those who are there for us when we are down. We let the prospect of instant gratification cloud our vision of the big picture. That bait looks good, but you have to trust your principles, not your emotions. We use this lesson with youth who always have someone trying to bait them with sex, cash, or drugs. This is similar to the story in the Bible where the devil offers Jesus Christ all the kingdoms of the world, but Jesus said in effect what Hasim should have said, "No thanks, I already have a better deal."

That breakfast experience later helped me walk away from a five hundred thousand dollar contract to run a program that had no chance of working. However, because other groups took the bait, many youth were either killed or became killers. This would subsequently be the springboard for Title XVI legislation which charged D.C. children as adults. Our patience and hard work got us a deal nearly twice that much. We were able to hire people from the community and get real results with DYRS children. The message is simple — don't take the bait!

Another experience, also involving John Day of HOBO, makes the same point. John and some other black D.C. clothing designers like Madness Shop, We Are One, All Daz, just to name a few, took some bait and got pimped themselves. An Asian mass clothing producer, who they trusted, took their designs and ideas and reproduced their clothes for very reasonable prices. This helped John and the others make a lot of money. That was the bait.

What they didn't know was that the manufacturer in Asia was learning from their business and stealing their designs to hustle them. Their big mistake was giving all their intellectual property to someone without requiring him to sign non-compete, confidentiality, and disclosure agreements. He started a clothing line called Visionz and underbid their prices using their styles and similar designs and used D.C.'s hottest band, TCB to be the face of his clothing line just like HOBO used Big G and the boxers I brought to him like William Joppy.

This caused many of the stores to close down and put others on the verge failure. That's when I stepped in to help by starting the Unity Clothing Association and getting all the stores to organize against Mr. Cohn because he would not play fair. I told Polo and the TCB Band what had happened and they stopped promoting Visionz clothing in return for being paid by the Unity Clothing Association. We also put the word out at the Go-Go concerts and eventually killed Vizionz.

I have great admiration for how the Asian community sticks together to create new businesses, I have had very positive relationships with many Asian business owners including Mr. Park who was a standup businessman in the Petworth neighborhood for nearly three decades. The sad thing about this was that I could not get all the black store owners to trust each other like Asian business owners do so they could put their money together to order shirts and supplies in bulk.

Their orders helped empower a company called Luz Tee that national Retailer DTLR (Downtown Locker Room) later picked up. Luz also treated them poorly. At the end of the day, they could have all been Luz Tee's. All I was trying to do was get them to put their money together and order the shirts in drums from a Chinese company to keep down their costs. They would have had a quality blank shirt that had the D.C. style that Luz eventually stole. They could then wholesale it as another business and as a capital investment outside their stores.

This mentality goes back to the first recorded homicide. Jealousy, envy, and lack of trust would not allow these brothers to come together and ultimately, they killed each other off just as Cain murdered his brother, Abel. Rob from Shooters Sportswear got frustrated and bought the same equipment as Mr. Cohn. He is one of the few still in business making his own clothes as well as clothes for schools and businesses.

My son and father, Ronald Starks-El, in Manhattan with former Heavy Weight Champion Hasim Rahman (l) and former boxing champ Derrell Coley (r).

I share these experiences because I'm not ashamed to say that I got pimped a time or two myself. In some cases it was by people who didn't give a damn about me, but in many cases, I was wronged by people who I called friends. They didn't care about themselves or me. What should I have expected? I teach youth and adults that if a deal appears to be too good and comes too easy, think twice because that's not how things work in the world. Nothing comes easy and, as Booker T. Washington said, "You can't get something for nothing." Everything worth having has a price. Are you willing to pay the price or will you continue to take shortcuts and set yourself up to be the sucker who takes the bait!

With my son Ronald with Don King in Manhattan, New York before William Joppy-Felix Trinidad fight.

Wearing Hobo gear with first black Fly-weight Champion and Boxing Hall of Fame inductee Mark "Too Sharp" Johnson.

5

A Mayor's Old School Ass Whoopin'

Nothing in the world is more dangerous than a sincere ignorance and conscience stupidly.
                                                          –Dr. Martin Luther King, Jr.

One politician is purposely misleading. He is a classic example of an old school politician who might have started out with good intentions some thirty years ago who turned into a corrupt politicians and poverty pimp in disguise. That politician is Vincent C. Gray. The other politician was aggressively naïve, inexperienced, and wanted to serve his community, but did not know or want to abide by the rules of the D.C.'s old school political game. He seemed totally unaware how honest mistakes would be used against him. That politician was Adrian Fenty.

Adrian Fenty became the mayor of the District of Columbia and immediately began to make positive things happen but at the same time he made stupid mistakes. One example was early on when he withheld Washington Nationals baseball tickets from an already hostile City Council. So, rather than his good work as mayor being in the spotlight, unnecessary distractions like baseball tickets were the highlight on his weekly Fox 5 News appearances.

I will give you several examples of how then Chairman Vincent Gray, Harry Thomas, Marion Barry, and Mary "Holier Than Thou" Cheh, Yvette Alexander, and a few other council members teamed up to give Fenty an old school ass whooping. They knew once they got the toothpaste out of the tube, well-meaning Adrian Fenty would not be able to get it back in. By the time the truth came out it would to be too late for him to be vindicated. They knew the people would not read between the lines and they could use perception to tear him down!

Why would they want to tear him down? Once again two words will explain this: contracts and power. These men and women did not want to relinquish even an ounce of power and Peaceoholics, and I, as its public face, would get caught up in this spider web of collateral damage as Marion Barry would later call it. Two years into his term we saw how the beef between what I would call the City Council Corrupt Seven and a naïve mayor turned ugly. Mayor Fenty was busting his butt to uplift the city. Was he doing it to perfection? Absolutely, not! But I knew it was better than any of the corrupt seven would do who wanted his power!

We took it upon ourselves to resolve this beef by meeting with council members and the mayor. Councilmember Michael Brown told us they were worried about us. He said, "You guys are the only ones who give him credibility in the hood!" Tommy Wells said we were like public figures and people listen to us so we should stick to what we do best! Mayor-for-Life Marion Barry, who is a brilliant political scientist, told me one day outside of Ballou Senior High School that they were going to destroy Fenty.

Barry said, "They had taken a poll of council members Mike Brown, Kwame Brown, and Vince Gray to see who had the best chance of beating him. Then they were going to drop a story on Fenty every month so by the time the election rolled around, he would be bleeding to death from all the stab wounds in his back." I debated Marion Barry during the campaign and, from the feedback I got, the people who saw it thought I won, but of course, the "Mayor for Life" jokes he won.

On May 15, 2009, we met with Vince Gray who said he and Mayor Fenty did not have a beef. Then he said, "We are trying to figure which side you guys are on." We told him we are not on any side except the side of what's right! Before you know it, tear gas and smoke screens were thrown all over Fenty and people like us who became, in Marion Barry's words, collateral damage. Most of the accusations were lies but they thought no one would care after the election. By the time the smoke cleared and we were vindicated, it was too late. Vince Gray was the new mayor, we were all but out of business, and my name and reputation were smeared.

Everything that came out showed we were clean and, at worst, could have done better administratively, but there were no finding of corruption of any kind. It was also clear who was corrupt but the fact that the council hires the people who investigate them, they get to choose who to bother with these politically motivated investigations that cost District residents hundreds of thousands of dollars for nothing and there's not a chance they would be corrected if the U.S. attorney and FBI didn't find a reason to penetrate this platinum mess! All of this from a council that refused to apply its own ethics rules to itself. These are the people who think they are entitled to govern us! Not over my dead body!

Once these attacks started, I did everything in my power to expose these crooks as they met behind closed doors to do whatever they could to ensure I could not feed my family. This is a principle in the art of war. I was told by a respected journalist if you mess with the king of the jungle, you better take him down or you will regret you ever took him on. In fact, Civil Rights Republican Harriet Tubman said it best, "Never wound a snake; kill it." During this time, I would flashback to a lesson taught me by a civil rights icon that if you do the right things for the right reasons you will get the right results, so I was confident Vince Gray would have his day. I would stay at it even if it had grave consequences for me. Look at the YouTube video called "Don't Leave Us Fenty" which was collaboration with rapper Big Wax and a production company called the Connoisseurs. This video accurately predicted everything that would happen if Gray was elected.

Dorothy Height and Maya Angelou

Given that 65 percent of African-American women voted in the 2008 presidential election, you probably wouldn't want to appear to have disrespected two civil rights icons. Vince Gray and his allies, once again, beat a politically naïve mayor in the game of politics. It all started when the Fenty administration decided not to renew the lease with Cora Masters Barry at the Washington Tennis Center. I must say this was an excellent program. I was familiar with it through a family member who participated in it.

I asked the mayor why the program didn't stay at the Tennis Center. This was one of the battles I didn't win and something we did not agree on. I even attended the rally held to keep the program open and I told him I was going to do so. This is what I meant when I told Vince Gray I was on the side of what is right. I never hesitated to disagree with or take a stand against Mayor Fenty or anyone else.

I knew this mistake could ultimately cost him the reelection because women in America are deciding factors in elections especially in urban areas. Vince Gray, Cora Masters Barry, Marion Barry, informed the media Mayor Fenty refused to meet with Dorothy Height and Maya Angelou, two iconic civil rights leaders, about keeping the Tennis Center open. Of course, I thought to myself, "What the hell is he doing? You can't publicly disrespect these women." I remembered as a child Dorothy

Height used to sit in my aunt's living room for strategy sessions and to socialize.

After weeks of negative press about this matter, I actually asked him, "What the hell are you all doing, why aren't you all meeting with these women?" I later found out none of it was true. It was all misinformation deliberately put out by the mayor's enemies. It was brought to my attention it was the two women who canceled the first two meetings. Then the last time they wanted to meet for two hours and the mayor could only do one hour.

I also found out Maya Angelou wrote a letter to Mayor Fenty stating that she was at peace and didn't feel disrespected. She did not want her name to be used in any negative way for other people's purposes. I asked them, "Why haven't you all gotten this letter out to the media? Do you know what this is going to do with black women?" Washington Post columnist Courtland Milloy later wrote that the mishandling of this situation all but eliminated Fenty's change of winning an election in which black women would be the deciding factor.

Dr. Angelou's letter of September 10, 2009 reads:

Dear Mayor Fenty:

This letter brings best wishes for you, yours, and your dream. I want you to know that I have not spoken to the press and it was never my intent to bogart or jam you against a wall.

I agree with the biblical encouragement to be a peacemaker. I want to be there and I am also a peace bringer. I do not wait to arrive at a destination to make peace, rather, I bring it with me when I leave me home.

Please know that my intention in the matter of the sports facility was to be a bridge over which opposing agents could cross and find peaceful solutions.

I know that my name has been used in varying ways, but while I am a friend of Mrs. Cora Masters Barry, and a supporter of her great efforts, I in no way meant to be a threat or a negative figure to you in this matter.
I pray that this letter conveys my best wishes to you.

Joy!

Maya Angelou

Maya Angelou

September 10, 2009

The Honorable Adrian M. Fenty
Mayor of the District of Columbia
Wilson District Building
1331 Pennsylvania Avenue, NW, 5th Floor
Washington, DC 20004

Dear Mayor Fenty,

This letter brings best wishes for you, yours, and your dream. I want you to know that I have not spoken to the press and it was never my intent to bogart or jam you against a wall.

I agree with the biblical encouragement to be a peacemaker. I want to be there and I am also a peace bringer. I do not wait to arrive at a destination to make peace; rather, I bring it with me when I leave my home.

Please know that my intentions in the matter of the sports facility was to be a bridge over which opposing agents could cross and find peaceful solutions.

I know that my name has been used in varying ways, but while I am a friend of Mrs. Cora Masters Barry, and a supporter of her great efforts, I in no way meant to be a threat or a negative figure to you in this matter.

I pray that this letter conveys my best wishes to you.

Joy!

Maya Angelou

Maya Angelou
MA/fho

2240 Valley Road, Winston-Salem, NC 27106

For some reason, Mayor Fenty didn't feel as though it would make a difference and if he put the letter out, it would be disrespectful to these civil rights icons. He allowed me to put the letter out which was far too late and not the same as if it was coming from him. Nikita Stewart, a Washington Post writer, did a story on it, but it was only posted online! This was a major win for Gray in the pursuit of victory because Fenty didn't understand how important it was to address this matter. It also did not help that Ms. Height died shortly before the election.

Councilman Harry Thomas

Harry Thomas called for what seemed like a hundred hearings on the Parks and Recreation Department contracts awarded to Mayor Fenty's fraternity brothers Sinclair Skinner and Omar Karim. Harry gave the impression this was "contract steering" or whatever terms he could come up with to suggest corruption and make the mayor look bad. This had the effect of making black people envious and white people mad about the use of tax payer dollars. All this happened when Harry Thomas was stealing hundreds of thousands dollars as kickbacks from money designated to combat youth violence in his ward.

Skinner was a Fenty campaign organizer. Omar Karim, who managed the project, had graduated from Howard University with dual degrees. Karim is one of two hundred black men in America who graduated with a double degree in law and engineering. He made the cover of Black Enterprise magazine.

Sinclair Skinner meant well, but didn't do Mayor Fenty any favors by not telling him when he thought the mayor was wrong. In my estimation, Sinclair would back off instead of pushing the issue to help Fenty see he was making a mistake. It wasn't that Skinner wanted to intentionally harm the mayor; it just seems to me that he was afraid to challenge him. It is true that many of Adrian's political wounds were self-inflicted, but Skinner's style didn't make things any easier. Sinclair wasn't a likeable guy, he labeled Jim Graham as "Grahamzilla, the black business killa." In hind sight it seems as though everything Skinner said about him is proving to be true.

However, Fenty's and Skinner's weaknesses aside, what Harry Thomas did to those two men was one of the most grave injustices and abuses of power I have ever seen by an elected official.

It didn't seem to matter when an ally of Councilmember Jim Graham, chairman of the Metro Board, seemed to get every contract to build on top of nearly every Metro station in D.C. No one said a word about this until the Sulaimon Brown episode started peeling off the layers of corruption like an onion and Eric Payne's lawsuit gained momentum by revealing classified information.

This Metro land is prime real estate, and yet, the recreation contract hearings dominated the news for months. Payne's credibility would be attacked, but had the resources to fight back with sweat equity since he himself was a lawyer. He filed FOIA (Freedom of Information Act) petition, which showed proof that they tried to destroy him because he would not play ball.

Until recently, no one seemed willing to unseal another one of Jim Graham's scandals. No councilmember would talk about it and no reporter dared to write about it. Was that because they were afraid of the consequences of challenging Graham? When Colby King did write about it, Graham referred to him as Hitler. I consider Jim Graham a gay gangster in a suit who has done more to hurt our community than the gay gang *Check It* ever did. Most of those awarded Metro contracts were honorable people.

What is so interesting and sad about this whole thing is nobody said a thing about all the white friends of Fenty or Gray who got the majority of the contracts. Black or white should not matter, but apparently it does. Skinner was the target of this double standard which is one reason why some conscientious and well educated blacks still accept corruption in D.C. politics.

Neither Councilmember Harry Thomas, other council members, nor any media outlets, except the Washington Times, addressed developers like W. C. Smith who received $500 million in city contracts. It also bothers a lot of people that Smith rarely sub-contracts to black developers or minorities in the District of Columbia. Why the double standard? Why the scrutiny of Omar Karim and not of Smith?

I used my online magazine "The Other Side," to get the truth out to my four thousand subscribers. To their credit Attorney General Peter Nickles and Jeff Anderson of the Washington Times and the Washington Post editorial board all investigated and corroborated my interpretation of events. Unfortunately, by the time the smoke cleared in this case, the election was over and Vincent Gray was the new mayor. The good news is that Adrian Fenty was cleared of all wrongdoing and Harry Thomas is in jail where he belongs.

Councilmember Mary Cheh

Now we come back to City Councilmember Mary Cheh who you read about in regard to the fire truck for the Dominican Republic. Ms. Cheh represents the city's richest residents, supported the candidacy of Vincent Gray and has mysteriously avoided being exposed for her unethical practices. She was another one who was critical of former Mayor Fenty and his contract practices. For some reason, it didn't seem to matter that Fenty got things done with schools, recreation centers, parks, and libraries in all eight wards. All people like Mary Cheh cared about was that out of more than fifty thousand contracts awarded during his tenure, a couple of them went to two of his friends.

Seems like a lot of people came from Chicago and Texas with our last two presidents and benefited from their friendships? It is only natural that a mayor or president would know some people who would be competent to do some work for the government. The question is whether or not it was done in an ethical, fair, and competitive manner.

The hypocrisy of Mary Cheh is that she was guilty of doing some of the same things she accused Fenty of doing, but none of her colleagues on the council said a word. I have already documented that Councilmember Cheh's friend Claire Blotch was awarded a multi-million-dollar project (parcel 69). As reported in the Washington Business Journal, Ms. Cheh did not recuse herself or make their relationship public knowledge. She held roundtables and voted on this project which was for 500,000 square feet, which included a fire station.

Nothing will ever be made of this because Ms. Cheh is a good politician. She is an ally of Jim Graham and she was smart enough to not call for hearings on Harry Thomas. Best not to be too curious about what Harry Thomas had in his closet when she had her own skeletons in the closet! When a small article was written about this in the Washington Business Journal, she raised hell and tried to tear down the reporter.

Fenty's staff did not want to expose this and it was a big mistake as far as public perception. He could have exposed Gray, Thomas, Graham, and Cheh and put them on public notice that they were not above the law. It was naïve of the mayor to think he did not have to tell his side of the story. He was a political novice, but to his credit, he did not believe in tearing people down. This is an admirable trait, but at the end of the day, it might have cost him an election he should have won.

Now, it is Adrian Fenty who many praise around the country while the corruption of the Gray campaign and administration are bringing shame on our great city. A story by Bruce Johnson of WUSA Channel 9 in Washington, D.C. revealed President Obama himself wanted no association with D.C. Democratic leaders, particularly Mayor Gray.

Councilmember Yvette Alexander

Councilmember Alexander herself came under fire and was investigated for what turned out to be something unimaginable. She spent less than 5 percent of her constituents' services fund on the poorest citizens in her Ward for whom the money was designated. These funds were to be used for utility bills, rent, funerals, and things of that nature! This is not surprising given that it comes from the same woman who told a group of her constituents in front of the Wilson Building, "I do not like people who drop out of school and don't elevate themselves."

That's fact, not propaganda, but she was saved by OCF (Office of Campaign Finance) because they did not conduct an audit and never made her produce receipts. She was fined a mere four thousand dollars. She hid the fact that she paid a consultant from a company that did not exist and used checks from her constituents' fund. She even had the nerve to send the checks to his home address and allegedly used the constituents fund card to buy alcohol in Stan's, a downtown hot spot!

This is all totally illegal and unethical but this is how things are done all too often in the Nation's Capital. Crooked politicians can tear down good people while at the same time protecting themselves from responsibility for their deliberate illegal or questionable acts. Ms. Alexander would later shed tears on the City Council Dais saying during a hearing, "Any of us could be walking out of here in handcuffs."

I won't let her get away with this as I prepare to make certain people hear the truth during my campaign. If I can withstand an audit, she, as an elected official, should be forced to pass the smell test, too. Win or lose I will follow the lead of A. Phillip Randolph, a great Civil Rights Republican who said, "Nothing counts but pressure, pressure, more pressure, and still more pressure through organized, aggressive, mass pressure." I worked with the people in the community like Jeri Washington and Lisa Shaw to bring this topic to the surface and will work with them to get the truth out just as I did Vince Gray and Harry Thomas. They were so busy putting their feet on people's throats, they did not see they were off-balance and easy targets!

There would be other scandals on the council involving both white and black members. What hurt was to be attacked by the same people who had previously touted the work of Peaceoholics and my service to the community. I had become an enemy to people I had once loved and respected.

People like Gray, Thomas, Cheh, and Alexander expect you to either be silent about their corruption or to become corrupt yourself. When Vincent Gray met with me privately and told me to pick a side, he was speaking for all corrupt politicians in D.C. An honest politician would have been satisfied with my answer that I was on the side of what is right. I know Adrian Fenty still respects me because I supported him, but I never hesitated to tell him the truth as I saw it either publicly or privately. If I thought what he was doing was not good for the people, I spoke up.

Politricks Come Home to Roost

The Bible says that vengeance belongs to the Lord. I am not God. My job is to keep fighting the battles and to let God bring victory for the people and justice to the corrupt politicians who are enemies of the people. In the spirit of "what goes around comes around," I offer the following evidence for your consideration.

Exhibit 1

During Vince Gray's campaign, he showed my picture in a television ad as a $10 million crony for Mayor Fenty. On the campaign trail, he said disingenuous things like, "I'm going to stop play for pay politics and I'm going to eliminate the Peaceoholics gravy train!" Yes, little ole Ron was so much of a threat that I was attacked in a campaign ad. It did not say we received our first direct city funding from Jack Evans, a white City Council member who appreciated our work years before Fenty became mayor. Go back to Mayor Anthony Williams' State of the District speech in 2006 and listen to him praise Jauhar, Peaceoholics and me for working tirelessly in our community. Why did they praise us? Why did they fund us? It was because we were the answer to problems that few others could solve, not because they loved us.

Gray's accusation that we were part of "play for pay" doesn't make any sense. We legitimately received funding for our work. It was precisely because we would not play ball in return for being funded is what made Gray and his cronies hate us. We did not funnel a percentage of the funding we got from the city back to politicians as kickbacks for earmarks. We earned the funding we received with results, we did not have to promise, nor would we ever promise kickbacks in return for funding.

The real problem for Team Gray was that results like ours did not just get us funded. Our results also gave us credibility with the community. The Gray campaign understood they had to make this attack ad against me because people in our communities were listening to me. I went on television and did what nobody in the Fenty Camp could do. I beat Marion Barry in a Debate on Fox 5, but I did it making it clear I have always had great respect and love for him for what he did as mayor for the people of D.C.

I also whipped Mo Ellibee in a debate on a News Channel 8 Talk show. He and his wife were political consultants for Hillary Clinton and for the Obama campaign. We debated a second time and he had to acknowledge I was right about Vince Gray and even criticized his old boss. I had a cousin in their camp who told me they had meetings about me every day to figure out how they were going to deal with me. Why? For one, I joined Team Fenty and we registered many new voters.

The Go-Go Coalition initiative that I helped create registered more new voters through Go-Go music events and videos than Fenty's campaign did through the entire campaign. Unfortunately, we could not use it to our maximum advantage. We had it set up to take thousands of people to the D.C. Stadium Armory Complex to a big Go-Go after they voted but a week before the election, the campaign received a letter from the Justice Department telling us we could not do this. Of course, it was okay for Vince Gray and his shadow campaign to feed seniors on the bus, tell them who to vote for, take them to the polls and pay them off with ten-dollar gift cards. They got away with it and, Vince Gray won and is the mayor, for the moment anyway.

Within a few months of taking office, scandals and rumors of scandals came in waves and have not stopped since. Columnists immediately began questioning the new mayor about things like the fence built around his property tied to a local developer and supporter. I heard through a friend of mine that he had a conversation with one of the contractor's employees who bragged about the fact that they did much more than just build the fence at Gray's house. I used that information in my role as a strategist for Mayor Fenty.

Vince Gray told a sitting councilmember that he blames me and will never forget that I cost him fifteen thousand dollars in legal fees to defend himself against allegations about the illegal work he had done. Remember that it was Vince Gray who first politicized the work of Peaceoholics by telling me that I had to choose sides. Destroying me and Peaceoholics is a personal vendetta for Vince Gray for the black eye I gave him.

One article cited fallen leadership and embarrassment for the city and called for Gray to resign and for Fenty to come back. Most notably was the Sulaimon Brown hiring scandal in which Mayor Gray's ally and friend Howard Brooks paid Brown to attack Mayor Fenty. The Gray shadow campaign wanted Brown to stay in the race just to bash Fenty. Brown also said the mayor knew and was a part of what Gray called

"Pay-to-Play" politics. Gray disingenuously claimed he would stop that practice.

It was exposed in the Washington Post that Gray tried to steer $10 million from the United Medical Center to Loraine Green's boyfriend, Howard Brooks. Loraine Green is a longtime friend of Gray and a key advisor. Brooks ended up wearing a wire for the feds in their investigation of the pay-to-play campaign. Now prosecutors have asked he be spared prison because he is what Gray's friends call a snitch because he was part of organized corruption and trying to save his own skin. Don't be surprised if you read about him or a scapegoat of his going to jail.

Exhibit 2

I advised Mayor Fenty's campaign to expose Harry Thomas' corruption because the media would not address Gray's troubled past. They refused to ask why the Department of Human Services went into receivership under Gray's leadership. The Thomas hearings were all political maneuvering and were more damaging than anything in the campaign besides the Dorothy Height/Maya Angelou episode.

The news would finally break when Tim Day and the DCGOP exposed it and this time the people listened. I had talked about it during council hearings and in my online magazine, but people really needed to hear it from Adrian. He could have made this an issue but as I said before, he wanted to keep his campaign positive; this was a political miscalculation. When you are fighting against a bunch of gangsters in suits who specialize in misleading people, you have to fight back.

Keep in mind most of the media chose to believe what this crook Harry Thomas was saying about me rather than what I was saying about him. He was a city councilmember and I was just a guy from the hood who was a community organizer, activist, and had given everything to help the people. I reiterate what I have said before about D.C. politics, results don't matter. It did not matter that I was the co-founder and the face of a nonprofit organization that squashed forty plus gang beefs, employed hundreds of people, and got kids into and through college.

Harry Thomas entered a plea bargain and was sentenced to 38 months in a relatively luxurious prison. From what I hear is that he is doing a lot of crying! He shamelessly stole more than $300,000 from the city while the Trinidad neighborhood in his own Ward 5 was under siege. We assisted in stopping riots in that community after the Park Police killed what the community believed was an innocent man. Remember, fifteen people were killed while military-style roadblocks were put in place. It also has been exposed through an audit that he used sixty thousand dollars in cash to pay for an Audi truck for personal use, not to do the work of the people. Yet, none of the crooked seven was willing to speak out against him.

Exhibit 3

Councilmember Yvette Alexander used her power to call for an audit to put out the perception that our organization was doing something wrong. She was more invisible in Ward 7 than Casper the Friendly Ghost. I operated more like the councilmember fighting in City Hall for the people and finding ways to uplift the community. She made it seem as if I was doing something wrong because I was exposing Vince Gray's corruption. I was behind the scenes finding the truth and learning things only the FBI should be able to find out.

With Adrian Fenty, councilmember and future mayor of Washington, D.C.

Fenty's grassroots messaging would become awesome. We made it so people in many areas east of the river started getting the facts and not the fiction. Unfortunately, this initiative came late in the game and with the shadow campaign it was like playing against loaded dice. This was after candidate Gray alongside Yvette Alexander put out propaganda and lies stating, "Fenty does not care about black people and he only built dog parks for yuppies west of the river." How could he say this with all of the new recreation centers, libraries, schools, and parks Fenty had built east of the river? Gray also put it out that he was going to address the changes Fenty made to the public school system.

So, how did Yvette Alexander's chickens come home to roost? For one thing, as mentioned earlier, she was exposed for spending only 5 percent of her constituents fund money on its intended recipients who are the poorest and neediest citizens in her ward. We aren't talking about affluent Cleveland Park where few people need government help. Forty percent of Ward 7 residents receive some kind of government assistance. It is inexcusable that she spent less than 5 percent of the funds to help families pay for utility bills, funerals, and college assistance.

There were also illegal things done with the money, but once again, the City Council hired the investigators to investigate its own members. That's like a drug dealer being investigated by one of its runners! So this has yet to come out because she was never required to produce the receipts which would have proven campaign violations and misuse of funds.

There is a saying that people in glass houses should not throw stones. It was only a matter of time before these stone throwers destroyed the glass house of corruption they built. They threw stones at me and I fired them right back. That is all Mayor Fenty needed to do during the campaign but he tried to stay out of the mud and it cost him the election.

Adrian needs to learn from his mistakes if he plans to return to politics. I am not saying he needs to use dirty tactics like Gray and his shadow campaign. But when you are hit with false accusations, you have to counterpunch. In my case, it would have been wise to stay out of this, but Gray was a man I admired at one time. He just did not give me any options, so I had no choice but to come out swinging.

A Washington Post article entitled "Fenty's Terrible Week in Washington" cited a poll that showed two-thirds of District voters thought Fenty did a lot and was diligent. In spite of those numbers, he still lost. I believe in talent and results; it's great if a candidate is charming, but don't vote based on style points. It should be about the results they produce and whether they are more qualified than their opponents.

I realize we both lost big. We can't deny that. He lost the mayor's race, Peaceoholics was defunded, and my reputation was temporarily tarnished. For now, we both have the satisfaction of watching as the people who won the battle are losing the war. One by one, they are resigning in disgrace; some are marching off to prison and others are not sleeping well at night waiting for a subpoena or a knock on the door by law enforcement. Since these crooks and their politricks are being exposed, maybe the people can learn to take a closer look at the dog that brings them the bones.

Conclusion

There are plenty of politricks that have not been addressed here and there will always be corrupt politicians to come up with new and creative ones. If they spent more time finding solutions that work than they do thinking up ways to fleece the people, they would win reelection every time. For now, they seem to believe they are in office for the special interests and to enrich their friends, not to serve WE THE PEOPLE!

I want people to watch us all closely for the results we produce. I don't want them to be moved by a man's looks or style, but his character, deeds, and spirit. A prime example is Bill Clinton. He did a lot to help blacks in America, but he also did a lot of harm as well. With the stroke of his pen, he signed a law preventing people with criminal records to return home if their families live in public housing.

These laws are very damaging because you cannot build a healthy village, community, city, or nation without family. In many cases, the black girl will always have her mother's shoes to walk in, but too often, the black male will not have his father's shoes to walk in, unless he is following him to prison. A recent New York Times article reported that this was devastating to the black family and has enhanced generations of poverty in our communities. It is easy to find examples of the media blaming Republicans, but unless you do your own research, you will never know about the negative role of policies like those of Bill Clinton.

Vince Gray became mayor because black people were angry with Mayor Fenty. Gray is corrupt, but he can do the Electric Slide, but what price will we pay for this silliness? Only time will tell, but I'm willing to bet he will continue to take us backwards as long as he is in office. Sadly, while giving the illusion that the city is moving forward, the very people who put him in office are the ones who are suffering.

It seems like Gray and his partners in crime (literally) on the council, on his campaign staff, and among his supporters have all the juice. All we got were inflated traffic and parking ticket fees, speed trap cameras everywhere, oppressive regulations, and the loss of pride in D.C. politics. Mayor Gray took seven years to get his traffic tickets paid, but he expects the average citizen to pay in thirty days or the fine doubles. Now he holds endless press conferences telling us that everything is better now that he is the mayor when, in fact, things are much worse.

Once again, we have been set up to be treated like second class citizens. We look like fools fighting for statehood as our local politicians fight to silence those who stand up for the rights of the people and refuse to clean up the corruption among themselves! More than 140 years ago Frederick Douglass of the D.C. Republican Party said, "Regarding their political rights residents of the Nation's Capital are not really citizens, but aliens in their own country."

Thanks to Vince Gray and his cronies, our city has been set back in the eyes of many to where we were before home rule. The question is this: who should we blame and where do we go from here in our local and national politics?

Lesson Five

Weathering the Storm

If there is no struggle, there is no progress. Those who profess to favor and yet deprecate agitation are men who want crops without plowing up the ground, they want rain without the thundering and lightening, they want the ocean without the awful roar of its many waters. This struggle may be a moral one; or it may be a physical one; or it may be both moral and physical; but it must be a struggle.

—Frederick Douglass, Civil Rights Republican

It had been a long draining day when we left Oak Hill Youth Rehabilitation Center, in Laurel, MD. After two straight years of volunteering, helping them turn a hostile and unsafe environment into a miracle with Rev. Cole and the superintendent. The majority of the Oak Hill staff was scared to do what it would take to pull off this miracle inside this hostile institution. We had to defy all security rules in order to pull rival neighborhoods to the gym to hit the problem head on. This was worth the chance because all traffic in the institution was put to a halt. There was no school, food had to be brought to the dirty units, and no one was even allowed to walk to the cafeteria because nobody could walk to the cafeteria or school without a melee breaking out.

Two hours later, the youth left in tears, hugging their rivals, Barry Farms and Condon Terrace together in an institution, something that hadn't been done in twenty years. This miracle would save the institution millions of dollars by eliminating the need for staff overtime. Beefs inside the institution influenced and ignited conflicts on the street which also affected our community. As, always after we pulled off a miracle by the grace of God, we looked at how crazy we were for even taking the risk.

This gave us a temporary high. Jauhar and I walked out of the door with our mentees and trained mediator Big G, AKA Slim Charles from HBO's "The Wire." I got into my beat-up car in the dark and as I drove down the Baltimore-Washington Parkway my car cut off. I had run out of gas and had no money to buy any. It really hit me, I had basically spent nine years volunteering since coming home from federal prison and working out my redemption by pulling off miracles like the one we just did at Oak Hill and I didn't have gas money. Two years of working in Oak Hill with no compensation gave us plenty of awards but not a dime to pay the bills. This was a time when the gas in my house in River Terrace was off and I had to heat our bath water in the microwave for my son Tavon, who I was raising by myself. I did the same to give my daughter, Yasmeen, her baths when she visited.

Two days after this happened, "Reddz," a guy who I did some time with and who was real tight with Cornell Jones, a former drug kingpin, visited me. I met him outside of my house. He tried to convince me the answer to all my troubles would be to get pounds of weed from him. The first thing that came to my mind was Anthony Nugent, a brother who I loved so much and was incarcerated with. At one time in his life, he was a kingpin of the R Street Crew. Anthony left the game but had caught some bad breaks and had financial trouble. He had been desperate just like I was then. Anthony took five kilos of cocaine from a guy, a so-called friend, and was set up.

Nugent was given life in prison. I have never forgotten what he told me, "Moe, I would rather be a bum on the street than spend the rest of my life in jail." I snapped out of it and told "Reddz" I changed my life for good and I will never go back to destroying my family and community. I would rather be a bum on the street first. I really thank God for my experience with Nugent. It makes me realize how a word of wisdom to someone can really have an influence on a person's life.

That was all good but wasn't going to help stop my clothes and belongings from being thrown on the street as I was about to be evicted. At that point, I was three months behind on my rent. It had been two years since I held my last job as the Health and Physical Education instructor at the Village Learning Center Public Charter School. I called Jauhar and said, "Brother, I can't do this for free anymore." We put out fires in Ballou S.H.S. after the shooting and homicide in the Barry Farms and Condon Terrace beef. We put fires out in Oak Hill and we can't get a dime while all these ineffective people roll out of the institution with 22's on their expensive vehicles. My stuff is about to be out on the street. He said, "Let's call and tell them our plight. We can't do this for free anymore." We also remembered what Dr. Donald Johnson told us, "Don't forget, if they don't pay you for your skills they don't respect you." Rev. Cole got to work and said, "We have to have you all."

The head honcho, Mr. York, pushed for emergency funding for us, but it would take at least thirty days. Once again before Tommy Well's and Mayors Fenty's tenure it was understood that we had a unique talent when it came to this work. We were still desperate and needed cash fast or my belongings would be on the street. Jauhar wasn't faring much better than I. His bills were behind too. So, we went to see a pastor we worked with in various stages of the Million Man March and whose church I attended at that time. We talked and explained our plight of desperation and needs to Rev. Willie Wilson. He gave each of us $3,500. That was amazing to me. I don't know too many preachers who give money to the soldiers who struggle and work in the communities outside of their churches. There might be some, but there aren't many.

Thirty days later, we got our first government funding of $40,000. It came through a third party fiduciary while we awaited our 501(c)(3) certification. We were on our way. We went from $40,000 to over $15 million in government contracts in a seven year period. It reminded me of going from $150 to $150,000 in six months when I was a drug dealer except this time, it was done the right way. This is what we teach young people: life is about making choices and decisions with full awareness of both the negative and positive consequences.

Months later, I found out "Reddz" set up a host of people including a close friend of my father's from the old school. Reddz had mentioned my name and if I would have taken the same bait offered to Nugent, I wouldn't be talking about the miracle at Oak Hill or the miracle of how God provided through Rev. Wilson. These were all storms I had to weather in order for the flowers to bloom in my life.

This same lesson has once again allowed me to weather the storm in which people were given orders by top officials, including Vince Gray to annihilate Ron Moten. They almost did. I came very close to being homeless like many others we see every day in the streets of the Nation's Capital. I didn't steal to get back on my feet. I'm fighting through the storm and often feel like I am alone in a tornado. As always, I will never give up until the flowers bloom again because I've been in this familiar territory before. I know there is a way to get out a positive message for the people in our city who have been forgotten.

If you are not willing to go through the storm, then you are not worthy of the treasures that come from the pain of doing what is right. Weathering the storm is just another way to say you are willing to drink muddy water. Too many people have already given their lives for me to stop now just because there is no money and the winds and waves of the storm are raging. I always told our staff when they were being trained, "Dance in the rain until the flowers bloom."

6

Returned Citizens

With malice toward none and charity toward all….
—Abraham Lincoln, Civil Rights Republican

The Nation's Capital is often looked upon as a catalyst for change or even sometimes social experiments. What we did in D.C. to level the playing field for ex-offenders began with the symbolism of getting rid of the very term "ex-offender." I am an ex-offender myself and I know the challenges and how grateful I was to get an opportunity right after my release to work at Cease Fire Don't Smoke the Brothers. When I was at Peaceoholics, I held informal discussions with leaders of this population in D.C. on how to do more for what we called, not ex-offenders, but "returned citizens."

Out of those informal meetings, I helped co-found a group called Returned Citizens United. As President Obama said, "Words matter." Words are powerful and people who are labeled "ex-offenders" are being told their future is defined only by their past. So, we worked with and set up a kind of think-tank with a group of ex-offenders to change the way we refer to ourselves. We refused to use the term "ex-offenders" or "ex-convicts" to refer to a population that includes celebrities like Martha Stewart who are never labeled with those words. The meetings were initially held at the offices of Peaceoholics and gave birth to the concept of "returned citizens."

People with criminal records understand that we have to live with the immediate and long-term consequences of our actions when applying for jobs and living with people's natural caution or suspicion about someone who has been in prison. It was our belief that it is already hard enough to make a fresh start without being labeled as a felon or an ex-convict. For example, returned citizens who committed felonies lose their right to vote except in D.C., the right to public assistance, and the right to live in government subsidized housing even to move in with their own families.

We fought for everyone released from prison back into our communities, with the exception of proven sex offenders, to be officially referred to as returned citizens and not ex-offenders or felons. As a direct result of our efforts, the D.C. City Council changed the name of the D.C. Office for Ex-Offender Affairs to the Office for Returned Citizen Affairs and directed local government officials to use this terminology.

No returned citizen I know, including myself, wants anything other than a fair chance to get housing and a job. This does not seem too much to ask if it is really true we have "paid our debt to society." Eventually, flawed legislation was passed in D.C. to help returned citizens obtain employment. We still have a long way to go because laws are not always enforced, have too many loopholes, or have no teeth. We don't want to be considered heroes. What we want is to get a fresh start like those who left England for the "New World" and every other immigrant since then who has come to this great country with the hope of a better life. Even many of them were "returned citizens" in their home countries. Without second chances, there might not be an America as we know it today.

Citizenship is something African Americans waited a long time to achieve. Even "free" blacks were not given full citizenship in the Constitution. Our hope has always been in the "Idea of America," not necessarily the reality. That idea is expressed in the Declaration of Independence by the words "all men are created equal." With the mass incarceration of black men since 1980, our citizenship is again in jeopardy and we thought being called returned citizens would restore some sense of dignity and create hope for a fresh start. Our people unjustly provided America with 400 years of free labor. The majority of those who have been in prison simply want a second chance to make positive contributions to the same communities our crimes damaged.

Over the years, a number of people have tried to take credit for the phrase "returned citizen." Charles Thornton, one of the guys in the meetings, later claimed the name was his idea. This upset me because I had brought this man to the meetings. We had many local activists such as Yango Sawyer, Johnny Boy, Debra, Jerry, Cornell Jones from American Gangster, and Lynch-Bey who was a Lorton Prison and street icon, all at the table and were part of the group that came up with the name. This was one of several times others took credit for something I was part of and just outright stole our intellectual property.

This Charles Thornton was nominated to be the Director of the Office of Returned Citizens Affairs by Mayor Vincent Gray in return for campaign favors and not because he was competent to do the job. Unfortunately, he left the returned citizen population hanging because he was more caught up on having a position than standing up for the people he is supposed to represent! In short, he proved himself to be a true friendnemy!

When I approached him on his position on video visits, which I and most other D.C. residents opposed, he said that they were being done all around the country. Only Vince Gray, the new warden, and Charles Thornton supported the idea. This let me know that he was the kind of person who would do anything for a job even when it did not serve the best interests of those incarcerated or their families.

I soon learned to be careful who I invited to sit in on our meetings. We did not need back-biting crabs in barrel hindering the decision-making process because they are unable to put aside their own personal agenda. Once again, we went back to networking with more young adults, including a brilliant lawyer named Rodney Mitchell, who was a returned citizen, and a few respected elders who loved sharing wisdom with young men on the rise.

Rodney was the first director of the Office of Ex-Offender Affairs before its name was changed. We shot for the stars to achieve human and civil rights for returned citizens. We only made it to the clouds, but returned citizens in D.C. were in a better situation than the returned citizens in other American cities. We testified and advocated at City Council hearings, worked behind the scenes, held protest marches, and much more.

One protest really stands out in my mind. We helped organize a protest with Returned Citizens United in front of the D.C. Chamber of Commerce. I am not sure what CEO Barbara Lang was thinking but they came out with cookies and juice as if we were homeless or crack heads. All of a sudden everyone was chanting, "JOBS NOT COOKIES." I told her I respected her for doing her job very well, but now it was time for us to do our job.

When the legislation again came up for a vote, the majority of politicians did not just turn their backs on me or Peaceoholics, but on all returned citizens. Then City Councilmember Michael Brown, who promised to support our efforts to pass human rights legislation for returned citizens, voted against the bill when it came up for a vote. As I write this, news comes that Michael Brown is pleading guilty to taking a $55,000 bribe. FBI agents posed as a company who wanted Brown to assist them in obtaining CBE (Certified Business Enterprise) certification for disadvantaged minority businesses in D.C. Now that Mr. Brown faces the possibility of jail time, maybe we can get him to support the Human Rights for Returned Citizens' bill.

It was part of Barbara Lang's job to keep laws in place that stopped returning citizen from moving into certain housing even though many of the real estate developers she represented received hundreds of millions of dollars in government subsidies and tax abatements! But the bigger issues were that jobs and housing were being denied to returned citizens based on their criminal records. Statistics show that a lower percentage of returned citizens commit crimes on the job than those without criminal records.

Ironically, it was the disastrous Yvette Alexander, Amin Muslim, Barry Harrison episode I recounted in Chapter 3 that turned out to be a blessing in disguise. This was the event God used to bring about a change in the practice of denying jobs to returned citizens simply because their FBI background check or SBC shows they have a criminal record.

You will remember Yvette Alexander's constituent services director, Amin Muslim, called me and asked if I would please look out for his brother, Barry Harrison. He told me Barry had a petty drug charge and a twenty-year-old robbery charge on his record. His MPD background check did not come up with anything more. We felt like there was no reason not to trust Amin and the MPD report.

What Amin did not tell us and our SBC normally would have revealed was that Barry had served twenty years on a murder charge. Unfortunately, without that critical information, I accepted Barry under our Project Empowerment contract with the DOES program to institutionalize our Rebuild the Village Model® at Ballou, Spingarn, Cardozo, and Dunbar High Schools, and Hart Middle School. Barry was assigned to Spingarn.

I got a heartbreaking call one day informing me that Barry had been kicked out of Spingarn for a confrontation with a female student. However, it was the action taken by DCPS and Peaceoholics after the incident ended that had a positive result for returned citizens and DCPS students in D.C. DCPS decided to throw me and everyone associated with Peaceoholics out of all of the schools where we were providing services. This included the schools where we had contracted for the Rebuild the Village Model. We agreed that Barry had to be removed from the program. We had fired him ourselves, but DCPS decided to ban Peaceoholics, which was like throwing out the baby with the dirty bathwater.

At the same time, but unrelated to the Barry Harrison episode, DCPS began to review every employee's background and fired everyone who had a criminal record. That purged me and many of our Peaceoholics staff and interns. DCPS removed many of our staff without due process even though they had become productive citizens. Some had worked for DCPS for more than a decade. So, based on our standing in the Barry Harrison case, we fought DCPS and, after a long battle to have a majority of our staff reinstated, we won.

We were not fighting to have employers in the District ignore the criminal record of job applicants. We were fighting to have DCPS institute a policy and a process that would allow returned citizens the opportunity to show potential employers their past mistakes did not pose any more of a risk than the "clean" background check of any other employee. We excluded sex offenders and murderers from this process. We also did not want employers to be required to hire returned citizens whose crimes were related to the area of employment. For example, banks did not have to consider anyone convicted of bank robbery.

The result was that DCPS had to follow the law that prohibits employers from discriminating against job applicants for having criminal records. The only exceptions were those convicted of violent crimes against children, seniors, or animals or crimes related to the areas in which they would be working. So, when I talk about how many people got employment through Peaceoholics, those numbers do not include the hundreds of returned citizens who were able to stay on their jobs or who got their jobs back after being unlawfully fired from jobs in the District, especially by DCPS.

They later told us Jauhar and I could enter the building and work. We told them this is a systemic problem that needs to be fixed and this decision affected the 60,000 returned citizens in the District of Columbia. We also found out at the same time, DCPS was laying off staff in the schools with records before the Barry Harrison incident. So their fight was, indirectly, our fight and most of them never knew that if it wasn't for Peaceoholics and the Barry Harrison episode, most of them would have been terminated.

We called Rodney Mitchell and negotiated a deal that ensured children's safety but was fair to qualified individuals who deserved a second chance. As long as you have not committed a crime against children animals or seniors you would be reviewed on a case-by-case basis in which character references from churches, community leaders, school and your personal interview would be the deciding factors of receiving your clearance! The majority of our staff passed the test although we had a few disappointments among some of our most effective people!

This was another situation where it was not about us but about the people! We would also push for Metro Transit Authority to continue hiring returned citizen after negative media attention concerning a few bad apples who had committed crimes. Of course, these stories do not mention that this was out of hundreds of returned citizens hired by Metro. Many of these drive bus routes that are in sections of the city that are dangerous and avoided by many people.

Metro continued to hire returned citizens, but now there is a probationary period that has to be achieved without any new charges being brought. As our city continues to change, I wonder if the requirements with change for Metro like it did for MPD. This resulted in fewer and fewer blacks on the police force.

Things have only gone backwards under Mayor Gray who came to office under a cloud of scandal. His administration is now reviewing the staffs in agencies like the Department of Recreation and DCPS targeting people with criminal records. So, the hard work we had done was, to a great extent, poured down the drain by the man most returned citizens voted for or, more accurately, their names were stolen and used to cast fraudulent votes for in a corrupted election. We are back to square one. Very few from the returned citizen population are obtaining employment in D.C. We have gone from a proud Chocolate City to a Corrupt City whose city government is a punch line for late night comedians.

Time after time our elected officials have acted shamefully. For example, during my campaign for City Council, I had a debate on News Channel 8 with the incumbent Yvette Alexander moderated by Bruce Depuyt. By all accounts, I beat her handily on the issues. What was her response? In spite of directives for city employees to use the term returned citizens, this six-year City Council member was reduced to using third-grade name calling tactics by responding with, "You're a felon, you're a felon!"

When advocates testified before the City Council for the Human Rights Bill, they asked Ms. Alexander how she could be against the bill when Amin Muslim, her director for constituent services, is a returned citizen himself. Her response, "If I had known I probably would not have hired him."

It was a source of great satisfaction and pride for me that many of our returned citizens no longer came back into our communities and preyed upon our people. But it's even tougher for them today. There is both a lack of unity in the population and because of the lack of opportunities for those in need. For example, as reported in the Washington Informer, I worked with leaders such as Yango Sawyer to register as many as three thousand returned citizens to vote out of a returned citizen population of sixty-thousand. Imagine if we were to mobilize 20 percent of them. We would then have the political power to institutionalize incubator businesses to begin hiring more and more of the returned citizen population. This is one of many solutions that would work, not only in Washington, D.C. but throughout urban America.

Yet Mayor Gray claims things are better now. It is obvious to anyone who is being honest that there is a lot of work to do. The struggle goes on as each generation builds upon the previous one. I thank God however, that I was co-founded an organization that did something to create opportunities for returned citizens and to take away the hurtful labels that stripped them of their dignity.

Participants in a reenactment of Bloody Sunday on the famous Edmund Pettus Bridge in Selma, Alabama. Their T-shirts ask a very important question: "EX-FELON, DO YOU COUNT?"

Lesson Six

Speaking Truth to Power

Criminals are not the only people who abuse our communities and get away with it because of the silence of citizens. Politicians, whether corrupt or just naïve on the issues, do untold damage to our city and its neighborhoods. It is common for politicians to forget everything they promised people once they take their hands off the Bible.

Too often our elected officials cater to the special interests groups while fooling and deceiving the people into thinking they are working in their best interest. They abuse their power and stop progress for the majority of their constituents and only pay attention to the people who can help or hurt them politically. The problem is that too many people in our communities act like residents and not citizens. Our definition of residents is people who reside and defer to others to make decisions for them, which usually are not in their best interests.

Citizens vote, residents don't. Not voting makes you worthless to politicians who only care about you if you vote. They will hand a resident the short end of the stick and get a thank you in return. Politicians only worry about people who can hurt them, help them, or who yell the loudest. If they hand a true citizen the short end of the stick, the citizen takes the stick and beats the politician over the head and votes for someone else in the next election.

So, we understand why it's so instrumental for us to teach our community citizenship is the only direct path to happiness and equality in America. Sometimes, residents sit by and watch this happen before their eyes as if they have a severe case of cataracts. We try to turn residents into citizens by teaching them that silence, according to Dr. Martin Luther King, Jr., is a form of betrayal.

We always say politicians are like children, if you don't correct them when they make little mistakes, then those little mistakes turn into big mistakes. Their actions eventually adversely affect the very people, who didn't hold them accountable, citizens, residents, parents, children, and colleagues. Sometimes they can't get themselves out of the mess they have created and they need our help to keep them from destroying all the greatness God has in store for them.

I use Marion Barry as an example of how we let a great man tarnish his legacy by not correcting him and holding him accountable when he was wrong. We let his weaknesses minimize his influence and effectiveness in serving the people. He has always loved the people of the District of Columbia and was willing to sacrifice his life for us. But he lost his way and we just let him self-destruct.

Once at an early voting site during the heated Fenty-Gray 2010 election, the great master politician, Marion Barry, yelled in a loud, aggressive voice, "Hey, Ron and Jauhar, you can't be intimidating voters like that. You have to stop this!" That comment made it into a Washington Post article. Nearly six months later, we sat down with him and asked why he would do that to us. He said with a smile a campaign was going on at the time. "It's only politics," he said, "don't take it personal. You guys were just collateral damage."

I wish blacks would understand how we failed to be true friends by not being honest with this man who was once our greatest leader. We failed him by never challenging him whenever he strayed wrong. Speaking truth to power is not just a right we have as citizens, but a duty we have to God, country, and to those we elected to serve us in government.

The same is true for President Obama. It says a lot about how far America has come in our attitudes about race that so many whites and Latinos voted for an African American for president. But if having a black president means that I can't criticize him when he does not address our issues just because he is black, then we are judging him by the color of his skin and not the by the effectiveness of his policies. Our democracy only works if WE THE PEOPLE can hold our politicians accountable regardless of their color. If criticizing a black president makes a white critic a racist and a black critic a traitor, then I am afraid it might be a long time before Americans are willing to elect another black president. This attitude also has implications for Latino, Asian, Female, or others who aspire to the presidency.

The exception to the political incorrectness of criticizing a president unless he is a white male is that any and all invective, any of the vilest accusations, and personal attacks are acceptable as long as they are aimed at black, female, or Latino Republicans. Whatever you think of Marco Rubio, Sarah Palin, or Allen West's politics, many liberals and their media supporters engage in vicious personal attacks on them and no one accuses them of racism or sexism. The politics of personal destruction is outrageous behavior.

We need to have the same rules for everyone. First, speaking truth to power in a democracy should mean that any and all criticisms of policies are in bounds and should not be construed as racist or sexist. Second, speaking truth to power does not include personal attacks unless there is evidence of immorality or unethical behavior that would impact directly on a person's ability to serve in elective office.

This second one seems simple enough, but liberal Democrats are sneaky. They call anyone a racist who opposes any of President Obama's policies such as the "Affordable Care Act" (Obama Care). This has to stop if we are going to have an honest debate of the critical issues facing our great country.

Aristotle said, "To avoid criticism, say nothing, do nothing, be nothing," so we first must understand activism is a must. Stevie Wonder, the great singer, said to me in a 2009 phone conversation, "The activism from the grassroots was the only way that the Dr. Martin Luther King, Jr. holiday became a reality." Mr. Wonder was also the spark who started the movement and even though you're the spark, you may not necessarily be the person who finishes the mission or even get the credits for your works.

I also recently talked to Dick Gregory outside of his Rittenhouse Street apartment and I brought up the fact that I was upset I was not able to attend the 100th year birthday celebration for Civil Rights icon Amelia Boynton Robinson, the mother of the voting rights movement and I was sad her accomplishments have been overlooked. He said to me, "Sometimes when you are chosen by the universe, you don't leave any footprints behind." Most people don't know Mr. Gregory chose the people over fame. In fact, he was bigger than Bill Cosby but you will never catch him on 60 Minutes or with a billion dollars in his pockets but he will leave this earth with pride and dignity. He was one of the few famous leaders in the sixties you could witness being put in handcuffs supporting the children during the 1963 Children's March that helped end segregation. What happened to those types of leaders in Hollywood?

To those who live west of the river, I give you some words of wisdom to reflect upon. Dr. Martin Luther King Jr. said, "It may well be that, the greatest tragedy of this period of social transition is not the glaring noisiness of the so-called bad people, but silence of the so-called "good" people. Dante said, "The hottest places in hell are reserved for those who, in times of great moral crisis, maintain their neutrality."

Dr. King said, "It's hardly a moral act to encourage others, to patiently accept injustice which he himself does not endure."

Remember, when the powers rage at you, rage back, fight and don't be a coward, speak up when being oppressed or being denied opportunity to do for self. Remember the words of Winston Churchill, "Never give in. Never give in. Never, never, never, never—in nothing, great or small, large or petty—never give in except to conviction of honor …. Never yield to the apparently overwhelming might of the enemy." Keep in mind the words of Christ, "The truth shall set you free."

Fight on so your soul remains free and your spirit can lift your community and self to greatness.

Speaking at the historic Lincoln Theatre in Washington, D.C. at Peaceoholics' Change Agents Awards in 2008.

7

Citizenship vs. Snitching

The Negro must keep himself, his children, and his home clean and make the surroundings in which he lives comfortable and a attraction. He must learn to "run his community up" not down—we can segregate law, we can integrate by living. Civilization is not a matter of race; it's a matter of standards.
—Nannie Helen Burroughs, Civil Rights Republican

This is a topic we have addressed in our community on many occasions in forums, conferences, workshops, and PSA's. See also my Washington Post op-ed from Sunday August 19th 2007: "The Real Meaning of SNITCHING." The one thing I wanted people to understand was that there is such a thing as "snitching," but there is also such a thing as "citizenship." We do not condone "snitching" and we believe that "citizenship" is a necessity for uplifting our communities and our country.

We all must have a "WE THE PEOPLE," attitude and spirit, not "WE THE FOOLS." If the KKK did a drive-by in the hood, would you call the police? Is that snitching? I asked a group of youth that question at the Oak Hill Youth Reformatory in Laurel, Maryland in 2006 when we first took on this debate in the African-American community. All their hands went up as a "yes" for calling the police or for taking it into their own hands. But hands went down when I asked them, "Is it okay for someone who is not in the streets to call the police when an innocent person is gunned down in the community?"

We teach this to young people and go toe-to-toe with the hardest brothers on the street, with scholars, and with law enforcement on this issue. Our point is that the "street code" that applies to those in the wicked streets is the same as "code blue" for some police and the "code of silence" for corrupt elected officials. That code of silence is in full operation in the John Wilson Building in the District of Columbia. This blatant hypocrisy by people in public office makes it difficult to get the average person to take citizenship seriously.

Many of the City Council members and Mayor Gray have no credibility when it comes to the subject of citizenship. They are, as Jonetta Rose Barras puts it in a Washington Examiner article, "Pimps and Hustler's in D.C." How can they tell the community that reporting a crime is not snitching when they themselves won't call out their own colleagues like Harry Thomas, Jr. for stealing more than three hundred thousand dollars from D.C. children? Then there is Jim Graham who, when it comes to scandals, has gotten himself out of more tight places than Houdini. The same thing happens on the national stage with Jesse Jackson, Jr.'s colleagues not holding him accountable.

Some residents might say, "I don't want to risk my life or career by reporting a crime." I ask, "Didn't Dr. King do it for you? Didn't Dorothy Height do it for you?" "Didn't the four little girls bombed in the 16th Street Baptist Church do so and didn't Marcus Garvey do it for you?" Does my grandmother have to fear someone who looks like her more than her grandmother had to fear the KKK?

One of our immediate success stories was a call we received while we were on the nationally syndicated Russ Parr Show discussing what is and is not, snitching. A "snitch" is not someone who helps bring his peers to justice because he cares about the well-being of his community. A snitch is a rat's co-defendant in the "game," out to be free or to get a lighter sentence. The snitch often needs to fabricate or commit perjury to cut the deal. The snitch avoids paying the debt due to society or learning a life lesson, returning to a life of criminal activities. The rule in life, not the game, is "you reap what you sow," or "you made your bed, now lie in it."

If somebody robs your mother while she is walking down the street, an honest, law-abiding citizen has the obligation and right to ensure that justice prevails. We talked to a caller who stated that we motivated her to come forward because she had witnessed a murder. This was difficult for her because her brother had been killed and even though there were witnesses, the people who killed him were never brought to justice. She explained to us that she had promised herself that if she ever witnessed a murder, she would make sure the next family wouldn't go through what she and her family had to endure.

The catch was that the murderer was a friend of hers. It was very hard for her. She also explained that she went to the U.S. Attorney's office and they were insensitive and unprofessional. I called a friend who understands our "codes" and respect for the street but simultaneously, had respect for our interpretation of "citizenship." This murderer was brought to justice and I would later find out the victim was the son of Afro-American newspaper writer and community activist, Valencia Mohammed who is a friend of mine and had two sons murdered in D.C.

Some might say, "Them niggas are hot." I explained to them "we know what real gangstas are." I'm not a fool like the "Scarface" type. I'm the "Godfather" type. The Corleone's had relationships with the streets, doctors, lawyers and judges. "Scarface" was a fool and died with the words, "Say hello to my little friend." This young lady was not in the streets so the code did not apply to her, plain and simple.

In contrast, we had the U.S. Attorney's Office and MPD mad at us because we mediated a situation between Barry Farms and Washington View after four people were shot near Washington View and others shot outside Ballou Senior High School. Both hoods agreed to squash the beef. One person, who was shot, initially agreed to talk to the feds, but decided he wanted to let it go because we had resolved the beef and he felt he was just as guilty as anyone else in the game.

Squashing this beef prevented another shooting at Anacostia High School. The boys from Barry Farms warned they were going to finish what their boy started if we didn't talk to the other guy. The snitch in this case would have gotten the perpetrator arrested, but that would not have stopped the shooting about to happen at Anacostia and the Metro Station.

This is why it was so important for us to be in the schools because youth would tell us things they would not tell others and we knew and taught the difference between snitching and citizenship. Once we left Anacostia, things were again covered up by the schools because if they acknowledged any problems, they would be seen as not meeting DCPS standards even though the goal was to stop more violence. For some people it is all about just keeping problems out of the press. This is just a reality; people want to protect their jobs, especially in the current economy.

The reality is that sometimes you make decisions you think are best and even within Peaceoholics we disagreed about what was the best thing to do. Some staff felt the feds should never be trusted. We also had to keep our word to people or our credibility would be lost. Our word had to be our bond. The line between snitching and citizenship is not always clear to everyone. We tried to do what was right but only God can judge how often we succeeded. I know this: we saved lives, many, many lives, and we kept our word without violating the code as we understood it.

I also remember U.S. Attorney Albert Herring who participated in the forums telling us a story about a guy who was a part of "Murder Inc." a notorious gang, who allegedly committed several murders. They asked the defendant from Murder Inc., "Why did you kill the victim when you abducted him from Georgetown?" The murderer said he knew that if he killed him in Georgetown, people would tell, but he knew if he took him to the impoverished Southeast D.C. area to kill him, everyone would remain silent. The next time you want to play the race card, think about that story. Not only do we commit black-on-black crime, but we do not report crimes in our own neighborhoods and the cycle of violence continues. We miss the point when we fail to act as good citizens and then attribute the police failure to solve crimes as purely racism.

If someone is killed in Georgetown, there would be so many people ready to testify that you could fill a bus. Georgetown residents will not tolerate this kind of horrific act in their community regardless of the color of the victim and murderer. In our community, on the other hand, there can be a hundred people watching and you will be hard pressed to get two people to come forward. And when there are only two, it is easy to intimidate them. Just think about it; if twenty-five of the hundred came forward, the murderer couldn't intimidate that many. The murderer would be the one who is intimidated. We have to fix this, now! It is an embarrassment to the black community.

Murders would be drastically reduced if people knew that they couldn't get away with it. If you take a twenty minute ride from D.C. into the Hopkins Tancil Court Projects of Alexandria, Virginia, you don't hear of shootings every week or stabbings and fights every night. The people's needs are not being met just like in D.C. They are not being taught how to fish and are being set up to have generation after generation in the same predicament of welfare and poverty. But those neighborhoods do not have nearly the crime we do in our neighborhoods in D.C. Once again, they know better because even in poor areas of Alexandria, they know there will be consequences!

Dr. King said, "It is only a matter of time before silence becomes betrayal." It is time to understand that we are betraying our families and our communities when we let people terrorize us. We watch bad things happen to other people and remain silent. Crime is only a problem for us when tragedy hits home. Then we want everyone to get involved like good citizens. All of a sudden, going to the police is citizenship and not snitching when it is our child who was murdered.

I often quote this Sura from the Holy Quran, especially to my Muslim brothers. Sura 4 ayat 135, "Oh, you who believe, stand out firmly for justice as a witness to God, even as against yourselves, or parents, or your kin and whether it be against poor, for God can best protect both. Follow not the lust of your hearts, lest you swerve distort justice or decline to do justice. Verily, God is well acquainted with all that you do."

We worked hard to make this the code on the streets of the Nation's Capital and, to some degree, have succeeded. However, I say to my brothers that if you believe in this, but refuse to use law enforcement, then the only other option is to patrol and protect your community yourself. We did this when I was with Cease Fire Don't Smoke the Brothers to protect a community from a returned citizen who came back to the community and began selling drugs again after we helped him get his release.

We must stay still sometimes, meditate, and pay attention to what is going on. Things in America are changing so fast people must pump the brakes and stop giving people a pass because of the color of their skin, class, or titles. Dr. King said, "The important thing about a man is not the color of his skin or the texture of his hair, but the texture of his soul." Why am I so concerned about the confusion of citizenship with snitching? I am concerned that if we don't fix this now, we will look up one day and find we live in a country where WE THE PEOPLE are prisoners of fear in our own homes and communities.

We must stop the injustice, the genocide, and self-inflicted horrific crimes we allow our own people to commit in our communities without fear that we will hold them accountable. We have trapped ourselves in a dysfunctional system. We must stop being cowards. Why are we so afraid of being citizens that refuse to turn the other way when criminals terrorize our communities?

Why are we willing to risk the lives of our loved ones, especially our children, so the criminals among us can drive their cars with 22's or buy three-hundred-fifty-dollar Lebron James shoes after they have robbed somebody's mother, wife, or child walking home from school? We should also be outraged that very few shoe stores like DTLR (Downtown Locker Room) give back to the urban communities. They are pimps and cowards, too. Our people enrich their businesses and the community gets nothing back.

We must not be cowards. We must stand up and act like the men and women we were born to be. Jesus said, "Fear not." St. Paul tells us,

"God's grace is sufficient." Do we believe in God's grace or not? Don't forget about the children of Israel who had everything until God took it away and sent them into exile because they refused to follow his divine order. Let there be no doubt we are "reaping what we sow" when we fear the criminals or children gone astray more than we fear of the wrath of God. We cannot violate our core values without damaging our communities and our own souls.

Whatever our race, class, or political affiliation, we all know the difference between courage and cowardice. Dr. King said, "Courageous men never lose their zest for living, even though their life situations are zestless, cowardly men, overwhelmed by the uncertainties of life, lose the will to live." Are you a courageous citizen or just a cowardly resident? I hope you are a courageous citizen ready to stand up for the innocent rather than protecting the guilty. If you are a coward, if you are silent, then you are joining the criminals in the streets and in City Hall destroying our communities. That cowardice has resulted in burying your friends and family members.

When will we begin to act like good citizens? Are we so foolish to think that being a good citizen is for white or affluent people? When will we finally stand up against the criminal in the neighborhood and the crooked politician in City Hall who are both pimping our communities? Let's start moving mountains and addressing issues that expose those who have been living off the very people they live among and those who profess, under false pretenses, to have our best interests at heart.

During the Vietnam War, Dr. King chastised the people for letting the government spend $500,000 for every soldier who was killed and only fifty-three dollars on those living in poverty with the majority of those fifty-three dollars going to bureaucrats. I believe it was these words alone that got him killed but I know he died in peace because he had the courage to speak the words he believed his Lord wanted him to speak. Like Christ, he challenged the establishment and it got him killed. How dare we celebrate his life and then in our daily lives turn away from his example of courage.

People praised Dr. King for letting people beat him upside his head and telling people to keep the peace but he was called an extremist for doing what Christ would do when he spoke out against a brutal war! Dr. King later said, "I must admit that I was initially disappointed in being categorized [as an extremist]. But as I continued to think about the matter, I gradually gained a bit of satisfaction from being considered an extremist…. Was not Abraham Lincoln an extremist? 'This nation cannot survive half slave and half free.' Was not Thomas Jefferson an extremist? 'We hold these truths to be self-evident, that all men are created equal.' So, the question is not whether we will be extremists but what kind of extremist will we be. Will it be extremists for the preservation of injustice, or will we be extremists for the cause of justice?"

As long as we continue to protect criminals rather than act like true citizens and helping them before it is too late, we dishonor the memory of Dr. King. Many of our people claim to be Christ-like or believers in other faiths, but act like cowards. We talk about Christ's resurrection on Easter, but we skip his suffering. Remember, Jesus was praised on Palm Sunday, betrayed by one of his disciples and arrested on Thursday, tried and convicted in the middle of the night. None of his friends, followers, or the people he helped came to testify for him but there were plenty of his friendnemies willing to bear false witness against him – sounds like Vince Gray and company. When Pilate offered to free him, the same people who praised him on Sunday, cried out, "Crucify him!" By noon, he was hanging on a Roman cross, executed for telling the truth.

Too many of us are Palm Sunday Christians. We are good citizens with our words when the crowds are cheering but we turn into nothing more than residents and cowards when it comes to action. We become like all the folks Jesus healed and loved who abandoned him in his hour of need. No one came to his defense. No one was willing to testify on his behalf because they feared the corrupt politicians. When we refuse to testify against crime in our neighborhoods or when one City Council member refuses to call out another City Council member for corruption, we betray the legacy of Dr. King and the grace of God in Christ.

So, why would you fear the consequences of being "Christ-like" if you really believe in him and his teachings? Dr. King put it in words you might understand better than mine. He said, "When you stand up for truth and justice, sometimes it means being frustrated and when you tell the truth and take a stand, sometimes it means you will walk the streets with a burdened heart, or lose a job, maybe be abused and scorned, it may mean hearing your seven and eight-year-old children asking, "Daddy, why do you have to go to jail?"

How well I know this story! Dr. King said following Christ means taking up the cross. It means there has to be a Good Friday before there can be an Easter. Remember, no lie can live forever unless you let it. It's time for WE THE PEOPLE to enforce moral order in our communities so we can eliminate the many hardships we have brought upon ourselves because of our complacency and lack true citizenship.

We must remember all children are born innocent and have to be taught to practice citizenship. If Tony is punished and mislabeled as a snitch for telling on little brother Jimmy for disobeying Mommy's rule to not eat cookies without her permission, then both Tony and Jimmy will learn the wrong lesson. Tony will learn that being a good big brother means letting Jimmy do anything he wants to do or to be called a snitch. Jimmy will learn stealing is okay and that Tony can be intimidated by being called a snitch.

We teach our children to be passive conformers. If WE THE PEOPLE continue to be silent while oppressors, who come in all colors, races, classes, religions continue to crush us, our communities and country continue to decline. This silence in the face of injustice is a breeding ground for what Malcolm X called the potential for an explosion in the sixties just before the riots. Once again, Frederick Douglass said it best, "Where justice is denied, where poverty is enforced, where ignorance prevails, and where one class is made to feel that society is an organized conspiracy to oppress, rob, and degrade them, neither person nor property will be safe."

We have created Hell for the poor by making them unwilling or afraid to hold politicians accountable and to hold accountable the very criminals who are destroying our neighborhoods. We have devastated independence and independent thinking. Instead of helping the poor learn how to fish to feed their families and to become good citizens with a voice, we say, "Take this fish, shut up, and vote for me." (You can substitute gift card or turkeys or crony jobs for the word "fish").

Martin Luther King, Jr. once said, "Riots are the voices of the unheard." Throughout America, poor people are being trampled on because of the recession. If we continue to stifle the voice of the voiceless, there is going to be another explosion in America far worse than the 1968 riots. Remember, most of the Petey Green's are dead or have been destroyed, so it will be hard to tell the unheard to stop once they get started. There aren't any present leaders like Dr. King, so who will stop it when it comes? Who will have the courage that Christ or Muhammad had in the desert?

I hope we take action so we won't have to answer this question again in the future. I hope those who have achieved the American Dream stop sleeping on those who have not yet achieved it, that both the Haves and the Have Not's will wake up and pay attention to our message.

Gandhi once said, "Never underestimate the little people. If you don't believe me, try locking yourself in the room at night with a mosquito, shut the windows and door then turn out the light and see what happens to you!" It is time for the little people to take action.

Pay close attention and you will understand you can be the spark of change! Those mosquitoes are the people of Egypt, the people of Syria, or the people of Vietnam who beat our ass, the Latino people who orchestrated the Mt. Pleasant riots in Washington D.C., the riots in Attica Prison, the 1968 riots that went on after Dr. King was assassinated while I was a seed about to be released into my mother's womb. Margaret Mead Once said, "Never doubt that small group of thoughtful, committed citizens can change the world; indeed it's the only thing that ever has."

A seventeen-year-old girl with a baby in her arms was chased down and killed in Benning Terrace, also known as Simple City! We had been coming around looking for Blocker to squash a beef and the community pleaded with us to help. The Williams administration also asked us to try to do something. The people were numb and in shock as expected when a seventeen-year-old girl was gunned down with a child in her hands.

We used part of our model for working with the girl gangs and other community epidemics our city was having in 2005. We took eighty people including youth and adults. About 70 percent of those were youth. In our experience, if you give youth a chance, they will take a stand. We taught them citizenship and about taking responsibility for their communities and how to hold their elected officials and the people in the community accountable.

The youth and adults came up with great ideas. The adults put together a plan to paint and clean up on the weekend. The youth brought me to tears as always! They drafted a proposal for soon-to-be mayor, Adrian Fenty. He met with them and promised he would help. Legislation was passed by the City Council to do a study. What we don't need is another study! We need to vote passive politicians out of office. Studies and not action are what we get for not practicing citizenship.

Things got better and people became more like citizens than residents. The young people started a group called the Youth of Benning. We had to stretch our budget to do this work, but we managed as always. Our staff knew this was not a job, but a ministry. While most would sleep at night, our phones would ring and the staff knew that if a youth told us they called and no one answered, someone was going to be out of a job.

The Washington Post did a story on this community project titled "Out Of Grief Comes Hope." Later, we were devastated because our budget was cut a year or so later and we could not keep our people in the community or fund the activities that were bringing the community together. Once again, we used money for this project designated for other use. We were using our best judgment to stretch available funds to do more. This is technically considered misappropriation of funds. We freely admit this but it was done in order to get this community on its way to self-efficiency, which is the key to rebuilding the Village Triangle in One Model. Unlike Vince Gray and Harry Thomas we did not use the money for our own personal benefit.

This supports Chris Rock's theory that "Ain't no money in the cure!" Any poverty pimp including Jesse Jackson, Jr. can tell you that. The community returned to shambles and the same cycle repeated itself. Every three to five years a group of black boys would be rounded up and hauled off to prison with conspiracy and murder charges. The community had no hope and was dependent on the government plantation owners. Too many parents were waiting around for a check on the first of the month while our government provided no real programs to set them free with real jobs and real paychecks.

Part of our model was to do community retreats. We did one of those retreats for one hundred grieving residents of Benning Terrace after Lil Cindy's assassination. The youth came up with the idea of a group called Youth of Benning and drafted a proposal for a recreation center that the city promised to build, but never did. The parents got engaged and held community clean up events and organized monthly meetings for the residents to take ownership of their community.

This project was on its way to being a great success. The city was always coming to us and asking us to help when tragedy struck because the politicians did not know how to bring healing in the community. Unfortunately, we were not funded to do everything we were asked to do and so there where situations like the one at Benning Terrace when we admittedly used funds from other projects to provide the services we were asked to render.

Once Vince Gray and his cronies were successful at cutting off all of our funding, projects like the one at Benning Terrace suffered and eventually stopped. These programs need to be nurtured and cultivated over a long period of time. Sadly, if things don't change, Benning Terrace residents will never be empowered to do for themselves what Jack Kemp's program enable Kimi Gray to do at Kenilworth Parkside.

Eventually they will all be moved out by HOPE VI bulldozers making room for gentrification.

We brought ninety-nine year-old civil rights icon Amelia Boynton Robinson to D.C. to talk to the community and youth after the horrific South Capitol Massacre. This was the episode in which the stealing of a cheap bracelet led to three shootings in two days of inconceivable violence in which nine youth were shot. Two were females and four of the nine died leaving permanent scars on so many lives. Her words of wisdom to us were: "Listen to God when he talks to you. Some people call it conscience, some people call it the Holy Spirit, and some people call it your soul, but just know when it's God and when he tells you to do something, listen to him and do it. Don't sit around waiting for something to fall out of the sky for he has given you everything you need to succeed and the only question is will you take it?"

My fellow citizens, please, listen to God in your hearts. Take back your city and country from the people who sell drugs to our children and at the same time make sure they have opportunities so they won't have to sell drugs when they return from prison? Will you rid your city of crooked politicians like Mayor Gray and Yvette Alexander? Will you vote for people because of their history of serving the people and keeping their word to you or will you continue to vote blindly for the symbol of a dumb ass donkey or a stinky ass elephant because that's what you have always done?

Remember, we have the power to make every bad situation a good one and every good situation a better one. The ball is in your court, what are you going to do? I close with this thought that people from other countries often risk their lives to become American citizens. They have to pass a test or they are denied citizenship. They understand and value citizenship in America. They come here with nothing, and in most cases, go on to live a great life in America. They amass influence and financial security as they build strong private and public institutions in the pursuit of happiness. My fellow citizens, go and do likewise!

Are You a Citizen or Just a Resident?

In our eyes, there are two types of residents. There are those who reside, but don't get involved with issues that affect their communities or their offspring. These are the ones who don't do anything and then whine and complain when they are mistreated. Then there are those who we call Re-si-di-zens, those who only advocate for policies of their own

244 | Drinking Muddy Water

interests and not the interest of everyone as a whole. The poor are crushed in America because of this. These are the type of people who see their neighbor's house on fire and can't be bothered to pick up a bucket and throw water on it. We must teach these types of Re-si-di-zens what Dr. Martin Luther King taught during the Civil Rights Movement that what affects my neighbor directly affects us all indirectly.

Thomas Jefferson said, "All tyranny needs to gain a foothold is for people of good conscience to remain silent." If the founding fathers had remained silent in the face of tyranny, we would not be the United States of America. They were true revolutionaries. They passed on to us a living Declaration of Independence to which they each pledged, "Our lives, our fortunes, and our sacred honor."

The following is from the Declaration of Independence:

> We hold these truths to be self-evident, that all men are created equal, that they are endowed by their Creator with certain unalienable Rights, that among these are Life, Liberty and the pursuit of Happiness. — That to secure these rights, Governments are instituted among Men, deriving their just powers from the consent of the governed— That whenever any Form of Government becomes destructive of these ends, it is the Right of the People to alter or to abolish it, and to institute new government, laying its foundation on such principles and organizing its powers in such form, as to them shall seem most likely to affect their Safety and Happiness.

The most damage is done by those who remain silent or only object in a whisper to ensure their comfort while others suffer unnecessarily in many cases before their very eyes. These are the people who have become conformists, they don't want to piss anybody off because they are comfortable with their jobs, cars, houses, and for this very reason, over five-thousand children shut down Birmingham, Alabama when they filled the prisons up to help Dr. Martin Luther King, Jr. win his first battle in eight years. Today, we see the same thing; material possessions, fear, and the lack of the will to sacrifice in the best interest of humanity are the main reasons for silence and inaction.

I am amazed at the cowardice of some of our people after the price many of our ancestors paid, such as Emmitt Till, Nathaniel Turner, Harriet Tubman, and Martin Luther King, Jr. In fact, King said it best himself, "He who passively accepts evil is as involved in it as he who helps perpetrate it. He who accepts evil without protesting against it is really cooperating with it." He goes on to say, "Cowardice asks the question, 'Is it safe?' Expediency asks the question, 'Is it politic?' but conscience asks the question, 'Is it right?' and there comes a time when one must take a position that is neither safe, nor politic, nor popular, but because conscience tells one it is right."

In the District of Columbia, we have two cities in one. West of the river, where the majority of the affluent and upper middle class live, and east of the river where the majority of the poor and some middle class live. I want to note what I'm addressing here isn't always a racial issue but an economic class issue in many cases, what my father calls economic segregation. Things sadden me on both sides of the river. Here, where I am east of the river is where you will find the highest population of poor residents, but they don't get engaged in things that will decide their well-being or children's future.

On the west side of town, they generally practice citizenship when it is in their own interest. But when black boys and girls are gunned down blocks away, it's as if they are in two different worlds. When a congressional staffer is robbed on Capitol Hill, it is always a news story, especially if the victim is a young, attractive, white female. I am not suggesting this should not be a story. I am just appalled that if a young black male is not only robbed but gunned down a mile away in Anacostia, the life expectancy of the story is less than a day. I also think we are fools if we expect the press to care about our young men dying, if we are not willing to step up and hold people accountable.

We believe they should study, Dr. Martin Luther King Jr. who said, "An injustice anywhere is a threat to justice everywhere." This is why homes in more affluent neighborhoods all across America are being burglarized and robbed more than those in poor neighborhoods. The poor have nowhere else to turn these days and most people who have been around for a while know there was a time when predators were more reluctant to go outside the "hood." Now it has spread to the so-called good communities where it gets the attention of the press and an outraged community. It is up to everyone to be a part of the solution for what goes on in the wider community.

The other thing that saddens me is how hard it is to get some of the parents east of the river to show up at PTSA meetings. They will line up early in the morning at a downtown Foot Locker to buy their children popular two-hundred-dollar Nike shoes, but when I was the vice president of Ballou Senior High School PTSA, we had to have gimmicks to get them out in big numbers. We got a great crowd when we invited Sugar Bear and EU to perform live at the meeting. What does this say to people on the outside and, more importantly, to our children about how much we really care about their safety and education?

This school, like many east of the river and beyond, really needs their parents' and community's support because their funding has been cut by the regional office. We need more than residents, we need citizens. At times, some classrooms have a student to teacher ratio of forty to one. This is a grave injustice that shouldn't go another day without outrage and advocacy from within the community, starting with the parents.

Ballou Senior High School still has a long way to go, but by any standard of measurement, it has come a long way in regard to safety and academic performance. If the parents got involved, can you imagine how things could be? We've gone from being the laughing stock of D.C. to being the pride of the District of Columbia and with the parents' help we could be the model for the nation. To do that though, we need more residents to become true citizens.

I will close with my August 19, 2007 op-ed, "The Real Meaning of Snitching," that appeared in the Sunday Outlook section of the Washington Post:

A hundred people gathered at Washington's Scripture Cathedral in May, many of them teenagers from the surrounding O Street NW neighborhood, where a murderous street feud had terrorized the community. Our anti-violence group, Peaceoholics, had convened a forum to ask "What's Snitching and What's Not?"

Snitching -- and its sibling, witness intimidation -- is much in the news these days, the result of a series of high-profile killings and shootings both here in the Washington area and elsewhere. But there are a lot of myths and misconceptions about it, not just among people in the community, but also among law enforcement officials and the media.

Trying to break the ice at our forum, I threw out a few questions: If someone shot your mother during a drive-by, would you have a problem with that? Would you want something to happen to that person? Would it make more sense for you to be locked up, or would you like the shooter to be incarcerated?

There wasn't much of a response until a young man came forward. "I ain't no snitch," he said. "But I'll help the community."

Nobody wants to be a snitch -- not even in a forum that's supposed to define what exactly snitching is.

My job is to try to bring peace to the community. But I'm also realistic: You are never going to get black people to agree to snitch. The reasons are rooted in history and culture, and the realities of so many inner cities, where human life is cheap.
But as someone who has been on the other side of the law, what I will say is that if you work at it, you can persuade witnesses to violent crime to come forward.

For those of us who live in high-crime areas, there's nothing new about witness intimidation — criminals threatening or even killing citizens who could testify against them. But several recent incidents have brought wider attention to this issue.

In Newark, witnesses have fingered the suspects in 14 recent killings, but prosecutors have not charged them for fear that the witnesses who identified them would be hurt or killed. Rap artists and gang leaders in Baltimore and Boston have recently begun campaigns urging city residents to "Stop Snitching." The rapper Cam'ron was interviewed on "60 Minutes" about why he refused to cooperate with police after he was shot in the arm in Washington during a botched car-jacking in 2005.

And last week, Prince George's County prosecutors blamed witness intimidation for their failure to win convictions in two homicide cases. In the fall of 2005, Lakita Danielle Tolson, a 19-year-old mother and nursing student, was killed outside a Temple Hills nightclub. Nine months later, Eric S. Holland, 18, was killed in a crowded schoolyard. Law enforcement and family members believe he was targeted because people (wrongly) thought he was cooperating with police on the Tolson case. Large crowds were at both shootings, but only one witness agreed to testify in both cases.

I've told the young people at our snitching forums that if they see someone killed, it's their obligation to help make sure that the killer is punished. The government works for us, and together we can hold it to higher standards.

But words and connotations are powerful. And to many of us, the word "snitch" brings to mind a distant memory of a house slave telling the master when another slave tried to escape. We're a long way from the days of slavery, but the adversity that those of us trapped in communities with little money, education and police protection share has forced us to create our own codes and coping strategies.

Russ Parr moderating one of our many well-attended "What's Snitching and What's Not" forums at Howard University's Blackburn Center.

Exercising my citizenship by testifying alongside Vincent Shirraldi and Chief of Police Cathy Lanier on best practices to prevent youth violence.

One of many marches Peaceoholics organized to teach young people the importance of activism and citizenship. This march was part of the annual Unity on the Borders March conducted with D.C. and Maryland elected officials in partnership with Rev. Tony Lee of Community of Hope AME Church.

Lesson Seven

Friendnemies

In our early years we made the statement, "I'm not going to let nobody rock me asleep!" This meant not letting anyone trick me into thinking they care about me and then rob or set me up. I'm going to expand on that and how this idea evolved into a new term called friendnemies which is broader but just as serious!

Here are some of our definitions and examples of friendnemies:

1) In reality they are people who are only around you because you have something they want.

2) They can't hurt you because they are scared to tell you the truth because they are scared to be out of favor or are only around as a tick to suck all of the blood out of you, often leaving you with sickness and death.

3) You can do something they cannot do or are afraid to do so they get close to you so that they can use you, steal your dreams for themselves, and move on when they no longer have any use for you.

4) Somebody who professes to be your friend but when you aren't looking, they are stabbing you in your back or talking about you because they are jealous of you and envy your success.

5) Last, but not least, there are those who you care about or who know your commitment to helping people and they use you to fight their wars and, if they get rich, they turn their backs on you when there is no longer a need for your advocacy or spirit.

Having an organization everybody was talking about and wanted to be a part of was like getting bears with honey. But we found out when the honey was gone, only 25 percent of the people around us were there for the movement. Many of these people were never given a chance before to use any of their skills. Many of them did not know they possessed any skills at all. In fact, a few of these people would turn on you the minute you took the honey away from them. After you have given them chance after chance to improve themselves, they still are not grateful. In the art of war, the enemy relies on these types of people to defeat you by taking away your honey, more specifically, our funding.

One secretary thought because she had a big butt, it meant she did not have to show up to work on time or help keep the office clean even though I was the co-founder and would do the very things we were asking her to do. A woman we respected who was trying to help her asked us to give her a chance. After we laid her off, she was mad as hell and refused to look at all the good we did for her. Instead, she just talked about us and spread rumors about us attempting to destroy us.

It did not help that her family was politically connected. She later had the nerve to use us as a job reference and she and her politically connected family became angry because we would not lie and say she would be a great hire! Well, I did try to help a little by saying if she ever got to work on time she had the potential to be a good employee. Then there are those people around you who profess to be your friends who are just there for the ride and are scared to tell you the truth because they worry about being out of your favor.

I saw this happen firsthand with Mayor Fenty who had some so-called allies who only worried about what they could get and would be quiet and let him self-destruct as long as they could continue to benefit from him being the mayor. I was like, "Man, won't you tell him that stuff is crazy? Tell him to give that man the baseball tickets. This is making him look like a fool." They would act as if it was funny and would ride him like a pony even though they were helping drive the people away from him, people who once liked him and were starting to see the mayor in a bad light.

Don't get me wrong, I believed there were more important things than baseball tickets and even had my friend, Big Wax produce a song rapping about people worrying about baseball tickets while children are dying; however, this was a bad move and it was bad politics! Fenty was doing a hell of a job in most cases but these friendnemies are people who you better look out for because a man is as only as strong as his strongest critic. Men will help a wise man destroy his greatness! Ask Marion Barry, I'm sure he would agree.

There are those who can't do what you can do or are scared to try themselves. These people will ride your coattail as long as they can and then will steal all of your secrets, good or bad and use them for their benefit as soon as they get a chance. One guy would always come to me trying to find a way in. He had plenty of money but could not get any attention or credibility. Finally, I took him to a meeting with other returned citizens who were trying to give back to the communities they had once destroyed. Not all of the men wanted him there. You will remember that he showed himself to be a friendnemy early on when he took credit for coming up with the term "returned citizen" to replace ex-offender, which simply was not true.

Then you have those who say they are your friends, but have the twin diseases called jealousy and envy. These are the people who will smile in your face and, as soon as you turn your back, they are putting a knife into it! They despise seeing another person make it. In the black community, we call it the Willie Lynch Syndrome or crabs in a barrel.

In politricks I call it Lobsters in a Barrel. Lobsters in a Barrel is when you take a stand and fight for people you believe in or even consider friends, but realize after the battle is over that you are the only one with bruises. It turns out that the people you fought for don't really give a damn about you! The reward is a few crumbs as though that makes up for all your losses and sacrifices on their behalf. This is the nature, not only of D.C. politics, but of all politics.

If I was in the streets and put a good dude in harm's way and caused him to lose a million-dollar deal, then I would owe him for as long as it takes to undo the damage. The shame is that what I lost was not money that was intended to help me but to help the people in the community. That kind of honor is rare these days. I take it as a lesson learned because we did it for the right reasons but I have learned that you need to think twice before you put what you have on the line for businessmen, politicians, or your boys in the hood!

Real leaders sacrifice for the people, which is something I will never regret! I have learned friendnemies don't always have to be bad. As long as you know who and what they are, you can keep them close and in front of you just like you do an enemy! The Godfather said, "Keep your friends close, but your enemies closer." I guess friendnemies need to be kept close enough to keep a close eye on them.

With D.C. homies while serving time for a drug
conviction at Allenwood Federal Correction facility.

8

Hurt People Hurt People

If corrupt politicians think they can defeat a man of principle who helps uplift his community by using their power to unjustly harm him, they don't know the same God I know!

—Ron Moten, Civil Rights Republican

Hurt people hurt people is a saying we got from a great civil rights leader. In our work we would often see the truth of this phrase. It goes a long way toward understanding the mystery of why our youth are committing the most heinous crimes. But it's really not that hard to understand once you realize this wall of terror is a defense our youth put up to hide deep wounds of their own terrorized souls. It is a sad fact that a high percentage of abused children grow up and abuse their own children, mates, or others in society.

Let's be clear, hurt people hurt people explains, but does not excuse, the violence. When a person has an addiction to violence, the first step to recovery, just like with drug addiction, is to accept responsibility. The second step is for a friend, counselor, pastor, or someone from a community organization like Peaceoholics to help youth understand why their use violence to solve every problem. Violence, like drugs, numbs the pain of poverty, grief over the death of a parent, abuse, failure, heartbreak or any other problem.

Another basic principle of human behavior is what we don't work out, we act out. Our urban children in particular are both witnesses and victims of emotional, physical, and sexual abuse and violence committed by the very people who should be protecting them. Don't get me wrong, there is as much emotional, physical, and sexual abuse in communities like Potomac, Maryland as there is in the Anacostia neighborhoods of Washington, D.C. but it is not as public, not as "on the street." Another difference is wealthy families and schools can afford to get counseling for their youth. In poor communities, this work is left to the church, community advocates, and organizations like Peaceoholics.

When it comes to children and youth, behavior is more caught than taught. When children grow up in safe and caring home and community, they try to create that same environment as adults. Unfortunately, it works the same way when children live in fear of the very people God created to protect them. When children are betrayed by the very people they should be able to trust, they protect themselves any way they can, which includes acts of almost unspeakable violence.

Remember, we are not talking about the same intensity or frequency of emotions we all feel periodically. We aren't just talking about anger, but rage, not just disappointment, but bitterness, not just fear, but terror. We are talking about these emotions eating them up day in and day out, year after year from the day they are born. Fortunately, not every child turns to violence, some turn to having faith in God. Some are mentored by good role models, some turn to music or some other positive outlet for their emotions. That's how we re-directed the gang members when I was with Peaceoholics and what I am still doing with them now.

Many of these youth have been victimized in more ways than a mind can fathom. This can be a wicked world that is unkind to our children who are violently assaulted, sexually molested, neglected, and see young gunmen fire bullets that kill their friends and family members. These actions rip holes in their souls. These experiences repeated over and over again would make the strongest of us numb, very similar to the PTSD (Post-Traumatic Stress Disorder) suffered by our soldiers when they return from war. When trauma is unresolved, our children often turn to violent behavior and develop low to no respect for self or others.

Our organization once attended an assembly at Hart Middle School with Kenny Barnes, founder of ROOT Inc. in Washington, D.C. We were partnering with the schools' social worker, Ms. Bojoli. She was one of the few white women I've seen who children and families from war zones such as Condon Terrace love, trust, and respect more than they do most blacks who do similar work in our communities. Racial stereotypes on all sides are hard to overcome, trust me, she earned every bit of it. She wasn't just putting in her two years of "service to the poor little black children" like so many others who have come into our communities only to disappear as fast as they appeared. She wasn't there just to enhance her resume like we see in programs like Teach for America. The Teach for America program would work if the its teachers had the same commitment as Ms. Bojoli or my first grade teacher, Ms. Webb, or Ms. Watty Lewis who taught me at Alice Deal Middle School.

One event in particular made me believe prayer was needed in schools. After we partnered with ROOT, Inc. founder, Kenny Barnes, we were in an assembly at Hart Middle School. In the assembly, Kenny asked everybody who has had a friend or family member killed or injured by gun violence in Washington, D.C. to raise their hands. 90 percent of the hands went up out of about one hundred students.

Then he asked how many of them had received counseling afterward. Maybe five hands went up. I know we need prayer because "hurt people hurt people" and the old saying in therapy goes, "what you don't work out, you act out." We have a generation of urban children who are going to act out the hurts they have experienced. Why not spend a little money to help them process their trauma now rather than pay a much higher price in more lives lost and hundreds of thousands for incarceration when they go out and hurt other people? This lack of counseling is the norm in our children's world unlike the children of Columbine or other schools in affluent communities after their youth are affected by acts of violence.

Mr. Barnes asked over two hundred youth how many of them had been victims of gun violence or had a family member or a close friend who were victims. Every hand went up. Sadly, being neglected or molested could be substituted for gun violence and still all the hands would have gone up. Then he asked how many of them received any counseling after any of these experiences. Fewer than ten hands went up and the room was silent as a kind of emotional numbness set in as we realized how abandoned and alone those kids must have felt.

This would not be the case in affluent Montgomery County, Maryland middle school but it is the reality at too many of the schools in America's urban communities. In that numbed silence, I thought to myself, this is why this middle school has produced more killers and have more children murdered than any school in the city. Tragic evidence that hurt people hurt people, that what you don't work out, you act out, and that behavior is more caught than taught.

Ms. Bojoli called and asked us to mentor a student named Marcel. He had been seen outside the school stashing a Mac-10. Marcel had a troubled past and lost many friends before he went to Oak Hill Youth Correctional Facility, a place where reform meant recycling our youth until they were ready for the big house. Marcel never received any counseling services and we told them not to release him because we knew he was not ready to go back to his community where wars were going on. His father and grandmother told them he was not ready as well, but Vincent Shiraldi, the internationally known reformer, released him without telling us.

His mother was incarcerated at the time so she was not there to help his transition. Although she had her own problems, she would have made a difference in his life. It wasn't long before Marcel was murdered and his body and the body of a friend were dumped on the Suitland Parkway. This was right on the route the Secret Service motorcade uses when the President goes to Andrews Air Force Base to fly on Air Force One. I thought it was an interesting contrast to imagine the President of the United States looking out his limousine window and seeing Marcel's body disposed of like human litter. In a final irony, Marcel died with a R.I.P. t-shirt with the picture of one of his murdered friends on it, tied around his head with a friend who was deposed in the same manner.

This was a big story. Marcel was later featured in the Washington Post as he was, allegedly, tied to four homicides. Congressman Tom Davis (R-Virginia) was on the D.C. Oversight Committee and wanted to know why Oak Hill did not listen to the Peaceoholics who told them it was not safe to release him. He told us himself that he was not ready to do the right thing. He needed to be ambushed with services and not bullets and rushed back into the same situation expecting a different result. That's the very definition of insanity, right?

When the Massacre at Columbine happened, those children received help for years just as they would in more affluent local communities around D.C. like Montgomery or Charles Counties. Counselors are brought in to help students in those schools for as long as needed in response to a student being killed in a car accident or a mass murder like in Newtown, Connecticut. Unfortunately, children in urban schools like Marcel rarely get help for even a day when they lose a friend. All they get are R.I.P. t-shirts to die in themselves. Those who are brought in to help are often in culture shock and the children feel like the helpers as the "specialist" gets accustomed to the horrific realities of poor urban schools and communities.

What we are clear on is that if these children hold the pain inside and receive no help, it's just a matter of time before the community pays the price in some shape, form, or fashion. It's a bomb waiting to explode. In the meantime, many students start self-medicating with drugs or with the rush of hurting others just as they have been hurt. They do not think about the repercussions for their horrific actions while we distance ourselves from any responsibility for what is happening to our children.

Let's look at the numbers. We held an emergency town hall meeting at First Rock Baptist Church on "The Correlation Between Unemployment and Violence. We learned from an official of the Washington Hospital Center MedSTAR Trauma Unit that this one hospital treated 4,003 people from 2006-2010 for intentionally violent inflicted injuries. More than 1,458 were from gunshots, over 1,300 for stab wounds, and more than 1,200 from assaults.

Blocker was a little boy who at the age of fourteen had reputation that would precede him around the Washington Metropolitan Area. Both of his parents died, his sister was deaf, and his brother was killed by a rival crew who told Blocker he was next. Ask yourself what you would do if this happened to you. It is easy to figure out what Blocker decided to do next once you know his medication of choice was a gun. He needed guidance from a professional counselor, a church, mosque, or synagogue, but what he got was a gun from the people he looked up to on the streets.

While we were trying to hunt him down before it was too late, he used the gun to protect himself and to address the guys in the community who were accused of killing his brother. He went through Kenilworth in broad daylight on an ATV 4-wheeler, ambushing the community just as his brother who he loved so much was gunned down. We later found out he was locked up for shooting at a Maryland police officer in a car chase and we made our move on him once he was transferred to Oak Hill.

We worked with him but he too was released against our advice before he was ready. In fact, we raised hell because this young man had come a long way. He was even honored by the Association of Black Trial Lawyers for his progress. We arranged for him to speak while he was out on a home pass (we have pictures with him at event with a suit on and speaking in front of the Association of Black Lawyers). We helped move him along and he assisted us with bringing peace to Oak Hill as he converted nearly the entire compound to Islam and, for a change, he practiced the art of peace he followed as a child before unfortunate tragedies came into his life.

Blocker was charged with a serious crime in Maryland. He served three years in the penitentiary. Just weeks after his release, Blocker was charged with a double homicide in which the car was set on fire after the passengers inside were shot. Now you tell me, if Block was found guilty of committing such a crime, is he the only one who is guilty? Maybe some of us belong behind bars for contributing to a systemic pattern of neglect. Blocker must pay the consequences if he is guilty, but we all share some responsibility, but not guilt for his actions.

Then there is BJ who is an example of a child who was severely traumatized and did not get the counseling services needed to bring healing. BJ was a leader of the once notorious Hobart Crew. The Hobart community was known for being a troubled neighborhood. It earned its reputation when Anwar "Big G" Glover of D.C.'s Backyard Band and former star of HBO's hit series The Wire was on the streets of Hobart. The reason Big G made it was that we were part of a group of people who surrounded him with loving support so he could heal from all the hurt inside him and stop hurting others or always having to watch his back. Helping him deal with his demons and his past showed us that no one is beyond help as G has gone on to become a productive member in our society even after everybody had written him off. .

These days he has his own nonprofit organization that helps keep young folks like BJ get out of harm's way. BJ learned to shoot the basketball the way his stepfather did, but then he experienced something no child should ever see! His stepfather was gunned down right before his eyes by a rival crew at Bruce-Monroe, BJ's neighborhood playground.

Of course, neither BJ nor his siblings ever received the counseling services he needed. They were suffering from PTSD as much as any of our soldiers returning Iraq or Afghanistan and children such as those in Newtown, Connecticut. We have learned that left unaddressed, PTSD causes everything from nightmares to road rage, domestic abuse, durg addiction, and violent crimes including homicide. The scientific research on PTSD shows what is obvious to common sense and close observation, "Hurt people, hurt people!"

My point is that we have war zones in many of the neighborhoods in our cities where children are traumatized everyday by the violence and the fear of violence. They see their brothers and sisters gunned down, dying of drug overdose, and being taken away from them to prison. It's time we gave these children and families the same help we give our brave soldiers and, to be honest, the same help that children who come from "better" communities, wealthier communities whenever even one student dies from a car accident or twenty die in a mass murder.

Now let's look at BJ and Tee when they were leaders of Hobart and CTU. Their rivalry resulted in shootouts in broad daylight between Hobart and CTU which could no longer be tolerated because gentrification was bringing more affluent whites, blacks, Latinos, and gays into the community. We got a call to come to a press conference called by Mayor Adrian Fenty, Councilmember Jim Graham, and MPD to let the people know it would be addressed. This is the same Jim Graham who later turned his back on us even though we helped him whenever he called on us.

We made sure that Al, one of our key staff members, and Greg, one of the few good roving leaders working for the Department of Recreation, were in attendance. Al had a lifelong relationship with the community and had been shot in that neighborhood himself back in his wild days. We knew city leadership would listen to him and we, along with other staff, were there.

After the press conference we told them what we needed. First, reopen the recreation center. That's where we would start programming with targeted youth such as BJ and other leaders so they could be trained to be youth intervention specialists. Second, we needed funds to help support families, engage parents, run retreats, and take trips. We managed to negotiate this beef between adults like we did between gangs.

Reopening the recreation center did not come without a fight. The school where the recreation center was housed was largely Latino and run by a Latino principal who it seemed did not want the black children to have access. We fought with Jim Graham's office, other Latinos, and the community to have it opened for these boys because, as Dr. King once put it, "What affects my brother directly affects us all indirectly."

Our work with BJ was showing positive results until our funding was stopped by politicians who were more worried about their own ambitions for power than they were about the BJ's and Tee's of the world. Tee was another young man from a similar background that we helped who tried a drive-by through Hobart while on a motorcycle. We were able to enroll Tee into Benedict College where he stayed for two years. He later returned and married another youth who we worked with.

BJ was in his final year at Roosevelt and had become one of the best peer mediators in our citywide Street Commission. We successfully converted and trained gang leaders like Tee and BJ as paid mediators. This does not mean they were all perfect; it's a process, but it helped us stop the violence. How? Their peers would listen to them before they would listen to the police or even Peaceoholics. Tee and BJ squashed the beef Hobart – CTU beef wherever and whenever they could, even in the mayor's box at Wizards games in the Verizon Center. They did countless one-on-ones, retreats, and mediation with core leaders from both sides.

As we were doing all of this great work, our funding stopped and A-Ball, one of their associates, who was in prison when the truce occurred, came home with bad intentions. He began terrorizing the communities where we had squashed the beefs while he was gone. He was giving drugs to the youngsters around Hobart. It was inevitable that things went back to normal and BJ was charged and convicted for killing A-Ball, his one-time friend. In a twist of fate, BJ allegedly murdered A-Ball in the same place his stepfather was murdered.

The same fate awaited BJ's little brother who was working with people in government at age fourteen. He practiced good citizenship by testifying at several council hearings. He was even questioned at a City Council hearing they even questioned him about changing the law so he could legally ride his dirt bike at the age fourteen. But when the program was shut down because we lost our funding, he was charged with killing a white college student, Neil Godleski, who was riding a bicycle from work. He allegedly robbed Godleski and, according to his friend, stood over him and said, "It's like butter baby."

He is now facing thirty-two years to life. This case drew more attention than all the murders that happened in his community. This is another case of the victim, his family, and the perpetrator being let down by a broken family and a dysfunctional juvenile justice system. The people running the system are incompetent. They see rehabilitation as a way to get rich while appearing to help people. True rehabilitation only happens when both the client and family are strengthened along with improved social and economic conditions in the community.

We had no funding to do the work now. The recreation center was later closed and demolished to make room for future development. So the black children in the hood who were left without our help or a recreation center and became little men left on an island to deal with urban warfare in a way that has become all too familiar. So, to add insult to injury, the powers that be asked Peaceoholics and the other groups who were defunded to please step in and stop the brutality.

What most people do not understand is that it takes time to create a truce through cross-fertilization and for it to become more permanent like the Choppa City–Woodland truce that lasted for six years. This was not the case with the Hobart – CTU truce and once BJ was in custody, it was only a matter of time before the beefing started all over again. This time an innocent girl, Lucki Pannell who we mentioned earlier, was killed as the beef reemerged.

A CTU youth allegedly shot her with a stray bullet that was intended for a Hobart youth. Then an innocent man was killed at the Caribbean festival in front of thousands of people in a shootout. He was caught in the gun fire of two crews in broad daylight. This incident resulted in this great cultural event enjoyed by tens of thousands of people never being held again. This is one of the side effects of not having Peaceoholics around anymore. After our funding ended, after everyone got their petty revenge on Peaceoholics and on me, the murders, violence, chaos, and the gang beefs broke out again, but this time worse than before.

It hurts to see the lack of attention given to the children caught in the violence of the war zones in our cities. We as a nation rise to the occasion for isolated incidents and high-profile cases. We fail to deal with the root cause of evil and blame guns, which are inanimate objects with no mind or emotion of their own. It is time to pay attention to the hurt in the lives of those who pull the triggers. Trust me when I tell you, "Hurt people hurt people!" It is not a game and it's a shame nobody cares until it's too late and violence, mayhem, and murder come knocking at their own front doors.

I will close this chapter with a story that comes full circle for me. It illustrates how children in our urban war zones who are traumatized by the most horrible violence can find healing and live productive lives. William Killebrew is a great example of what can happen when a child with PTSD does get the help he or she needs. I think William's story will inspire you as well as give us all hope that "hurt people don't have to hurt people" if they are surrounded by love.

At age six William Killebrew was violently raped by his mom's neighbor. At age ten he watched helplessly as his brother and mother were gunned down in front of him by the mother's ex-boyfriend who took his own life but not before making ten-year-old William beg for his own life. The next day William witnessed his grandfather shoot the next door neighbor.

This shocked and terrified him for years. He abused drugs and even tried to commit suicide. What saved William from the self-destructive forces of the evil he had witnessed was that, unlike BJ, he got three-and-a-half years of intensive professional counseling. He also had family and friends who wrapped him in love to bring healing to his damaged soul. Peaceoholics did its best to do the same thing for BJ and his siblings and it was yielding positive results in his life and the life of the community, but when our funding was stopped, BJ's soul was sucked back into the dark side of urban America.

Even with counseling and a loving support system, the battle William Killebrew had to fight was difficult and heroic beyond words. I have heard him speak and I know he credits both the counseling and the love and support of others for saving his life. William went on to graduate from college. He is now a consultant to the Department of Justice on these very issues, he has spoken in over 120 countries and has been heard by an estimated 145 million people. He has established the William Killebrew Foundation and has appeared on the Oprah Winfrey Show with Dr. William Cosby.

Now here is the twist in the story that makes William's story so very meaningful to me personally. You might recall from chapter one that when I was a little boy, my sister and I narrowly escaped from a man named William Marshall who was beating my mother. I called that my first kiss with death because we saw on the news just two weeks later that William Marshall had killed a mother and her son and then took his own life in a situation exactly like ours, but with a tragic ending. Well, that mother and boy who were murdered by William Marshall were the mother and brother of William Killebrew who was forced to beg for his life before Marshall killed himself.

In cases like BJ and Tee, it is true that "hurt people hurt people." But it doesn't have to turn out that way if we will get these children the counseling services they need and then surround them with love for as long as it takes to heal them from the evil they have seen and then like William Killebrew it can truly be said that "hurt people, help people."

William Killebrew speaking at Peaceoholics' and Anthony Williams' Youth Truce Day at Freedom Plaza

Lesson Eight

Never Too Late for a Father's Love
Generational Forgiveness

I was in the Oak Hill Youth Center with a group of incarcerated youth asking them a common question, "How many of you have your father in your life?" Out of twenty youth, maybe four hands went up. Then I asked how many of them love their father. Most responded with a negative gesture. Then I asked them how many of them practice abstinence and they looked at me like I was crazy because they often get stripes for being able to conquer a woman with bad intentions.

Then I asked them why they can't forgive their fathers for being absent in their lives while they are out doing the same things their fathers did. Just like their fathers, they do not take education seriously and attempt to screw every woman who walks past and have no intention of being with her. I then let them have the truth, "You say you love your mother but you disrespect her when you treat women like that after she has given you such unconditional love without your father at home."

I explained that this mentality produces households in our communities where 80 percent don't have a father. This is a lesson I had to adapt for myself late in my life because I was just like them for much too long. I still struggle with abstinence until I get married. I had a lot of animosity towards my father because I felt he left my mother hanging and played a role in my mother's slide into mental illness and drug addiction as she unsuccessfully tried to raise me and my sister with no help from him.

I want to be the one who breaks the generational cycle of absent fathers. My father went through the same thing and had the same habits as his father. For me to stop this cycle there had to be some healing and, once I humbled myself to do that, a lot of good things happened. My father was there for my children while I was out saving other people's children and there is no way I could have accomplished what I did without him.

I'm proud to say this played a great part in ensuring my twenty-four and twenty-one year old sons did not follow our footsteps. One is a volunteer firefighter, football coach, and works a full-time and part-time job and just became a proud parent. You have to drag him away from his daughter. The twenty-one year old works full time in the John Wilson Building, has a part-time job, and is a full-time college student. He also recently started his own t-shirt line. The cycle from the cradle to the prison has been broken for my family and now we can focus on building institutions for generations to come.

Three generations of black men are spiritually and physically connected in a positive way. Just think, this might not have happened without my father. Maybe the success stories would not have happened without him being there for my children when I needed him to be. I let young men know wherever I go that good things can happen if you just forgive your father and see what God will do. I really thought I didn't need a father, but I did, and so do they! Not forgiving our parents just sets us up to be miserable. Unforgiveness is a cancer that eats at the soul. It's not worth it! Let it go!

It is important that parents also forgive their children. I am so grateful to my father for expressing his forgiveness to me for all the damage done by my own anger at him. Jesus said to the religious leaders of his day who were accusing a woman of adultery, "Let him without sin cast the first stone." One by one they all walked away. Since none of us as either children or parents is without our faults, the only way to live is to forgive each other.

9

Confronting Bullying and Gun Violence Before they were Buzz Words

It's easier to build strong children than repair broken men.

—Frederick Douglass, Civil Rights Republican

In 2006, Peaceoholics was in seven out of eight wards working to defuse or prevent anything that could start violence in the schools. We identified youths who were instigators and we also created safe passages for children who were scared to walk to school because of neighborhood conflicts, peer-pressure, taunting, and assaults due to sexual preference. We were vigilant to spot gang violence and the new thing called cyber-bullying which would often lead to gun violence. All of these are forms of what is today called bullying. It's the new buzz word.

When I was growing up, a bully was more like a person who tried to take someone's lunch money, but things have changed. By 2006, something unimaginable happened. Rock Star Games released several versions of the violent video game, *Grand Theft Auto*. This game trained our children to steal cars and kill people just as the military uses simulation games to train our soldiers to fight and kill our enemies in war. Police departments use simulators to train their officers to protect the citizenry, but it also trained ex-LA cop and cop killer Christopher Dorner.

We were especially concerned about the minds of children who have little to no overall parental guidance or after school supervision. Our own youth agreed that these games destroy their minds. Some of these children have mental illnesses like the Sandy Hook Elementary School shooter who reportedly sat in his basement playing violent video games.

Then, to add fuel to the fire, Rock Star Games announced it was about to release a game called *Bully*! We knew the effect this game would have, not just on urban communities, but children everywhere. Behavioral scientists tell us that anything we do for thirty days in a row, changes the way we think and act. We knew this problem was not unique to children in poor urban communities, but also affects children in rural and suburban America as well. Playing one of these games a few times may not immediately turn a good kid into a bully or a mass murderer but it's the repetitiveness that's damaging and fosters long-lasting effects.

We talked to our youth in our program about the problem and they came up with an idea of making awareness signs and they thought it would be good to write letters to Rock Star Games. As you would expect of a company that glorifies stealing and bullying, Rock Star Games did not respond to the letters from our children. So far, we had failed to bring down Rock Star Games or even to have them acknowledge the children.

None of these failures caused us to give up teaching the children to stand up to bullies without becoming bullies themselves. Cyber-bullying and video game violence might have been relatively new, but African Americans have a history of being bullied and fighting back with nonviolent action. We decided to use that history to teach the children how to fight bullies today.

All black children learn the name of Martin Luther King, Jr., so we introduced them to people who actually marched with Dr. King and fought the bullies of racism and discrimination. So, as part of the Civil Rights Tours that I mentioned previously, the children were trained by people such as Amelia Boynton Robinson, Rev James Bevel, the man who organized the children to end segregation, and Pastor Gwendolyn Webb, who was one of the children in the 1963 Children's March that ran racist Eugene "Bull" Connor out of Alabama.

We gave the children, who Rock Star Games ignored, an opportunity to learn at the feet of the heroes who fought on even when Martin was in jail. They lost a lot of battles, but segregation was eventually outlawed with the passage of the Civil Rights Bill of 1964. The bullies lost because good people, black and white, never quit in their nonviolent struggle. The children learned that no one wins every battle in the war against bullies. They were taught that it is not losing, but in giving up, in surrendering, that you lose your soul, your humanity. Civil rights leaders stood up to Bull Connor, I stood up to the Vincent Gray and the corrupt seven, and the children stood up to Rock Star Games.

The tour also took them to Tuskegee University to visit the gravesites of Booker T. Washington and George Washington Carver. They learned from the lives of those two great men the importance of exercising our rights as citizens. They began to understand that real power is not in fists or a gun, but in using their minds and spirits to uplift people. Now with these lessons learned, we were ready to continue the battle against Rock Star Games.

We were all convinced these games were affecting this generation just like the movie *Scarface* had affected my generation. I knew many men who died or went to prison with the attitude of the famous line by Al Pacino's character referring to his gun, "Say hello to my little friend." So, with a whole new mentality and confidence we boarded our little freedom fighters on buses just like the ones we watched in our civil rights documentary called "The Children's March." We headed up I-95 to the New York headquarters of Rock Stars Games to protest and demand attention to this issue.

Our freedom ride and protest outside the New York headquarters of Rock Star Games gained national and local attention. It was covered by the New York Post, the Washington Post, Nightline, Miami Herald, and many more. Our youth felt empowered like never before. They admitted to us that before this experience, many of them thought there was more power in a gun than in activism in the name of the truth. Other groups also protested and put pressure on Rock Star Games which caused them to delay the release of *Bully*. It is our belief that the delay was not just to wait for the protests to die down, but to alter the original content of the game. We claimed a small victory even though the game is still bad for the minds of American youth.

We had other small victories as Senator Hillary Clinton temporarily joined the fight against the makers of these violent games. Locally, Councilmember Jim Graham took a stand with us and held hearings on the issue. He helped legislation to make it illegal to sell video games to minors that are not rated safe for children. Unfortunately, that legislation never made it out of committee. This was another lesson for our children. It is not always enough to just be right. Bullies come in all shapes and sizes and in Washington, D.C.; the biggest bullies are the K Street lobbyists.

The powerful lobbyist groups for the video game industry held a dinner for Hillary Clinton at the Washington Hilton on Connecticut Avenue. They also met with Jim Graham. Our courageous children got a lesson in politics when both Graham and Clinton backed down after some arm twisting by lobbyists for the video game industry. I guess it takes more than a village to raise a child, it takes courage.

With Youth protesting outside the New York City headquarters of Rock Star Games, the maker of *Bully* and *Grand Theft Auto* video games. This is where civil rights activist seeds were planted in our children.

In NYC speaking at a protest against the *Bully* video game. I am surrounded by over a hundred youth activists that we bussed up from Washington, D.C.

Violence on the Screen, Violence on the Streets

On December 28, 2012, the Washington Post ran my op-ed on the relationship between screen violence in videos and movies and how that contributes to violence on the streets.

It was obvious that the violent games desensitized these youths to violence. But I didn't really need them to tell me this. The focus groups brought back memories of when I was growing up. I was just as easily influenced by the entertainment industry. Many of my friends either wanted to be like Michael Jordan — or Scarface.

Did we idolize Jordan because he was the most exciting basketball player of all time? Or could it have been because he showed up in pretty much every other commercial on television? Scarface was a different story. Tony Montana — Al Pacino's character in the movie of that name — was admired for how he rose in the drug game. I saw the influence firsthand when some of my friends began saying, "Say hello to my little friend" — Montana's famous line — before committing acts of violence similar to what they saw glorified in the film.

Abraham and I knew we had to do something with what we were learning about the negative impact of violent media. With the support of civil rights activists, we set out to train youths who were once members of rival gangs to become activists. During our sessions with them, we discussed the impact of violent video games. They came to see themselves as change agents with the power to stop this poison from reaching their peers.

We had some successes with our work and started attracting media attention. Adrian Fenty and Jim Graham took the lead on D.C. Council legislation aimed at stopping violent and sexually explicit games from getting into the hands of minors. But once the powerful lobbyists from the video game industry got involved, it all went nowhere.

Now we have seen the horrific massacre in Newtown, Conn., and we're having the same conversation all over again. For District residents, the violence displayed in Newtown is all too familiar. In 2010, five young people were killed and nine wounded in the South Capitol Street massacre, only a few miles from where our president resides. Data show that murder is down in the District, but this is misleading to some degree. Since 2005, thousands have fallen victim to assaults, stab wounds and gunshots — all of which our children act out daily in video games that grow more violent all the time.

As you can see, we were on top of these issues long before they became buzz words. Now bullying and gun violence throughout the country are on steroids and affects all races, classes, and communities. Young people are committing suicide because of ruthless bullying both in person and online. Children are bullied for how they look, for what they believe, for being gay, or for being too smart or too dumb.

Isn't all violence against innocent people bullying? There are all kinds of bullies on the streets of our cities waging urban warfare against law-abiding citizens. The most notable example is the violence that is happening in the city of Chicago where at one point twenty people were being killed on average every week. Even with some of the strictest gun laws in the country and a mayor who was President Obama's Chief of Staff, they seem helpless to stop the violence.

I see the same political imbalance there as we have in D.C. Whenever one political party controls a city the solutions will all be slanted to one side. If the Chicago politicians think gentrification and more gun laws will solve their problems, they need to take a good hard look at the Nation's Capital. It is true that gentrification will change pockets of the population and reduce the number of people committing homicide, but it does not address the root problem. Homicides are down in D.C. but burglaries and robberies are up and, to no one's surprise, the victims are increasingly those in the wealthier gentrified areas.

Neither will more laws address the root problem of violence in our cities. Laws don't stop bullies; bullies either ignore laws or find a way round them or are willing to suffer the consequences if caught. Our politicians drive right past the problem in order to get to solutions that don't work. Why is there no outrage over the murder of more than a hundred young black men every year in the District of Columbia? The 2010 South Capitol Street Massacre saw nine people shot including an innocent little girl in just one incident.

Appropriately, the mayor showed up immediately when Jason Anthony Emma was tragically and brutally shot thirteen times on Capitol Hill where more affluent and influential people live. It was this incident that moved Mayor Gray to call for the hiring of more police and an even greater police presence on Capitol Hill. Unfortunately, as is typical of Mayor Gray, it took a month for him to show up at the site on North Capitol Street where thirteen black people were shot.

We mourn the death of one person killed on Capitol Hill and for the heartbreaking deaths of twenty children at the Sandy Hook Elementary

School and those killed and wounded in the Aurora, Colorado movie theater shootings. We should weep for all the victims of bullying and gun violence. But we must ask ourselves why more is made of twenty people being killed in an isolated mass murder than twenty people a week being murdered for a string of multiple weeks in just one city.

It makes no sense to reserve our sorrow just for suburban middle class killings simply because what happens in Newtown, Connecticut in one day takes a week to do in Chicago. After a week of young black men being murdered in every big city around the country, we never hear the words, "Things like this aren't supposed to happen in Chicago, D.C., St. Louis, insert your city here?" The reason for those words not being spoken is that "things like this" are expected in our big cities.

The sad truth is that we were on top of this issue as early as 2006. We predicted the violence would leave urban America and touch everybody because *all* of our children were being trained by various forms of violent entertainment and social media with no one paying attention. In each of the last four massacres outside of our large cities, all of the killers played violent video games. But nobody would listen to black voices speaking from Washington, D.C. because they believed their white picket fences, college degrees, and big bank accounts insulated them from this kind of violence. Now it isn't just on everyone's doorstep, it is in everyone's house.

I am also impatiently waiting for the day when the bullying and gun violence buzzwords are not used for political posturing. No matter where you come down on gun control, it is typical of Washington to turn the issue of protecting our children in schools to a battle over the Second Amendment. We need to start dealing with the root causes of this behavior that are destroying our children and communities. No more knee jerk solutions such as tighter gun control.

Almost all of the gunmen in the massacres came from families and people who legally acquired guns! We have to deal with how our children are being trained to become bullies and murderers before things get worse. Let's make "hope" more than an applause line in a speech. We need to provide youth and young adults with real love and opportunities so they will have something to live for and think about before they pull the trigger.

The best thing about what we did with these children in the fight against Rock Star Games was planting activist seeds in over three hundred youth who participated in the rallies, protests, and civil rights tours. They saw firsthand the power they have to fight against bullying on Wall Street, Main Street, City Hall, and in our communities. We completed four successful trips to New York and we are so grateful to the Hill Snowmen Foundation for their support of our youth engagement projects. These are some of the life-changing experiences our youth no longer have access to in the Nation's Capital now that Peaceoholics has been destroyed by political bullies.

I am gratified for and proud of what we accomplished during those years. We helped young people address bullying and other forms of violence. They learned the science of activism from civil rights leaders who stood up to bullies alongside Dr. King. These bus trips also showed these youth that many of them act like bullies, too. When they first got on the buses, rival neighborhoods would not speak to each other because of existing beefs or fear of bullies. It was tremendously moving to watch this cross-fertilization process lead to peaceful relationships by the time we arrived back home.

I still pray for the day when there will be just as much outrage about the violence in my community as there was about Michael Vick abusing dogs. Why are the murders of young black boys and girls not worthy of the same outrage as we have over cruelty to animals? I can tell you the hurt I felt after I saw The Vick story in the papers and on television and wondered if America values the life of a dog more than the lives of my three sons or my brother who was kidnapped off the streets of Washington, D.C. and was shot in the head in a closet in Maryland.

It seems clear that God has brought us all to this crossroads at this moment in time, so let's work together on this issue, stop pointing fingers of blame, and help our children who have become both the perpetrators and the victims of bullying and gun violence. Let's find the courage to stop making the portrayal of violence profitable in video games, movies, and on television. The commercialization and the glorification of violence must stop, if not by legislation, then by the moral outrage of our citizens.

I went to the oral arguments at the Supreme Court where D.C. gun laws were being challenged. This is a tough issue for me having witnessed illegal firearms being brought into neighborhoods where they were used to commit murder. From that perspective, I remain in favor of stricter gun laws for those who illegally sell these weapons in our community. Now I have a more well thought out position due to several factors that reflect my own growth as a person and my commitment to true civil rights of the individual.

For most of my adult life, I have supported stronger gun laws. Until recently, I never connected owning a gun to the fact that my grandfather had a .410 over under shotgun. He was not a criminal nor was he a Republican or Democrat. To this day he does not think either party is really about the people. What he does believe is that he has a God-given obligation and a constitutional right to protect his family and property. But this was thirty years ago and it dawned on me that this change in our attitude toward guns coincided with the breakdown of the family.

In those days, 73 percent of black adults were married. We had family values that included the right of a man to defend his family. I have done a lot of soul searching on this issue because I don't want to be supporting anything that is going to cause me to have to go to more funerals of young black children and young black men. So, I don't take it lightly when I say that I am in favor of responsible gun ownership and the constitutional right of U.S. citizens to protect themselves.

The fact is that guns didn't cause violence back then and they don't cause it now. In the last few months of this writing, the Boston Marathon bombers used pressure cookers to kill and injure more than a hundred people and a British soldier was hacked to death with a meat cleaver. What is the solution to this kind of violence? Is it really to ban pressure cookers and meat cleavers? The same people who think that the problem in those cases were the evil perpetrators think the answer to gun violence is to ban guns.

Prohibiting guns won't stop gun violence any more than the prohibition of alcohol stopped drinking in the 1920's. Even if we outlawed all guns and stopped making them today, they would still be available to criminals through a massive worldwide black market. The problem is not the weapon in a young person's hand, but what is in the heart. If a person's heart is not changed, nothing else really matters.

Damon "Day Day" Sams, whose story we told in chapter two, was the subject of a Newsweek Magazine story on November 24, 2007 before he shot and killed twenty-one year old Ashley McCrae. You will recall that we thought we had Day Day on the road to responsible citizenship when tragedy struck. In spite of having left gang life, he still had an illegal handgun that he claims went off accidentally and killed Ashley.

Day Day had been with Lynch Mob and Ashley lived in the neighborhood where the 1-7 crew was active. The street outside of Ashley's funeral was turned into a shooting gallery as revenge was sought for her death. All of this gun violence happened in a city with some of the toughest gun laws in the country. If you think passing more gun laws to keep responsible citizens from owning firearms is going to stop criminals from having access to guns, you aren't paying attention to the slaughter of young blacks in Chicago.

Here is what Newsweek wrote about Damon "Day Day" Sams. Pay close attention to what Day Day says on the impact of gun laws. Remember, this article was written four years *before* he was sentenced to ten years in prison for murdering Ashley. The title is "A New Shot at History: The high court will soon examine D.C.'s handgun ban. In the meantime, life on the street carries on."

Here is the first paragraph:

> Washington, D.C., has the toughest gun-control laws in the country. For 31 years, it has been illegal in the nation's capital to buy, sell or own a handgun. Residents may keep shotguns or rifles—but only if they are stored unloaded, and either disassembled or disabled with trigger locks. Even so, Damon Sams doesn't spend much time worrying about restrictions on his right to bear arms. Now 19, the former drug dealer got his first gun, a .380 pistol, at 13, when he started selling marijuana and later crack on a street corner in Southeast Washington. "I wanted people to respect me and be scared of me," he says. He also wanted protection. As a kid, he'd seen his father shot dead in the street. He's been shot himself on two separate occasions. Now an aspiring rapper who works with Peaceoholics, a D.C. group that tries to get kids off the streets, Sams no longer has any guns, but he says it wouldn't be much trouble to get them, ban or no ban. "I wasn't tripping on D.C. laws," he says with a smile.

I also often carried an illegal firearm before I went to prison. I wasn't using it to commit crimes, but I was ready to use it as protection against people who owed me money or wanted to rob me. For me, using a gun was a last resort since I was taught that war is costly and you can't get your money from a corpse. I was also taught that human life has value, which is a lesson many youth today learn after it is too late.

I do not own a gun now, but if I did, I would not ever use it for evil. What changed my mind about gun laws? My heart is as committed as ever to peace, but we did not stop gang violence by taking guns away from gang members. It would be impossible to prevent them from getting guns, so we found ways to change their hearts.

I want to emphatically restate that I am absolutely against the trafficking of firearms. I support the tough enforcement of our gun laws for those deliberately pushing illegal guns to our youth, gang members, and anyone else who has bad intentions. There are two things that I am not for in regard to gun laws. One is legislation that simply results in the mass incarceration of minorities and does not address the real issues that cause people to obtain illegal guns and pull the trigger.

The second thing I am against is passing gun laws that by definition are going to be ignored by criminals and only obeyed by honest citizens who want a firearm to protect them from those who use guns to commit crimes and terrorize innocent people. The Second Amendment is short, simple, and unequivocal as to our rights:

A well-regulated militia, being necessary to the security of a free state, the right of the people to keep and bear arms, shall not be infringed.

"[S]hall not be infringed" does not leave a lot of room for restrictive laws. Those who want to keep chipping away at the Second Amendment should be careful about picking and choosing rights to infringe upon. You might not like the Second Amendment, but maybe you believe that the freedom of the press and speech are important human rights. Once you set a set a precedent for taking away the rights you don't like, you endanger the very rights that you do value.

One of the problems with being liberal is that it so often puts restrictions on the average person, but creates and elite class that is exempt from those restrictions. Look at all the big corporations that are getting exemptions from participating in the "Affordable Care Act." I thought Democrats hated evil Wall Street companies.

The same is true for gun control. The rich and famous in Hollywood who are always "shooting" off their mouths about the evil of guns, not only make movies of the most violent sort, but many of them have armed body guards. The anti-gun crowd does not want armed guards in our schools to protect our children, but in one of the Mecca's of liberalism, Washington, D.C., the black run District of Columbia Public Schools all have armed guards.

It is funny how blacks have rejected what our own people have stood for in exchange for free stuff from Democrats. Maybe these words from none other than Malcolm X will help me make my point. This is part of what he said in his 1964 speech at the founding rally of the Organization of Afro-American Unity:

Since self-preservation is the first law of nature, we assert the Afro American's right to self-defense. The Constitution of the United States of America clearly affirms the right of every American citizen to bear arms. And as Americans, we will not give up a single right guaranteed under the Constitution. The history of unpunished violence against our people clearly indicates that we must be prepared to defend ourselves or we will continue to be a defenseless people at the mercy of a ruthless and violent racist mob.

We assert that in those areas where the government is either unable or unwilling to protect the lives and property of our people, that our people are within our rights to protect themselves by whatever means necessary.

I repeat, because to me this is the most important thing you need to know. I already know it. "We assert that in those areas where the government is either unable or unwilling to protect the lives and property of our people, that our people are within our rights to protect themselves by whatever means necessary.

This is the thing you need to spread the word about among our people wherever you go. Never let them be brainwashed into thinking that whenever they take steps to see that they're in a position to defend themselves that they're being unlawful. The only time you're being unlawful is when you break the law.

Some liberals like to make fun of Republicans who rightly claim that the purpose of the Second Amendment is to protect the people from the tyranny of the government if the time ever comes that our rights are taken away from us. Is that a far-fetched idea? The spring of 2013 has brought to light some stunning government abuses of our right to privacy, long a liberal rallying call.

All of a sudden Democrats are defending the NSA (National Security Agency) collecting the phone records of every phone call and text and Internet web chat of every American every day. The use of security cameras in public places, traffic cameras, and GPS systems are opportunities for abuse by the government. If they can demand all of our records from phone and Internet companies, they can demand that they hand over GPS information on our cell phone locations.

We can be tracked everywhere we go unless we give up the use of our phones and computers. Security cameras are something we have no control of and they are becoming more and more in use in public places and not just in privately owned businesses. , and use security cameras that the government could also demand from phone carriers and Internet providers.

Do you really want to give up the right to own firearms or have the laws be so restrictive that it is too burdensome a process to go through? I know that many people who are anti-guns have guns in their homes because they know that when seconds count, the police are minutes away. Too many of the bad guys in D.C. are armed and too few of the good men and women who are good law-abiding citizens. It's okay for Lil Wayne to tell our children in a video to "go into the kitchen and kill my mom," but I can't have a gun in my home to protect my family.

If you are still not convinced then I suggest you take up the argument with the store owner who, and the clerks at City Beats shoe store. Then go to the barber shops and gas stations in Southeast, D.C. that are constantly being robbed and try to peddle your liberal anti-gun policies. Just don't go to there at night because the bad guys in D.C. know that you do not have a gun. It's a different story in Virginia where they have reasonable gun laws. There the bad guys know that they better be careful because many law-abiding citizens have concealed carry permits and might send them to meet their Maker if they try to rob them.

Lil Wayne is an example of my concerns about the power of those in the entertainment industry that send negative messages to our youth. Lil Wayne certainly has the First Amendment right to say whatever vile and disgusting things he wants to in his videos. I just wish he would think about the damage he is doing to our children. He always leaves out the part about dying young or how your manhood is taken away in prison where people like him have only done short stints in protective custody. While I defend his right to free speech, I deplore the fact that his speech is violent and insulting to our women and the institution of family with songs like "If I could f**k every girl in the world".

I wish those who want to take away my Second Amendment rights would think about the inconsistency of their position. It isn't just entertainers who are hypocrites. Some members of Congress who vote for anti-gun legislation to restrict the average voter's right to own a gun have concealed carry permits. Some have armed body guards and all of them work in the U.S. Capitol and have offices in buildings that are guarded by armed Capitol Police.

Thanks to memories of my grandfather's shotgun and my friend Malcolm from the often robbed City Beats shoe store, I began to rethink my position on gun laws. I hope for the safety of our citizens in urban communities that black folk especially will once again reaffirm the principle of defending both one's self and loved ones. No one should be required to own a gun, but it is foolish and unconstitutional to keep others from doing so. I hope that it never comes to American citizens having to be armed to defend themselves from their own government, but the fear of tyranny and the right of self-defense underpins the founding fathers' reason for the Second Amendment.

I close with the story of an historic summer camp in Lancaster County, Pennsylvania. Camp Oak Hill (www.campoakhilllpa.org) was founded by two African-American women in 1948 at a time when most summer camps for children and teens were closed to blacks. This historic black camp was named after the little village of Oak Hill that was a safe station stop on the Underground Railroad where it is likely that both Frederick Douglass and Harriet Tubman visited.

During the writing of this book, I was shown some 1951 photos of black rifle instructors teaching black teenage girls marksmanship on a rifle range. The idea was for them to learn steadiness, concentration, discipline, and responsibility. The camp program also included horseback riding, ballroom dancing, boating, tennis, and swimming.

A 1952 photo of African-American girls at historic Camp Oak Hill summer camp leaning marksmanship with rifles.

When I saw these photos, I began to ask myself how we have gone from black children being taught the responsible use of firearms at summer camp to denying law-abiding citizens the right to even own a gun. That would include denying my grandfather the right to own a rifle to protect his family.

Having read the story of my earlier life, you know that I am well aware of the dangers of legal and illegal gun ownership. I am not here to tell you how you should vote or what you should believe about gun laws or any other issue. What I am trying to do is to get black voters to think for themselves and not just assume that the liberal Democratic Party agenda is necessary the one that is consistent with historic African-American values. I am only asking you to consider that there may be some answers to bullying and to gun violence that are different that the typical liberal reaction of banning guns and taking away our rights . Let's start finding solutions and voting for the politicians in both parties who actually address the reasons that our children engage in such destructive behavior.

Lesson Nine

Birds and Their Nest

One of my favorite and most enjoyable lessons to teach is one that we received from civil rights icon Rev. James Bevel. Rev Bevel is known for making many great contributions to the Civil Rights Movement in the South. Rev. Bevel was especially noted as one who organized children to help end segregation. He is a philosopher who would often use illustrations when proving his theories. In one of his teachings he compared birds to people and questioned which one was smarter in regard to building the institution of family. His contention was that birds were so much smarter than many of us and when he finished no one could argue with him. I have used his lecture as a way to teach our youth and know-it-all men like me about building strong families.

First, we ask if it is a good thing or a bad thing to be called a birdbrain. Most people agree that it's a bad thing because birds have tiny brains. Then we ask if they have ever seen the common brown bird called a wren. Most say yes, they have. Then we ask "What actions do female wrens take before they lay their eggs, in other words, before they have babies? The answer is usually, "I don't know." Only one out of a hundred answer; "She builds a nest." That is a very common answer, but it happens to be wrong.

The female European house wren does not build a nest. She goes out and evaluates the nests of the male birds. In other words, she seeks out who she believes would be the best provider and uses that as the basis for choosing where she will lay her eggs. The male wren will often build as many as twelve different nests until he finally builds one that meets the approval of the female! Wow, now those are some pretty smart and demanding birds for having such small brains!

Then we ask them to compare that to how 80 percent of the females in our communities find their mates. Do they wait to have babies until they find a man who can demonstrate that he is a good provider with the intentions of building family and institution? Do they get married first? Are the mother and the father of the babies involved in raising the children, caring for them? Do the father and mother participate in the institution of marriage? This is one answer our youth get correct. "No, most don't care who the father is, many just want to have babies."

We see smart birds look for life mates yet we settle for playmates that are not ready to be parents. Our girls don't value themselves enough to demand a man show he can provide a suitable "nest" for the mother and baby. He just needs to have a working sex organ. I know this very well because I was one of those men. It's interesting how our people often use the term "crib" to describe where we live because far too many of our men are just irresponsible babies and not real men. Most of us are just looking to have our immediate sexual needs satisfied. If a baby is the result, it becomes the sole responsibility for the girl to worry about.

We lay our eggs without building a nest or even worst we lay eggs in someone else's nest, who is not the father. That's like a bird laying its egg while flying, splat! So, who is smarter in this case, the female bird that makes the male build up to twelve nests to prove he is a worthy provider and committed father, or 80 percent of our girls who don't demand anything of the male who gets her pregnant? Maybe being called a birdbrain isn't so bad after all.

Now, let's be clear, it's two sides to this coin. It isn't just about our girls having babies without first getting married to a good "nest builder" who will provide for his wife and children. We ask the male youth how many of them are as qualified as the male wren, with his birdbrain, to make a baby. Many of them have already gotten girls pregnant, but not one of them can raise their hands and claim to be as smart as a male bird who busts his butt to prove he will be a good father.

Rejecting the institution of marriage and two-parent families results in the brains of our children being splattered on the streets of our neighborhoods in Los Angeles, Philadelphia, Baltimore, Birmingham, and even in our beloved President Obama's backyard, Washington, D.C. I only have to think about my brother or the children of the South Capitol Street Massacre of 2009 to realize the price we have paid for disobeying God's law, and having babies outside of marriage.

This is something we must focus on. I believe we must spend more time focusing on teaching our people about family and marriage! It's the easiest and the best way to solve so many of our problems. This is one reason being a Republican is more consistent with the values of our people and, most Americans. Whatever your view on gay marriage, while gays in America fight for marriage, we fight against them and, at the same time, either turn a blind eye to or engage in adultery in violation of the very institution we say we believe in and should believe in so strongly.

My view on the Defense of Marriage Act, gay marriage, or the gay lifestyle, is that everyone deserves to be treated with dignity and respect as human beings. We teach that it is best if children are raised by a mother and father. God ordained the institution of marriage from the beginning of creation. In the book of Genesis, he said, "A man shall leave his father and mother and cling to his wife and the two shall become one flesh." He also said to them, "Be fruitful and multiply."

While I have great compassion for women and girls who face unwanted pregnancies, both pre-birth and post-birth abortion of innocent children are crimes against humanity. What I mean about post-birth abortion is the abandonment or abuse of children who are unwanted, but not aborted before birth. Post-birth abortions cast children into this wicked world without support and proper guidance. These children often grow up to produce much of the terror we see in urban America. Both sides on the abortion issue should work together to promote and teaching the value of the institution of marriage instead of constantly fighting a battle in which no one wins and the big losers are the children.

There is no statistic more out-of-line with the traditional values of the black community than this: seventy-two percent of black children in America are born to unwed mothers. Our generation is to blame, our churches and religious leaders have let us down, we have let ourselves down, and we have let our children down. Our Democratic Party has let us down. Black people have moved away from our pro-family mission. This is one of the reasons I am now a Civil Rights Republican. Not that the Republican Party knows how to deliver the message in a respectful and understandable way I think we have lost our way just thinking and taking the same route for the last forty years. We have gotten away from what made us strong and a respectable force to be reckoned with, strong family values. The policies of Republicans might not always be consistent with family values, but it is easier to fix the policies when the Party claims to be pro-family than to fight the Democrat policies that at times make fun of the idea of family values.

I have said time and time again that I am not under the impression the Republican Party is perfect. What I do know is one party supports policies that encourage our poor women to have new baby every few years to keep the welfare checks coming instead of empowering them to achieve the American Dream. A true government safety net, or springboard, would not encourage our young girls to have more children outside of marriage. That violates everything the black community, the black church believes! This practice also teaches men like me, that it is just fine to utilize our women as playmates versus as queens, who have a divine purpose.

We must understand that when we choose to be playmates instead of building a family, we increase the chances of negative emotions between the parents, feelings get hurt and it becomes less about the children. I now fully understand that my seed is sacred and every man is morally responsible for where that seed is planted and for the children that it produces. Women should feel the same way about the sacredness of the womb and receives the seed only from the right person for the right reason and to be responsible for the children that it produces.

When a woman uses her womb does not guard her sacred womb or a man does not take responsibility for the children that come from his seed, a lot of foolishness results. As part of this foolishness, mothers sometimes try to punish the father by not letting him see his children. This hurts the father, but also the children. Again, unless the courts determine that the father is somehow a danger to his children, he should be allowed to see them without duress and extensive court hearings.

Some women do abandon their children due to drug addiction or other problems, often times, single mothers bear burden of raising our children alone. Both mothers and fathers need to work these things out without the government getting involved. The government did not make us get in the bed and we should not need the threat of legal action to take responsibility!

When we have sex with multiple partners, drop our seed, and just move on, the females we impregnate have to carry the burden of parenthood or face the moral dilemma of whether or not to get an abortion. Whether a man is fighting the demons of self-gratification, going to prison, alcoholism, workaholism, drug addiction, or any other vice, children need both mommy and daddy. Let's man up, men!

I can personally attest to the negative impact that broken homes have on children, not just by my life experiences as a child but also through the challenges I faced with my children's mother. Those stories are enough to fill a separate book of its own. I'm just so happy we were able to eventually work out our issues however there was one situation which was hell for me.

I would like to take moment to look deeper into a messy relationship that I participated in during a time in my life when you would think that I would know to be better. Below you will find two letters that were written during that time. These letters clearly show that I too, was really caught up in a messy situation. Once that relationship ended, from that point forward, I was determined that it would be my last episode of this practice of this insanity. After all that was done by her, I once considered some wise advise to try and become a family with her and our two children. However, I found it very hard to do considering the recurring conflicts and serious trust issues that I held. Although our family unit will never be, I truly wish her well in all that she sets out to do.

Both letters were sent to the media by the mothers of my two children that I referenced above. She also sent them to my opponents in my City Council race. That was my "Herman Cain" moment. I was surprised when I received calls from the media. They informed me that I was being portrayed as a deadbeat dad when anybody who has ever been around me knows I've been there for my children. At one point, I was operating as a as a single parent with one of my boys with no support from the mom until he was old enough to take care of himself. Sending those letters was her way of getting back at me. Did I say it was perfect? No, but I've never ran away from my responsibilities. The first letter was intended to destroy my name and reputation because she was upset at me by her own admission.

The second letter was her retraction of the first letter. Her issue with me was that I did not want to be with her. I was foolish enough to think that if I told a woman that I did not want to be in a relationship or have children by her, and only wanted to have sex, and I thought because she agreed to the terms...silly me, I actually thought things would be just fine. We see so many people's reputation taken down from this type of madness. All due to their playmates acting out of emotion, why... because they were just that, a playmate.

In this case, it's difficult to take back stories like that once they are out there. It can affect a person forever. My opponent Yvette Alexander really took advantage of that situation. There were representatives from her camp at the polls telling people about the false content of this letter and in some cases showing constituents the email. To this day I don't know how much all of this hurt me but I can only imagine. With all the things I know about my children's mother, I could hurt her career and life, but what would that accomplish? I certainly wish she had thought about it before she committed this grave transgression against me.

I had to forgive her for trying to destroy my personal life and professional career because I was happily in another relationship with the intentions of getting married. I wanted to move on, but just when my life was in a better place, she again acted out of desperation. She found my address, came to my house, and wreaked havoc. This is the emotional roller coaster you get on when you treat each other as sex objects and not husband and wife building a positive institution.

I knew that I could never allow myself to be put in a compromising position. When a person is willing to destroy you, they will do almost anything. I have forgiven her because I have accepted the role I played in it all, but forgiving someone does not mean having trust. This is a relationship I truly regret and need all the prayers I can get so I will always do the right thing by her for the sake of our children. I have nobody to blame but myself for the insanity that I participated in. Let this be a lesson to all the black men and woman out there! We have to stop playing a role in this craziness.

The First letter:

Subject: I have been silent about Ronald Moten long enough....I am finally speaking up and letting the truth be known.

I am the mother of Ronald Moten's two youngest children (five and three) and I have kept silent about his blatant hypocrisy surrounding his image for almost six years. The truth is he isn't accountable with his children that he has with me. I never said a word publicly because I hoped, desired, and wanted him to be the man I know he is. If someone is going to run for public office and be a paid public servant, then they need to be living a credible, authentic, life when no one is looking. If a candidate is going to represent a community, then before he makes any speeches about what others should be doing in the community he should make sure his household is in order. It is not in order, nor does he want it to get in order.

He is saying he is a Republican, but Republicans number one rule is "personal responsibility" but he doesn't take credit for his role in anything. It's always my fault. This goes as far back as the Peaceoholics days, he has played games with denying them, to this day he continues to state that I "set him up" when I had these children. He will only take them to certain events, b/c as he informed me "it doesn't look good with me having these two small children with you." I have placed him in the child support system before and I'm in the process of doing so again. I have many stories that I allowed to happen as I sat by waiting, and hoping for him to change.

Some people are aware of the hypocrisy, but they never say a word because they were/are benefiting off of his "image" or connections, so many keep silent and "keep it in the black community". I could have continued to be silent, and watch him act one way in public, and a completely different way behind closed doors. I've had enough of the lack of responsibility and accountability for two of his five biological children. This doesn't negate what he does with other youth in the community, as he is very involved with children across the city. His own children he will not be able to show proof of providing for either of them for most of their short lives.

I recently tried again, to make things work and give him a chance to step up and be a responsible father again as he has done at times, but when I realized he was still playing games with the public and our children....I stepped away from his campaign, and told him I was fed up with his "refusing to get a job, or even put his resume out there to people". After six years of the games, lies, and deception, I'm speaking out and placing him back in the child support system, where I also had him when he was "running" the Peaceoholics.   Enough is enough.

The Second letter:

2 Timothy 2:23-24

[23] Don't have anything to do with foolish and stupid arguments, because you know they produce quarrels. [24] And the Lord's servant must not be quarrelsome but must be kind to everyone, able to teach, not resentful.

I am emailing because I want to retract the statement I sent out earlier about Ronald Moten. As, I read this scripture I know that I wasn't kind, and I was resentful and very hurt. I sent the email out with the intent to attack his credibility and hurt him. A sister warned me that "karma would come back with this". I chose not to listen to her and other elders about my email. She was correct in that "I was trying to attack his credibility and in turn, I will now be looked at with less credibility". We reap what we sow.

I know that I'm required to turn this around b/c I was unloyal [sic] to someone I love and consider a friend. We all have disagreements and we all can look at our lives and remember when "we did something or said something that we wish we never did". I regret that I used this tactic to try and destroy a man that I love, respect, and care deeply about.

I placed the Bible verse, because I was angry and we had some challenges going on with us, as everyone does. He is a great provider and he and I have experienced financial difficulties within the last year-and-a-half, (as you all know with his business being annihilated).

I consider him to always have my back and out of anger "I chose to forget all he has done".

He gave me the money for a car, he paid my security deposit for where I live, so many other things and he attends our daughters school so that we can read to the class together. He just participated and paid for our son to play soccer out here in Alexandria. The black man and woman's relationship can be loving and wonderful when we are in sync together, and I humanly got "out of sync" in anger. I was convicted in my spirit to take back, what I sent out to the universe. Thank you for respecting our privacy and reading my email.

Now, at age forty-two, I pray I will finally get married to a woman who can complement my strengths and weaknesses as I do hers. I'm ready to marry and build a strong family institution! It is time for me to lead by example because, up until now, I realize I have played a role in creating the mess I am speaking about to others. While I have been there for my children as much as possible, I was incarcerated in my early twenties and at times, I got caught up in a few foolish relationship games with the mothers of my children, but overall, I thank God for keeping me in place so that our children had an opportunity to witness a positive and loving sex free environment.

I have worked with a lot of children who have witnessed their parents play relationship games. It's a recipe for disaster and adds to the destruction of our communities. These games deprive our children of what they deserve; being raised by a father and a mother in a loving and caring family. Positive families create a stronger community and institutional support systems.

Let this be a lesson learned so you don't forget what we must do to "Rebuild the Village" we once had. Men must learn to respect our woman and understand what a great Civil Rights Republican named Mary McLeod-Bethune said, "Next to God, we are indebted to women, first for life itself and then making it worth living." Our women must understand what she meant when she said, "The true worth of a race must be measured by the character of its womanhood." Rev. Bevel told us we will fall on our faces until we understand and live by this principle.

Toward the end of his life Rev. Bevel became an unfortunate example of what can happen in unhealthy relationships. This does not negate all the good things he did and said. However, it is a lesson I have taken to heart and, from his experience, I know that a man can never stop being vigilant over all of his actions right up until the moment he passes from this life. I hope and pray that I will do just that!

CIVIL RIGHTS REPUBLICANS

In 1893, the famous Civil Rights Republican, Carter G. Woodson published the classic book "The Miseducation of the Negro." He was known as the father of Black History. The premise of the book was that blacks need to be self-reliant and not depend on others to do for us what we should do for ourselves. According to Woodson, history shows that it does not matter who is in power. Those who have not learned to do for themselves and have to depend solely on others, never obtain anymore rights and privileges in the end than they had in the beginning. Woodson continues, when you have to control a man's thinking, you do not have to worry about his actions. You do not have to tell him not to stand here or go yonder. He will not have to find his proper place. You will not have to tell him to go to the back door, he will go on his own.

Carter Woodson

CAN YOU MATCH THESE CIVIL RIGHTS REPUBLICANS WITH THEIR PHOTOS?

1. **John Mercer Langston**, whose grave site can be found at the historic Woodlawn Cemetery in Washington's Ward 7, served as the first African-American congressman from Virginia. Hughes, the uncle of poet Langston Hughes, was also the first president of Howard University and the founder of the law school. The Langston Golf Course on Benning Road is named for him.

2. **Blanche Kelso Bruce** was also laid to rest at Woodlawn Cemetery was the first African-American senator to be elected to a full term. He is the only African American to have his signature on U.S. currency.

3. **Frederick Douglass** was an advisor to presidents, an abolitionist, editor, orator, author, and statesman. He lived in the Anacostia section of Southeast, D.C. and his home is now a national park. He said, "I am a Republican, a black dyed in the wool Republican, I never intend to belong to any other party than the party of freedom and progress."

4. **Mary Church Terrell** who co-founded the NAACP said, "Every right that has been bestowed upon blacks was initiated by the Republican Party.

5. **Nannie Helen Burroughs**, an educator, orator, business woman, and a religious woman, attended Dunbar High School in D.C. She founded the National Training School for Women and Girls. In 1976 it was renamed the Nannie Helen Burroughs School. She was a member of the National Republican Colored Women and has an Avenue in Ward 7 named in her honor.

6. **A. Phillip Randolph** led the march on Washington in 1963. He also organized and led the Brotherhood of Sleeping Car Porters, the first black labor union.

7. **Sojourner Truth** was an abolitionist and women's rights activist. Her famous speech was entitled, "Ain't I a Woman?" In 2008 she was became the first black honored with a bust in the U.S. Capitol.

8. **George Washington Carver** was a world acclaimed scientist, botanist, educator, and inventor. An agricultural genius, Carver helped lift American agriculture during troubled times.

9. **Harriet Tubman** freed more than 300 slaves, fought in the Civil War, and was the first American woman to lead an expedition into war.

10. **Booker T. Washington**, educator and founder of historic Tuskegee University where he taught blacks to build with their own hands. He even taught how to manufacture the bricks used to build the university. He said, "At the bottom of education, at the bottom of politics, even at the bottom of religion, they must be for our economic independence."

11. **Eldridge Cleaver**, the Minister of Information for the Black Panther Party who said, "You're either part of the solution or part of the problem.

12. **Jackie Robinson** broke the color barrier in Major League Baseball. He said, "Life isn't important except for the impact it has on other lives."

"If we use what worked in the past, it will save our future."
—Ron Moten, Civil Rights Republican

Why I'm running for D.C. Council as a Republican

By Ron Moten, October 21, 2011
Washington Post Op-Ed

Last month, Republican presidential hopeful Herman Cain created waves about his ability to attract blacks to the Republican Party. Blitzer asked why the GOP is seen as "poison for African Americans." Cain responded, "Many African Americans have been brainwashed into not being open-minded." I believe that the problem is much deeper and more systemic than that. I believe that most Americans attach themselves to a particular party and lose sight of the fact that all political parties belong to the people.

That certainly appears to be the case in the District. For 40 years, since the District achieved home rule, its government has been led by Democrats. But what has a purely Democratic agenda delivered for the city and its African Americans?

African Americans in the District have made tremendous progress over the years. We have gained high-level positions in government and organizing, and we effectively manage nonprofits that have built communities. But with these achievements have come some enormous costs. The greed and corruption of legacy politics have become entrenched. We have allowed a privileged few to act as kingmakers, crowning as a result generations of lackluster politicians who seem not to have the District's best interests at heart.

These politicians have consistently spent more money to educate our children but have consistently failed to provide a quality education. We've entrusted them with bringing jobs and businesses to the city, but they have continually neglected Wards 7 and 8, where unemployment rates have long been at inexcusable levels. They have declared war on poverty in our neighborhoods, introducing "new and improved" programs. But still Ward 8 has a poverty rate of 35 percent.

The question remains: Who is leading our residents on a path to prosperity?

A lack of political balance has created an alarming trend in our city. With only one cookie-cutter template from which to bring about change, we have created a local political class who all think, act and support the same platform. We seem to be afraid to change the status quo. We support corrupt leadership and blame the messengers who expose the truth, rather than facing facts and withdrawing our support.

It doesn't have to be this way. I see real opportunity for the District and all of its residents to bring about the changes that have eluded us for so long. That is why I am running to become the next D.C. Council member to represent Ward 7. That is why I am running as a Civil Rights Republican.

Those who question my association with the Republican Party should look back on what it means to be a Civil Rights Republican. The fact is that African Americans have played a considerable role in shaping both major parties. Neither party has been perfect, but our involvement in each has brought about positive outcomes — for us as a people and for our country. Booker T. Washington and Frederick Douglass were Republicans. In 1870, when Thomas Mundy Peterson became the first African American to vote under the 15th Amendment, he did so as a Republican.

During the civil rights era, African Americans changed their allegiance when they saw the Democratic Party embrace their struggle for socioeconomic enfranchisement. (I doubt Peterson could have imagined an African American reaching the pinnacle of U.S. politics as a Democrat.) But it is time for this chapter to draw to a close. Our blind support for Democrats has left Washington politically stagnant. Our inability to secure voting representation in Congress, for instance, can be partially attributed to the lack of a balanced political spectrum in our city. If Republicans in Congress could count on a healthy debate in our halls of government, perhaps they would have less opposition to passing D.C. statehood legislation.

In the early 1900s, two thriving African American communities — Greenwood, Okla., (known as "Black Wall Street") and Rosewood, Fla. — were built upon Republican principles of strong family values, free enterprise and property ownership. Ultimately, both would be destroyed by the Ku Klux Klan — the terrorist arm of the Jim Crow Democratic Party. Now that we have some measure of political and economic success, I believe we can turn away from cycles of political and economic dependency and rekindle the spirit of Rosewood and "Black Wall Street." We can be the masters of our own destiny, rebuilding and strengthening our communities. By applying traditional Republican views, such as entrepreneurship, self-reliance and individual responsibility, many overlooked African Americans will find a real and successful way forward.

If our history of fighting for civil rights has taught us anything, it's that you don't have a positive effect on a society or a political party by sitting on the sidelines. You must become an active citizen and a formidable participant. My many years of community organizing have taught me that.

African Americans are not and have never been monolithic. Putting all of our eggs in one basket has left us powerless and vulnerable. Those who stood up and sacrificed to give us the rights we enjoy today would be marching right alongside of us to demand fair representation and change in the Ward 7 and accountability in the John Wilson Building. Come join the march for economic freedom. Come join the Civil Rights Republicans.

10

The Evolution of a Civil Rights Republican

It doesn't matter to me whether people are Democrat or liberal or conservative or Republican. I just think everyone has an obligation to think about what is going on around them – stand for something, care about something, don't be neutral.

—Jack Kemp

I was in Birmingham, Alabama, near the banks of the muddy Mississippi River, talking to a civil rights icon who worked with Rev. Martin Luther King, Jr. He told me he was a Republican, and had been all his life. He did not agree with all Republican policies or all Republican leadership. But he floored me when he pointed out that most of the people he fought against to end segregation like Bull Connor and George Wallace were Democrats. To my surprise he also informed me that the KKK was started by Democrats shortly after the Civil War.

It all made sense to me, every bit of it, but all I could think about was the seeds that were planted in my mind that all Republicans are racists. Every time I thought of Republicans, I had thoughts of Jesse Helms or Armstrong Williams. Helms eliminated Pell grants. These grants made it possible for inmates to get their degrees and return to society with additional education, better prepared for transition back into our communities. This really devastated me because I knew how much I benefited from taking college classes while incarcerated. I was also aware that the University of the District of Columbia once had a college program for inmates and 97 percent of those who obtained a degree never went back to prison.

Most African Americans consider Armstrong Williams a sellout because he speaks out strongly against liberal policies. I have now come to understand that Armstrong, like many black Republicans, have a much needed message to deliver, but they do not always know how to do so in a way that it can be digested by many blacks. They often come across as though blacks need the Republican Party and I believe that the Republican Party needs us. Black people need to be willing to stand up to the leadership of both parties. I think I have shown throughout this book that I will stand up to the leadership of either party regardless of the color of their skin.

My Birmingham experience opened my eyes and I realized that the Democrats have been no better to African Americans and, in many ways, worse than Republicans. When I became more exposed to the behind-the-scenes reality of D.C. and national politics, I felt like Ronald Reagan who, when asked why he left the Democratic Party, answered, "I didn't, it left me." In my eyes, the Democrat Party left me before I was born.

It left me when the Johnson administration enacted anti-black family legislation and disguised it as Great Society programs, which if it the programs were institutionalized correctly, could have been a continuous springboard and decades of quicksand. I'm convinced that the fundamental reason black people were able to defy all odds from slavery to Jim Crow was through its strong families. My ancestors built sound communities through institutions of integrity and success as have many newly arrived American citizens. These hard working folk do not fall for fool's gold. When the Democrat Party left the principles of hard work and responsibility, it left me. It just took me a while to figure that out.

The icing on the cake came when I saw firsthand how this liberal Democrat system of dependency rejects any policy or legislation that works to help poor people become self-sufficient and prosperous. Since a disproportionate number of black people live in poverty, too many of us blindly vote Democrat. So politicians in the entitlement party often take our automatic vote for granted, the "do-gooders" have their misplaced guilt soothed, and the black pimpocracy prospers from our poverty.

God help the black politician who bucks the Democrat machine. I supported D.C. Mayor Adrian Fenty when he declared no more business as usual; then I watched as the Democrats went after him and his supporters, including me. In chapter after chapter, I have recounted what was done to Peaceoholics in a city run exclusively by Democrats. It was this kind of experience that made me begin to feel more and more uncomfortable because I did not believe what I was seeing and hearing was the answer for the people I wanted to represent.

What those great Civil Rights Republicans taught me was starting to have an effect deep in my soul. They had warned me, "When a man goes against what he knows is true, it will drive him crazy." This is why many of them never became Democrats. It wasn't because today's Republican Party is perfect for black people, but its foundational principles and balance are something Democrats are missing, especially in the Nation's Capital. So, it was just a matter time before I decided to practice what I now understood and believed as a result of my time with those great gray-haired icons who marched with Dr. King.

I still often daydream about those conversations near the muddy waters of the Mississippi in Alabama and the walks we took in the fields of with those civil rights pioneers. I finally understood. I didn't agree with all Democrats or all Republicans, but I now understood that at my core I was a Civil Rights Republican like Frederick Douglass, Abraham Lincoln, Jack Kemp, Booker T. Washington, Nannie Helen Burroughs, and Harriet Tubman. It was time to advance their great works, which meant breaking the Democratic Party's stronghold on my soul.

What better place to do that than the Party of Lincoln? In spite of popular belief, Republicans allow much more diversity than Democrats. There are Jack Kemp, Ronald Reagan, Chris Christie, Log Cabin, Republicans. There are Rush Limbaugh and Tea Party conservatives. Republicans come in a lot of flavors and even though some of them are distasteful to me, each is grounded in the three principles of our Civil Rights Republican ancestors: freedom, opportunity, and individual responsibility.

Let me be clear, I am not going into this with my eyes closed. While I am proud to be in a truly "big tent" party, I still expect to be drinking muddy water fighting battles with Republican strategists. I simply do not think the Party still understands how to bring significant numbers of minorities into the tent.

One of my principles for violence reduction in our cities is that the antidote to the problem comes from the snake that bit you, that is, from the source of the problem. That meant training and utilizing former gang and crew members to help squash beefs. At first, not many people thought that was a good idea. They changed their minds when it began to work better than any other solution that had been tried. Even God used "the venom from the snake that bit you" principle to spread the Gospel through the whole Roman Empire. He took Saul of Tarsus who was persecuting Christians and putting them to death, changed his name to Paul and made him the greatest evangelist the world has ever known.

The same principle holds true for increasing minority participation in the Republican Party. Black voters from urban neighborhoods are not going to respond to the same voices as main stream Republican voters. For instance, take Armstrong Williams and Artur Davis who are both having a significant influence on behalf of the Republican Party in certain black populations. But as intelligent and articulate as these men are, I respect Artur Davis for the fact that he himself told participants at a D.C. GOP event that it's the Ron Moten's who are going to have the greatest impact for the Party in the black urban community.

However, I am encouraged by the fact that the RNC (Republican National Committee) has recently hired some people that send a strong signal that the Party is moving in the right direction. As part of the GOP minority outreach, the RNC just hired Amani L. Council to the newly created position of African-American Communications and Raffi Williams as Deputy Press Secretary. Unlike black CNN Republican contributor, Crystal Wright, I choose to trust that these efforts are not just token actions, but the first steps of many. What the RNC may not realize is that this kind of inclusiveness will not only increase black voter involvement in the Republican Party, but involvement those white Independents who have hesitated to vote Republican.

It is important to point out that being a Civil Rights Republican does not mean that Democrats are the enemy. As long as I'm involved in D.C., politics, I will collaborate with Democrats wherever we find points of agreement in order to get things done for the good people of the District of Columbia.

As a Civil Rights Republican, I stand for the great historic principles of the Republican Party and our political ancestors like Frederick Douglass. It does not mean I agree with every flavor of Republican or support every Republican candidate or policy. On economic issues, I am a Jack Kemp Republican and I disagree with how President Obama is handling the economy. Still, I am not ashamed to say I voted for President Obama in his first race. The difference between me and most blacks who voted for the first black president is that no one owns my vote. No Democrat can just take my vote for granted including Barack Obama.

On the other hand, I am not like some conservative black contributors to the media, who voted for President Obama, and then regularly tear him down publicly. Such is the case with the aforementioned Crystal Wright who can't seem to make up her mind what or who she supports. When convenient, Ms. Wright believes that if you are a Republican, you have to vote for only for Republican candidates. I disagree with that. How can I tell black Democrats to stop voting slavishly for all Democrats if I am a slave to voting for all Republicans?

It is also curious that Ms. Wright asked the DCGOP why they were holding the Ward 7 Republican primary debate in a Denny's on Benning

Road, NE. For those of you unfamiliar with D.C., the location of the Denny's is in what Ms. Wright probably considers "a bad neighborhood in the heart of urban D.C., where the community has more than 93 percent Democratic population." To add insult to injury, she sent out an email stating, Republicans should not support me because I was supporting Obama. That statement was far from the truth as my exact words were; I'm going to vote for the best candidate just like I'm asking everyone to do. Maybe, if Ms. Wright had the heart to come into the community she would have heard it herself.

As one of the two candidates in the debate, I applaud the DCGOP for having the courage to hold an historic first Republican debate in the heart of an underserved and over incarcerated urban community as I proposed.

We were honored to have Mr. Colby King, legendary Washington Post columnist, moderate the debate. He seemed to enjoy the setting and hanging out with the good folk in Ward 7. It was an exciting event. One can only call it hypocrisy when Ms. Wright criticizes the GOP for not reaching out to blacks and then questions why a Republican debate was in a neighborhood that is almost 100 percent African American.

Washington Post columnist Colby King (l) moderates the first ever Republican primary debate at the Denny's in Ward 7 between me and Don Folden (c)

By all accounts, it was said that I won the debate in front of a packed house filled with Republicans and Democrats. I went on to win the nomination and was later endorsed by the Washington Post against my

Democrat opponent in the general election in a liberal town. It seems that voters did not consider Ms. Wright to be very credible when she warned fellow Republicans that I could not be trusted because I supported President Obama. It is that kind of thinking that has kept blacks from becoming Republicans.

It is true that I voted for President Obama in his first race. I believed in him. Now, four years later, I really can't tell you three things he has done to make life better for African Americans compared to what he had done for others. I can tell you what he has done for the LGBTQ and Latino communities. That is all well and good, but it is clear that Mr. Obama and the Democratic Party are convinced that the black vote is so secure that our agenda is not a top priority. When We Act Radio hosted an event at Busboys and Poets, I stood up and talked about this with some Democratic scholars and friends. They agreed with me and then said, "You're right, but we still can't vote Republican."

You will never hear me say I will or won't vote for someone because of party affiliation. Chris Christie and Ben Carson would have had my vote rather than Obama if one of them had been the Republican nominee in 2012. However I supported Chris Christie by write-in because Obama and Mitt Romney just couldn't convince me to push the pen for either one of them. In most cases, I will lean toward Republicans, but as an American and a Civil Rights Republican, my vote will go to the candidate whose policies I judge to be based on the principles of freedom, opportunity, and individual responsibility, not political party or color.

The main point I want people to understand is that Obama and Romney are both men who put their pants on the same way. It's not about a donkey or an elephant. It's about going more than skin deep and seeing who is going to represent your interests and the interests of the country. Romney can be "stiff as cardboard" and Obama may be able to "sing like Al Green," but neither of those factors determined who I voted for on Election Day.

Even though I do not agree with many of Obama's policies, I still love and respect him as our president. My vote was based on policy, but my respect is for a person's character, not whether we agree or disagree on politics. I hope others would respect me for the same reason. In fact, one thing smart Republicans know is that many black Republicans voted for Obama for two reasons. First, they wanted to cast a vote in the election of the first black president. Second, they were motivated by how surrogates for the John McCain campaign attacked Obama.

That being said, I'm one of a growing number of black folks who will no longer take the bait held out by personalities like Bill Clinton. He was like Emperor Nero, but instead of fiddling while Rome burned, he played the sax while his policies were burning down the hopes and dreams of blacks and other minorities more than any other president since slavery. The same goes for Mayor Gray of Washington, D.C. He does the Electric Slide while taking our great city and its black citizens back twenty years.

I often ask myself whether President Obama is trying to do the same thing when he sings Al Green's hit "Let's Stay Together" while doing nothing for blacks and much more for our gay and Latino citizens. To their credit, they worked hard for what they got, but nobody worked any harder to elect President Obama than blacks. In fact, for the first time in American history, blacks turned out to vote in a higher percentage than whites.

Ask yourself if you can come up with two things President Obama has done to make your life better for black people. We worship the ground he walk on, meanwhile, black unemployment sky rockets and black entrepreneurship is shackled by massive regulations. Both the NAACP and the Congressional Black Caucus have recently put out official statements pointing out that blacks are worse off now than when President Obama took office.

Democrats are always offering hope and change, that was not original with Barack Obama, he just delivered the message better than Al Gore and John Kerry. Now, after almost four years of excuses and negative results, more blacks than ever are ready to swap promises of hope and change for results and jobs. The truth is that Republicans can deliver the goods, but not the message. Black voters turned off by Mitt Romney whose problem wasn't that he was saying all the wrong things, but when the opportunity presented itself, he always said the right things the wrong way for the ears of black Democrats and other minorities.

Men like Ronald Reagan, Bill Clinton, and Barack Obama are testaments to the importance and power of the messenger, not just the message. I think I am the type of Republican who can deliver the Republican message, not only to other blacks, but to all Americans including those in the dependent class who truly want to get off government assistance and work.

It is obvious from the outcome of the 2012 election that most minorities experiencing economic hardship don't realize that Republican

Party principles and policies could turn America around for everyone. My message to the Republican Party is that our principles are just what the country needs and, in many cases, the only route to true recovery for America. Now, let's get the messengers out there who know how to communicate those principles and policies to the various constituencies who typically vote Democrat.

My message to black people is that affirming Republican principles is not enough. We need representation in both parties, not just the Democratic Party that has taken our votes for granted for all too long. We need greater balance in party affiliation and to be willing to vote for the best candidate. When you need a plumber for a sewage problem, do you care if the plumber is a Republican or Democrat or do you only care if they can get the job done right and on time? Only a fool would care about the plumber's political party over his plumbing skills. This blind allegiance is how we have always elected our D.C. officials.

General elections hardly ever matter in D.C. The "real" election is in the Democratic primaries because no Republican has a chance to beat the Democratic candidate. Imagine what would happen if there was a Republican alternative that actually had a chance to win because blacks in D.C. weren't owned by Democrats. That kind of competition would start getting some real action from our Democratic politicians. What if blacks voted for the candidate, regardless of party, who would come in and clean up the sewage of corruption that has tarnished the reputation of our great city? Why do we keep voting for the same people in the same political party that has destroyed opportunities for African Americans to pursue happiness in freedom and individual responsibility?

I labeled myself a Civil Rights Republican who Democrats would vote for once they heard my message. My 2012 campaign for the D.C. City Council seat in Ward 7 was waged against all odds where over 90 percent are registered Democrats and only 3 percent are Republican. Even though I was out spent 14 to 1, I received 12 percent of the vote. Although I did not win, my candidacy proved that black Democrats will vote for a Republican. About 2,600 votes were cast for me by people who had never before voted for a Republican. This was 12 percent of the vote in Ward 7 which only has about 3 percent Republicans. We soon found out that the Republican database was embarrassingly out dated. We knocked on door where Republican voters were supposed to be living and were told again and again that the person had died or moved. Not surprisingly, no one in the house was an Independent or Republican. I'm thinking it might be time to update that database.

When I walk around the community people say, "You are the first Republican I ever voted for." They don't say I will be the last. This was a winnable race. I appreciate the support I got from the DCGOP, but I hope that the RNC was paying attention. Sometime an old fashioned ass whoopin' is just what is needed to wake up our leaders. We got attention that was never given to a Republican in non-at-large race for a seat on the City Council. The only problem is, outside of core DCGOP members, the attention came from the media and the Democrats who were afraid as they saw my momentum gaining. My growth caused the Democrats to extend greater support to their candidate.

We registered more blacks as Civil Rights Republicans than anybody had done in Ward 7 in more than thirty years. I received more votes than any Republican ever in Ward 7 and held the first ever Republican primary and debate in the ward. During both the primary and the general elections, we had many black Democrats turn out for events like those that I helped organize or convened and conducted myself. These included events with Jill Holman and Ralph J. Chittmans, Sr., both are elected D.C. National Committee members. We collaborated on these events to teach the history of blacks in the Republican Party. The events were jammed packed and many people who attended, left with a more positive perspective on what it means to be a Republican.

We showed them we cared and how Republican policies would help them if we were elected. We also showed them how an imbalance of support for the parties was hurting them, such as, forty years of one party has seen 40 percent of our people on some sort of government assistance. We wanted to help them understand that without talking down to them in reference to the 47 percent as Romney spoke of. We were saying it's time for more of us to be like the top 2 percent.

Republicans such as Patrice Lancaster and Democrats like Tyrone General, a Vietnam veteran, worked with me because they believed in my message and they knew I cared. I remember talking to Chuck Thies an NBC news contributor who told me that his father voted for different parties based upon how the issues affected him. For instance, he voted for McCain last election and Obama in 2012 only because of the social security issue. I told him I didn't vote for Obama or Romney, I wrote in Chris Christie because the other two turned me off. Neither one was talking to my interest or had a strategy to uplift the people I serve on a daily basis. I was interviewed by both Mike Debonis of the Washington

Post and James Wright of the Washington Informer about not endorsing Romney for president.

I will always cast my sacred vote. Too many of my ancestors died for me to have that right, but I don't give it away based on party, race, or personality. It is not good for African Americans to have a president whose policies we cannot criticize simply because he is black. I am perfectly capable of loving someone and disagreeing with them at the same time.

I think we all got a good lesson from Dr. Ben Carson when he spoke at the National Prayer Breakfast while standing right next to the President and Vice President. He was polite, thoughtful, respectful, and articulate in giving our president some advice, and yet, he was still chastised for honestly speaking his mind. Whether or not you agree with what Dr. Carson said, my point is that Dr. King died so that every black man and woman, not just the ones who are liberal Democrats, would be free to speak the truth as he or she sees it.

Getting blacks to vote for Republican candidates is only one side of the equation. Implementing these policies will take fixing a few things within the Republican Party. Even with its faults, the Republican Party is in many ways forty acres and a mule ahead of what the Democratic Party has to offer our people. African Americans have always cherished the values for which Dr. King died: freedom, opportunity, and individual responsibility. Without the balance that makes us a force in both parties, we are just being played for fools and the eagle will never soar.

Our self-defeating and foolish devotion to one party in a two-party system makes us look like chumps. D.C. has now had more than forty years of home rule under exclusively Democratic Party politicians and the results are not all good and balancing the eagle in D.C. would make things better for everyone. The same is true of the nation as a whole after four years of Barack Obama because we have not challenged him to be the best he can be for us. What else should black folk expect? Competition improves performance, but we don't make Democrats compete for our votes. Remember how we had to pay for AOL before competition like Yahoo launched its' site? Same thing if you use a business perspective for once.

Right here, in Obama's backyard, in this virtually all black Democratic Party controlled city, African-American voters act as though there is a new Jim Crow law that says we have to vote for Democrats regardless of how corrupt and ineffective they have been. We desperately need a Rosa Parks of party affiliation who refuses to sit in the back of the

Democrat bus whose destination is the land of unfulfilled promises of hope and change.

I got tired of sitting in the back of the Democrat bus and being told it is the only bus available for "real" blacks. After talking to those old timers of the Civil Rights Movement in Birmingham, I was convinced to never again have my vote taken for granted just because I am black. That's why I dared to put my picture on the cover of this book alongside the pictures of legendary Civil Rights Republicans. Not because I hope to match their great achievements, but because I hope to live up to the depth of their commitment.

Imagine the buzz when word got around that I was seriously considering becoming a Republican. Before my decision was final, I was summoned to meet with a community activist and political insider named Lisa Shaw. We met on the roof top of the Salvation Army Community Center in Southeast Washington, D.C. We could see the city spread out before us including the Capitol dome, the Washington Monument, and the Frederick Douglass house. It is one of the best views in the city. It was an awe-inspiring moment.

Lisa is a true friend, not a friendnemy. So, I respected her opinion when she told me she did not like what I was about to do. She was also honest enough to say she understood why I wanted to leave the Democratic Party. She begged me to become an Independent if I was determined to change parties. That way, she argued, I would still have a chance to win an election in this Democrat-dominated city. She said all of this while agreeing with the all the Republican Party principles I was sharing with her.

I explained to her that all of my life I have gone against the odds and won because I went with what my spirit told me to do. Being an Independent gave me no principles to stand on while the Republican Party had what I think we need as a people. As a matter of fact, they are the basic principles black Americans have held for generations. I was tired of watching helplessly as other minorities moved to the front of the bus on the back of what Dr. King achieved for us while we went to the back of the bus.

I admitted to her that there are some things that needed to be fixed "over there" as well, but how could that happen with people like me on the outside looking in? I know the language of the streets and I have been a lifelong Democrat and I am convinced that I can make the case why African Americans and other liberals should at least be willing to vote for the best candidate even if it is a Republican. I am not naïve enough to think there will be a mass exodus of blacks to the Republican Party.

I did my best to explain to Lisa that I really believe that the issue is not about choosing between Democrats and Republicans. Let's be honest, that decision has already been made for most African Americans who are told in so many ways that you are really not black if you vote Republican. It comes down to what I was taught growing up, "Do the right things for the right reasons and you will get the right results."

My decision was final, I officially boarded the Civil Rights Republican bus with Abraham Lincoln, Frederick Douglass, Harriet Tubman, Jack Kemp, Booker T. Washington, Dr. Martin Luther King, Jr. and all the unknown Republican civil rights soldiers who stood beside Dr. King and stood up to the racists and segregationist of the Democratic Party. Here's the best part, it's a helluva big bus; there is room for everyone!

I don't pull punches or sugar coat the truth and that has caused me endless pain and hardship in both my private and public lives. But that is who I am; I am a fighter. I fight for others and I have no regrets. When I was a child, I fought for my Uncle Edward, who was three years older than me and twice my size. I have fought for inmates to be called *returned citizens* rather than felons or ex-convicts after they did their time. I have fought to convince more than forty gangs, including the only documented gay gang in America, to stop their beefing and use their entrepreneurial spirit and gifts for something productive and positive.

I do not say all of this to hype myself or to be congratulated. My story speaks for itself. I am not interested in revenge. Those who lied about me and destroyed Peaceoholics are now paying the price for their actions. Indictments started coming down in early 2012 and federal investigations continue as I am writing this in 2013. They enriched themselves with pay-to-play money and abused their power to de-fund programs like Peaceoholics for political reasons. It is not my place to seek revenge. I am being vindicated and my story is being corroborated nearly every day in the Washington Post, Washington Times, the City Paper, and by an avalanche of indictments and convictions.

What was once was "he said, she said" in regard to the allegations made about me is now more a matter of concrete evidence in my favor. Many people in the media and in politics did not know who to believe or, maybe, they did not want to believe that so many of our politicians have been corrupted by power and money. If you have read to this point, you know I was praised for my work by every mayor and former mayor including my friend Marion Barry. It was only when I was backed into a corner and told by Vincent Gray that I had to choose sides that I had to take a stand against certain people.

The decision to refuse to be bought off was easy and I sleep well at night knowing I did the right thing. I don't claim to have ever been perfect. I would definitely change some things if I could go back in time, but my mistakes were always honest. What I care about most is that the people who believed in me and the work of Peaceoholics can now be reassured that I did not sell them out for power or money. As far as the members of the media and the politicians who were wrong about me, I hold no grudge and I really don't expect to get any apologies. They have to live with the part they played in damaging my reputation and destroying Peaceoholics.

All of that is now history and there is more history to be made. I still have a lot of life to live and I intend to use every minute of it serving the people, city, and nation I love. In the years since Peaceoholics was shut down, I have stepped back to look at the larger political situation. At some point, it dawned on me that everyone who attacked me, everyone in power in this city, those who defunded Peaceoholics, and those who stole money that was intended to help our children have one thing in common. All of them are in the Democratic Party.

The following quote by Malcolm X is interesting in light of the popular view among blacks that the Republican Party is racist and the Democratic Party is not.

> The white liberal differs from the white conservative only in one way: the liberal is more deceitful than the conservative. The liberal is more hypocritical than the conservative.
>
> Both want power, but the white liberal is the one who has perfected the art of posing as the Negro's friend and benefactor; and by winning the friendship, allegiance, and support of the Negro, the white liberal is able to use the Negro as a pawn or tool in this political "football game" that is constantly raging between the white liberals and white conservatives.
>
> Politically the American Negro is nothing but a football and the white liberals control this mentally dead ball through tricks of tokenism: false promises of integration and civil rights. In this profitable game of deceiving and exploiting the politics of the American Negro, those white liberals have the willing

cooperation of the Negro civil rights leaders. These "leaders" sell out our people for just a few crumbs of token recognition and token gains. These "leaders" are satisfied with token victories and token progress because they themselves are nothing but token leaders....

My father and our cousin Ilyasah Shabazz and recently murdered Malcom Shabazz (daughter and grandson of Malcolm X).

I don't share this powerful quote as a blanket indictment on all conservatives or all liberals and I don't agree with him that there is only one difference between the two parties. However, he does make the point that blacks should not put all their eggs in one basket. As one brother recently told me, when you put all your eggs in one basket, you better keep a close eye on that damn basket.

I would much rather deal with Republicans. Democrats say one thing privately and another publically like when Jesse Jackson was caught on an open microphone making a vulgar threats against President Obama's private parts. I prefer the Republican Party which is more prone to speaking its mind plainly whether right or wrong.

Both parties have really good people for the most part, but I prefer to be told to my face what people think about me or about black people in general. I don't like people or political parties that hide behind a mask of condescension and the soft racism of low expectations. All we have to do for the eagle to soar for all Americans including African Americans is to give it two wings to fly with and not just one. If we tip the scales to the Republican Party by just 15 percent, both parties will be more attentive to our concerns.

When I was finally taught real black history by those I met on our Civil Rights Tours, I realized a major reason for the black attitude toward Republicans is miss-education. I knew Abraham Lincoln was a Republican, but I had a huge blind spot when it came to the history of political parties before President Kennedy and the Civil Rights Movement of the 1960s. I subsequently found out that the American history I thought I knew since the Kennedy administration was not quite accurate either. Remember, if you do not know your own story, someone will tell it to you the way they want it to be.

I was totally unaware of the number of great black leaders that were Republicans. The first thirty black politicians in America were Republicans. The first black U.S. senator was a Republican. The first black congressman is a Republican. Colin Powell, the first black Secretary of State was a Republican. Even the first black female Secretary of State, Condoleezza Rice, is a Republican.

Something that really surprised me was the history buried at Woodland Cemetery in Ward 7 where I live and ran for a City Council seat in 2012. It wasn't until recently I learned that Blanche Bruce, the first black to be elected to the U.S. Senate and to serve a full term is buried there. The other historic figure buried there is John Mercer Hughes, the first black congressman elected in the state of Virginia, interim president and founder of Howard University Law School, and the uncle of famed poet, social activist, novelist, and columnist, Langston Hughes.

I have driven past that cemetery for decades without knowing who was buried there other than two of my very own grandparents. Most Washingtonians don't know about this treasure in our midst. For the last thirty years, local politicians have failed to support the preservation of this historic site. To our shame, the majority of supporters and volunteers who help keep Woodland barely operational are good white folk who seem to appreciate our history more than we do sometimes.

That is why I kicked off my campaign standing in front of the tombstone of Blanche Bruce. It is appalling the way D.C. government has treated this historic landmark, which has nine individuals buried there with "DCPS after their names. That is the kind of pride in being an educator we need to recapture. No wonder our schools are failing.

President Obama and other great men love to compare themselves to Abraham Lincoln at the same time that liberal historians write books about Lincoln being a racist. They say he fought the war and emancipated the slaves for political reasons. First, it did not turn out well for him personally and he was always aware of that danger, so that would not make him a very shrewd politician. But what if the historians are right? What does a slave care about the motives of a man if the man's actions set him free? A lot of us like Barack Obama personally more than we liked Mitt Romney, but if Romney knew how to create jobs, who cares about his lack of coolness?

Why do we think we have to vote for Barack Obama because he is a Democrat? Don't argue that it is because he is black. We seem to watch out for the Democratic Party even if it hurts us as a people. If it was about being black, we would not have put up with the way Justice Clarence Thomas was treated during his Senate confirmation whether we agree with his judicial philosophy or not. And don't forget who led that "high-tech lynching," the Democrat majority on the Judicial Committee and its star, and eventual Vice President of the United States, Senator Joe Biden. I always thought Dr. King died for the civil rights of all blacks, not just the ones who are liberal Democrats.

Who would you rather have making the decisions in the Oval Office, a Republican like Lincoln who makes political decisions that help our people, or a liberal who tells blacks what they want to hear, then takes us for granted and circumvents Congress with executive orders to help other minorities? I have no beef with other minorities, but I am fed up with broken promises to the black community!

The gay and lesbian vote was pandered too by administration support for same sex marriage and by instructing the Justice Department not to enforce the Defense of Marriage Act. There was an outcry from the black clergy over these actions, but how many of our people still voted Democrat anyway? I am the last person who can be accused of being anti-gay with all of my work with gay gangs. I am simply pointing out the inverted logic and to identify the double standards we have grown to expect from our paternalistic Democrat leaders.

What about jobs? President Obama signed another executive order making it possible for 800,000 to 1.2 million illegal immigrants up to the age of twenty-four to stay in this country legally even if they were not born here. This was payback for the Latino support for Obama in 2008. Black youth unemployment is 50 percent and he floods the job market with one stroke of the pen. Meanwhile, 97 percent turned out for our first black president. Where is our payback? Ask the Congressional Black Caucus who made sixty-one recommendations to the President for appointments in his administration. What does it say about the Democratic Party's grip on the black vote that a grand total of zero, zilch, zip, none of those sixty-one recommendations received appointments?

And don't insult my intelligence by pointing to the stimulus or Revitalization Act. The President put $3.4 million into the new Homeland Security Project right next door to the infamous Barry Farms Public Housing Complex in Southeast, D.C. Not one person that I know of from a housing project in D.C. received a job on this massive construction site. There were a lot of exciting words of hope and change spoken at the groundbreaking and press conference, but no jobs. Black people also initiated a protest on the construction site of the African-American Museum of all places to receive job placement.

Wasn't the President worried about losing black votes for his reelection campaign? Of course not, he knew our people would still vote for him even if the alternative had been better. I think if Carter G. Woodson, a great Civil Rights Republican, who is respected by Democrats and Republicans, was here today, he would probably write a book called *The Mis-Education of the Negro Voter!*

Yes, I am a Republican, but I reserve the right to vote for the best candidate. Once again, I am not advocating blind allegiance to the Republican Party. I just want to see the eagle soar with two strong wings. We must use our vote to balance black participation in both parties. As it stands now, the eagle is not soaring and we as a people are on the outside looking in. We have been rendered irrelevant regardless of who wins the election. We would have significantly more power if the black vote was divided more equally between the Democratic and Republican parties. As I stated, a 15 percent shift toward Republicans would create a massive sea change in U.S. politics. What are we waiting for?

My historical search was full of surprises. I kept coming across facts that contradicted the repeated untruths of white liberals and the black pimpocracy. Dr. King's niece, Dr. Alveda C. King says that both Daddy King and his son were registered Republicans; Dr. King saw more racism in liberals than in conservatives:

> Yes, racism still exists, but my experience over the years has been that it is strongest amongst those with a liberal or progressive agenda to push. I rarely see anyone on the Right being racist, but I see it on the Left on a regular basis. It seems to be part of the requirements of being on the Left to either push a racist agenda or to naively believe that it will somehow make things better.

When the 1960 Civil Rights Act was signed by President Dwight Eisenhower, it was only after it had been through a five-day filibuster by Democrats trying to stop it in the Senate. Senators in opposition included Lyndon Johnson who eventually signed the 1964 Civil Rights Act with one of our personal mentors, Amelia Boynton Robinson, the mother of the Voting Rights Act, standing right there beside him.

The 1964 Act was also opposed by Democrats. This time it was filibustered for fourteen hours by former Grand Wizard of the KKK, West Virginia Democrat Sen. Robert Byrd. "No" votes from twenty-two other Democrat senators failed to stop it. One of those twenty-two who voted "no" was Sen. Al Gore, Sr., father of former Vice-President Al Gore, Jr.

The more I learned, the more I began to wonder if liberals had hit us in the head with their lies so many times that we have collective concussion syndrome. The Mayo Clinic says the most common symptoms of concussive traumatic brain injury are amnesia and confusion. Sounds about right, too many black votes have forgotten who first opposed our emancipation from slavery, then segregated us with Jim Crow laws, fought against Dr. King and the Civil Rights Movement, ghettoized us under the noble sounding Urban Renewal programs of the 1960's and 70's, and closed the door to prosperity by luring us into womb to tomb government welfare dependency. All this reached its height under "our first honorary black president," Bill Clinton, who escalated the "War on Drugs" and instituted "three strikes you're out" resulting in the mass incarceration of millions of black men.

At the same time that the U.S. government wages war on drugs, they are encouraging us to drug our children with medication. They diagnose ADD, ADHD, dyslexia, and other learning disabilities and the prescription is always more medication. Our children are labeled with mental retardation and segregated in separate schools and classrooms, all in the name of helping us. I have seen this firsthand and have spoken out against it, but I am just one voice.

When I tell people Bill Clinton's policies were more harmful to black people than any other modern president, the black pimpocracy react as though it is blasphemy. Dependency-pushing liberals are horrified I don't dance to Bill Clinton's tune. Don't take my word for it, you can read about it in the book *The New Jim Crow* by Michelle Alexander. Yes, he did some good, but I won't buy into making an icon out of a man just because he can play the sax. Apparently, that is all it takes for some of my people to vote Democrat.

It happens even more at the local level. Marion Barry is famous for doing so much for all people in D.C., but lately in Ward 8 communities, it's all about the 2,500 turkeys he gives out from developers and other businesses every Thanksgiving to constituents. Combining this with his great past achievements, Marion is guaranteed winning the council seat until he decides to quit. In exchange for donating those 2,500 turkeys, the "generous" developers were allowed to modify their affordable housing agreements. The residents of public housing were modified right out of the opportunity for homeownership, but they did get a nice turkey for Thanksgiving.

Marion Barry had the city booming for all people during his first two terms as mayor. Since then, however, as a City Council member, his Ward 8 constituents have not moved forward. Once again, poverty ridden, undereducated, unemployment breaking an all-time high are handed the same lame slogan from the same people from the same old political party. So again, black people continue to ignore the results and worship at the altar of one party. When will Ward 8 voters and black voters nationally figure out that a great political cocktail has ingredients from the best that both parties have to offer?

Hey, I can take care of my own self-interest better than some political party. All I want from the Party are freedom and opportunity. I will take it from there by exercising individual responsibility. I don't need a nanny. That was the vision Jack Kemp, a true Civil Rights Republican had for America.

Compare Jack Kemp's vision and my vision, the Civil Rights Republican vision, to the lame and empty promises of hope and change, ten-dollar gift cards, and Thanksgiving turkeys. We have been brought off so cheaply and then we reward those who have cheated us. Harry Thomas received a going away party in a church after pleading guilty to stealing $300,000 from money designated to fight youth violence. He and fellow council members also forced the director of the Children Trust Investment Corporation to illegally maneuver around the law so that Thomas could throw a $110,000 Obama inauguration party in the John Wilson Building. Isn't the Wilson Building the very place that laws are supposed to be upheld and not broken? No wonder President Obama put them in the nosebleed section at the Democrat convention. How about making Thomas apologize to the families of the fifteen victims, killed in his ward where that the money he stole was supposed to help.

Liberal Democrats like Harry Thomas make KKK member and Democrat Senator Robert Byrd unnecessary. When was the last time you heard of the KKK pulling off fifteen murders of black youth in one community in such a short period? You won't, because they know there is no sense risking prison when they have Harry Thomas on the D.C. City Council. The KKK knows they have men who took money from youth drug addiction treatment and violence intervention programs while our children were being slaughtered.

Another thing that confused me was when Rev. Jesse Jackson said he was standing on principle by boycotting Budweiser and then, when Jackson suddenly ended the boycott, one of his sons got the lucrative Budweiser distributorship in Chicago. There is no mystery why his other son would think he could get away with embezzling over $750.000 for material gratification.

It's not just Dr. King's blood Jesse Jackson smeared on his clothes to make himself look like a martyr. When white liberal do-gooders can't win in the arena of ideas, they always call on good reverends like Jesse and Al Sharpton to cry "racism" and beg the government to "please, help us poor black folk." They are rewarded handsomely for being mindlessly dedicated servants of the Democratic Party. They receive highly paid and visible positions in the pimpocracy as long as they dance to the party-line tune. Sounds like Uncle Tom to me. Their lavish lifestyles are purchased with the blood of our children and ancestors.

Of course, folks in D.C.'s Ward 8 have been mesmerized just like I was by all Marion Barry did for us in the past. He will never be surpassed in that regard, but now constituents in Ward 8 are content to vote for him off the memories like a first summer job twenty years ago. Barry's summer jobs program was outstanding and a good reason to vote for him back then. The same people are still motivated to vote for him and for Vince Gray in exchange for Thanksgiving turkeys or gift cards. It is time for us to stop drinking the "Pimpade" because we are in danger of waking up in five years to a city where low and middle income blacks have been bulldozed out of the city by the developers who are not content to play for turkeys and gift cards.

All my research, logic, and common sense came together that day on the roof of the Salvation Army building. My friends begged me not to go so far as to become an evil Republican asking me, "Why not just be an Independent?" Once again, the problem with being an Independent is that it is a no-man's land as far as influence. Independent voters do have the same impact on elections as either of the two major parties. They do not have the same power to help our people as being affiliated with one of the two major political parties.

I have never been lukewarm about anything. God says in the Bible, "Because you are neither hot nor cold, I spew you out of my mouth." Cold water is refreshing and hot water is cleansing, but lukewarm water is good for nothing. No, I had to be true to myself and my principles and become a Civil Rights Republican.

The fact is I am a Republican because I believe in the core constitutional principles held sacred by Republicans: freedom, the pursuit happiness, and personal responsibility. Do I agree with every Republican or Party policies? No, I do not. When I was I Democrat, I did not agree every Democrat or their Party policies. Democrats confuse me and sometimes Republicans make me angry, but at least with Republicans, I don't feel like I am being manipulated or bamboozled. When liberals can't convince you, they try to confuse you.

How much sense does it make that over 90 percent of blacks give unconditional support to just one political Party in a country with a two-party political system? We have all of our eggs in one basket and there is no way to keep a close enough eye on that basket to keep the liberal foxes away. Our stubbornness in deciding to participate in only one party is self-defeating and, honestly, stupid. It isn't a strategy, it is just a habit. We play into the hands of the liberals who take us for granted and we keep coming back for more. The American eagle cannot soar with just one wing.

It comes down to making smart decisions in both our personal and political affairs. We need to lead a party and not just follow a party as we have as Democrats. The Republican Party has a long way to go, but it now realizes that it needs to be a party for all people and it is ready for black leadership. The problem is that when I looked at the delegates at the 2012 Republican National Convention, it did not reflect the reality of the Party's commitment to the black community. We need to do better and I can help make it happen.

I am now part of the change needed to communicate the commitment of the Party to our people. I, not long ago attended an excellent event put on by DCGOP at the Salisbury residence in Georgetown. The guest speaker was former Alabama congressman Artur Davis who spoke at the Republican National Convention. He did a magnificent job at both events and generated a lot of excitement in the Party. Afterwards, while I was talking with Congressman Davis, a very nice Republican woman came up to us and said, "Ron, you should take Congressman Davis with you to speak to blacks in Ward 7." Artur, wisely and humbly, said he thought that would hurt me more than help me.

I was so impressed with his sincerity and his understanding that different people in the black community are better at delivering the Republican message to different constituencies. Artur can really fire up the Republican base. I do a better job with blacks in low-income communities. I look forward to learning more from people like Congressman Davis and Dr. Ben Carson because together we have a powerful message for the Republican Party commitment to our people.

My challenge to blacks who always vote Democrat is to consider what happens when the White House or Congress or both are under Republican control? The answer is that we have no voice. We so blindly support Democrat candidates that when Republicans are in power, we have no representation, anywhere. Democrats know they own us and the only threat or leverage we have is not turning out in large numbers, but they know very well that we won't vote Republican. We should not allow ourselves to be shackled like that.

Even the CBC (Congressional Black Caucus) dutifully comes out of its political ghetto to dance to whatever tune keeps them in good favor with the Democrat leadership. They can be counted on when Harry Reed and Nancy Pelosi need a black member of the Caucus to yell, "Racism!" The CBC was sent out to walk through the Tea Party protest in front of the U.S. Capitol in hope of inducing violence or some racist remark. Don't get me wrong, I am not a Tea Party Republican, but it is beneath our dignity to be decoys for potential violence or racism. We all know there are extremists in both parties and no one should stoop to use or be used by others as bait.

I am longing for the day when we come together to focus on issues that will move our people forward. It was funny to be at the CBC and hear a guy in the audience ask Rev. Jesse Jackson when the CBC was going to put forth a strategic plan for African Americans to build institutions for the empowerment of our families and communities. He wanted to know why we were waiting for someone else to do it. No one had an answer for him. There is really no excuse for inaction when Democrats had the White House and both houses of Congress Obama's first two years in office.

If African Americans were a separate nation, our disposable income would make us one of the top twelve richest countries in the world. So, it is not just the politicians who are to blame for our economic condition, we are all to blame. We have the resources for economic growth. We don't need to count solely on government money to create a black economic boom in this country. We need strategy, leadership, and a focused purpose like the Latino and Gay communities that comes from a determination to push their agenda.

Here is my case against black loyalty to the Democrat Party. You be the jury. Remember, my case is not that the Republican Party is perfect or that all blacks should switch and vote Republican. My argument is first, the Republican Party has the history and a core set of principles much more compatible with the welfare of the black family than those of liberal Democrats.

Second, because we vote blindly Democratic in numbers that are so overwhelming, Democrats take us for granted. They own us and being owned is not something I or any other African American should accept. We are fools to be so completely sold out to one party in a two-party political system. Whatever happened to knowing how to play the game, to the political art of war? How did we let ourselves be co-opted by the Party of the KKK and those in our government responsible for conducting surveillance on our beloved Dr. King?

The Republican Party was founded in 1854 as the anti-slavery Party and stood in stark contrast to the pro-slavery Democratic Party. Democrats used the term "Black Republican" as a derisive term to describe the newly formed Republican Party. That is how closely the Republican Party was associated with anti-slavery. Before Abraham Lincoln was elected the first Republican president, Republicans like Harriet Tubman, Sojourner Truth, and Frederick Douglass were fighting for the abolition of slavery.

While the Democrat South was fighting for the expansion of slavery into the territories, President Lincoln laid the groundwork for ending slavery with the Emancipation Proclamation. While largely symbolic, Republicans reinforced the symbolism of Lincoln's bold proclamation through constitutional amendments.

Republicans pushed for the passage and ratification of the thirteenth, fourteen, and fifteenth amendments after the Civil War. These amendments abolished slavery, guaranteed citizenship to all persons born or naturalized in the United States including former slaves, and prohibited the denial of the right to vote based on a citizen's race.

Republican Representative Benjamin Butler and Senator Charles Sumner introduced the Civil Rights Act of 1875. It was signed into law by Republican president Ulysses S. Grant. This Act guaranteed everyone, regardless of race, color, or "previous condition of servitude," equal treatment in public accommodations such as public transportation and theaters.

The Act went largely unenforced when federal troops withdrew from the South. It was not until almost a century later that Republicans were able to secure passage of the Civil Rights Act of 1964. The bill was introduced by Democrat president, John F. Kennedy who found support from Republicans and opposition primarily from Democrats. Democrat Party icon, Sen. Robert Byrd filibustered for fourteen hours and thirteen minutes against the bill. The Act was passed and signed by Democrat President Lyndon Johnson. Republicans voted 82 percent for the 1964 Civil Rights Act compared to 63 percent of Democrats.

Speaking of Robert Byrd, the founder of the KKK was Democrat Nathan Bedford Forest. Several of the founders of the NAACP, on the other hand, had close ties to the Republican Party. So, while the party who has owned the black vote for over forty years was out lynching blacks, the Republicans who we teach our children to hate were passing constitutional amendments, both the 1875 and the 1964 Civil Rights Acts, and helping to found the NAACP.

We have the Democrat governor of Arkansas Orval Faubus to thank for deploying the Arkansas National Guard to prevent nine black students from entering Little Rock Central High School in 1957. We have Republican president Dwight D. Eisenhower to thank for getting those same black students, now known as the "Little Rock Nine", admitted to the school by ordering the 101st Airborne Division of the United States Army to protect them.

It was also President Eisenhower's U. S. Supreme Court appointee Chief Justice Earl Warren's court who made the 1954 *Brown v. Board of Education* decision that gave those students the right to attend the all-white high school. The showdown in Little Rock is considered a seminal event in the early history of the Civil Rights Movement and Republicans were on the right side of that historic event.

When Mayor Vincent "Electric Slide" Gray confronted me in his office and warned me that I had to choose sides, I told him that I was on the side of right. Just like President Eisenhower, I don't care what color or what party or how rich someone is, I just know right is right. That's why I can tell you honestly, I love Barack Obama and I love Marion Barry, but I'm nobody's stooge and if the truth is not on the side of Obama and Barry, then neither am I.

When the truth is on their side, I will be there to support them as I should because I will not be kept in a Republican box either. I will never return to the party I left because of differences in principles, but I will always support and acknowledge when the other party or its politicians are right. I learned that from Jack Kemp and Frederick Douglass, my favorite Republicans! We can no longer afford to think only about the party but only about working together for the good of the country.

I spoke about one great supporter of the black community in its hopes and dreams for prosperity who was Jack Kemp who died in May of 2009. He may have been the Republican politician most trusted by African Americans. Some would say blacks trusted him more than any politician in any party, period.

Jason DeParle wrote in the New York Times on February 28, 1993, "Kemp may be the only official to have won standing ovations in black ghettos by calling for a capital gains tax cut." The programs Jack Kemp introduced as George H. W. Bush's Secretary of HUD were the most innovative and empowering housing programs ever for low-income Americans of any color.

Just like Democrats got the Civil Rights Act of 1875 declared unconstitutional, Republican supply side economic guru Jack Kemp's programs were hollowed out by Clinton, but made to look like they are the same empowering programs as the original ones. They are not! Right up to the current administration the Democratic Party has gutted those programs and returned blacks to a government dependency mentality when it comes to housing and entrepreneurship.

Jack Kemp's HOPE-1 (Homeownership Opportunity for People Everywhere) program was designed to sell public housing to the residents. HOPE-2 was a program for low-income families to buy single units in multi-family rental property owned by HUD. HOPE-3 was created to help low-income families purchase single family homes owned by HUD. Note the common theme of home ownership, not just rentals.

HOPE VI was not Jack Kemp's program. It was developed as a result of recommendations by National Commission on Severely Distressed Public Housing, which was charged with proposing a National Action Plan to eradicate severely distressed public housing. Unlike Secretary Kemp's programs, HOPE VI does not bring hope, it displaces the poor. The Commission recommended revitalization in three general areas: physical improvements, management improvements, and social and community services to address resident needs.

The second Bush administration stopped funding the program, but the Obama administration funded it again. Only a small percentage of the displaced residents move back in after the new development is built and they do not own their units, they only rent them. Ownership, not renting is true empowerment. Renting is not what Jack Kemp had in mind with his HOPE programs.

Secretary Kemp's Enterprise Zones, for the most part, have been replaced by the Obama administration with Empowerment Zones. Notice how similar language is used to disguise the changed reality. Enterprise Zones are private sector oriented and focus on giving businesses incentives to locate in low-income areas. Empowerment Zones sound good but they are public sector oriented and focus on providing government regulated hiring and grants, which cause much of the corruption we see in the Nation's Capital today.

This chapter began with a quote from Jack Kemp saying, "It doesn't matter to me whether people are Democrat or liberal or conservative or Republican. I just think everyone has an obligation to think about what is going on around them – stand for something, care about something, don't be neutral."

I have done my best to stand for something, to care about something and not to be neutral. It is easy to let people label you. Right now, most black citizens of the United States have allowed themselves to be labeled as "bought and paid for Democrat votes." All I really care about is finding and fixing problems based on the principles of freedom, opportunity, and individual responsibility. When I was with Peaceoholics, it was always about results and I have the same determination to make that my standard when it comes to politics. I look back on the policies of President Johnson's War on Poverty and it looks like the war was lost. That was fifty years ago. Maybe we should stop being such stubborn donkeys and see what the elephant has to offer.

I have willingly sacrificed in order to help others and I have seen so much carnage in the streets, so much blood, so much death, so many tears. The KKK could not have devised a more insidious plan to eliminate young black men than getting them to murder each other. There is no outrage over this genocide whatsoever and if, God forbid, a Bill Cosby or a Juan Williams brings attention to this black genocide, they are attacked by other blacks. What I can guarantee is that Chicago Mayor Rahm Emanuel, President Obama's former Chief of Staff, will be re-elected by dutiful black Democrats even though he has not the first clue what to do about the mass slaughter of black young men in his city.

I am ashamed of the silence of the black community in the face of a dysfunctional educational system like the one in the District of Columbia. The school system was run for decades almost entirely by African Americans. Black superintendents were in charge for decades and were not held accountable for the mis-education and neglect of our children.

If you just go by how much money DCPS receives per student, you would say education is a high priority, wrong! It isn't the total amount of money in the budget that matters. DCPS received $29,409.00 per student in the 2009-2010 school year according to Andrew Coulson of the Cato Institute. A year at Harvard University is only a few thousand more and it is about what the Obama's pay every year to send their girls to the prestigious Sidwell Friends private school in Washington, D.C.

Simply by making sure we teach our third graders to actually read on third-grade level increases the likelihood of graduation by 400 percent and decrease the likelihood of future incarceration by one-third. The Annie E. Casey Foundation reported that students with below average reading skills in the third grade are four times more likely to drop out of school. Maybe K-3 teachers should be getting the big bucks instead of the administrators and politicians.

The sad tale of Michelle Rhee tells you all you need to know about our priorities when it comes to the education of our children. Michelle is the daughter of Korean immigrants. She was hired as the chancellor of DCPS. I'm sure she came into the job under the mistaken impression that for her Democrat bosses, i.e., the mayor and City Council, results mattered and that people really wanted change. If that was true, Peaceoholics would still be alive and Rhee would still have her job.

Unfortunately, it is also true that if Ms. Rhee had she not been tone deaf and culturally naïve to the culture and temperament of black Americans, she still might be in D.C. She needed to listen to people like the parents of Hardy Middle School where she made a great mistake by destroying a great program that was working. If I had gotten on the corrupt Vince Gray band wagon in the Wilson Building, Peaceoholics would probably still be alive.

In here zeal to improve the education of our children, she stepped on the toes of the teachers' union. Like I said, it is true that Rhee did make some mistakes. In some ways, she was a lot like Adrian Fenty in her political naiveté. She could have been even more effective and possibly kept her job, if she had surrounded herself with more people who were culturally adept at relating to black people. That aside, she got results and was highly respected everywhere except right here in D.C.

As I communicated earlier, the same deficiencies exist at both the 2012 DNC and RNC conventions. One party was singing the same tired old song to keep blacks happy sitting in the back of the bus. The Republican Party, on the other hand, had great words, but do not yet have a tune with the right rhythm to wake up our people. The RNC needs to incorporate some of the principles the great Civil Rights Republicans such as Nannie Helen Burroughs and Booker T. Washington. Republicans need to revive the memory and reality of Black Wall Street and Black Rosewood just as my Chinese brothers created Chinatowns throughout America or how Ethiopians recently created Little Ethiopia in D.C. on the U Street corridor.

So it was with Michelle Rhee who was summarily canned after three years and left after Mayor Fenty lost the 2010 election. She had succeeded in changing the culture of minimum standards and was aggressively addressing the systemic problems of DCPS. What was the sin that got her fired? She was against the practice of teacher tenure that prevented getting rid of poor teachers. All Hell broke loose because she threatened the status quo. I believe she made a lot of mistakes, but I would have rather beat her into shape than to return to a system that never listened to the community and parents, but always gave the impression that they were.

Why does all Hell not break loose in the Nation's Capital when our children receive a substandard education? I guess we can tolerate the educational abuse of our children by black leadership, but we won't stand for someone of another race getting credit for improving some things for our precious children or having the guts to at least try. We certainly don't demand our teachers be held to a high standard of excellence.

Part of the problem is that we have not given our teachers the support they deserve and need. Teaching gets lip service as a noble profession, but the truth is we do not really honor people who choose to be teachers. At the same time, we stand by as our children walk into dilapidated schools with raw sewage, broken windows, and lax security. The inadequate answer to a lot of these problems is to close neighborhood schools.

In Closing

I look around and sixteen years have passed, sixteen years of fighting and addressing all the gang beefs night and day, pushing students through college, and fighting the corrupt system. I am reminded of all of the stories of the civil rights leaders and how they were willing to keep "drinking muddy water" so I could pursue my dreams. Your family suffers in this work and you suffer from not spending time with your friends and family, but that is the choice I made. It helps me not regret my decisions knowing that my children are happy and proud that their father is an agent of change in the community.

If I have not yet convinced you to vote the truth rather than the party whether Democrat or Republican, let me leave you with the words of Malcolm X from his speech of January 7, 1965, "I don't think people should refer to themselves as leftist, or rightist. I think they should be whatever they are, and don't allow anybody to put labels on them."

The last eighteen months of my life have been like heaven and Hell on earth. I have learned who my friends are and I have learned from my mistakes. I have increased my understanding of the rules of the game of life. I am ready for a rebound from the attacks on my reputation and the death of Peaceoholics.

My personal rebound will also be a rebound for the people. I am not in this for myself or to simply clear my name. I am certainly not in it for the money. After all is said and done, I am still most grateful for the "spiritual wealth" I have received even though my pockets are empty. I would rather have empty pockets on the road to redemption than pockets overflowing with the money of corruption on the road to Hell.

From losing my dream house on the hills of Penn Branch, Washington, D.C., to putting my younger children on a poverty- like budget, to being blackballed from serving the people I love and need the most, to having people who called themselves spiritually connected either turn their backs or steal from me, I know in my heart I would not be ready for the next chapter of my life, nor would you be reading this book if all these things did not happen the way they did.

According to Buddha, "Sometimes, even when the cell door is flung open, the prisoner chooses not to leave!" What a tragedy. Never be enslaved to anything, to any person, or to any political party, only to God and to what is right! I am still evolving as a Civil Rights Republican and I invite you to join me in the movement to balance the eagle in America from the political parties to education, equality and opportunity for all who are willing to pay the price. Please don't forget what Booker T. Washington said, "You can't get something for nothing".

Making announcement of party change at the historic Woodlawn Cemetery where black Civil Rights Republicans Blanche Bruce and John Mercer Hughes are buried. Bruce was the first elected black Senator to serve a full term. His tombstone can be seen in the background. Hughes was the first elected black congressmen in the state of Virginia.

Leaving the Democratic Party to become a Civil Rights Republican just like Abraham Lincoln, Frederick Douglass, and Nannie Helen Burroughs.

DCGOP Committee Chairwoman Jill Holman joins me to conduct a Black History event on contributions by black Republicans such as Harriet Tubman, Booker T. Washington, and John Mercer Hughes who was the first Black Congressman elected in Virginia.

My youngest son, Asante, running at a press conference, will be the next generation of Civil rights Republicans as we awake those who were asleep and bring political party balance back to the black community.

First day of early voting in the 2011 Republican primary is joined by the first Republicans to vote for him. Moten went on to win the primary with over 65 percent of the votes.

With Jo Ann Emerson, U.S. Representative for Missouri's 8th congressional district and a great friend of the District of Columbia. Rep. Emerson is married to a Democrat, which shows we can live together and love each other even still work together to encourage personal responsibility and to ensure freedom and equal opportunity for all Americans.

Lesson Ten

The Streets, the Scandals, the Politics

In the three-and-a-half years since I left Peaceoholics, the Nation's Capital has become a model of dysfunction, neglect, deception, and abuse that is typical in urban America. One of the symptoms of dysfunction is that we blame everyone except ourselves, successful business people, corporations, racism, Wall Street, and of course, evil Republicans. This is really being out of touch with reality since almost all of our governments and school systems in our urban areas are run by liberals.

This refusal by our political, societal, and spiritual leaders to accept the blame for the violence, poverty, poor education, and low morals, teaches the rest of us to do the same thing when it comes to our personal failures, it's always someone else who is at fault.

This has resulted in children who do not think it is cool to be smart and if people are successful, it is not from hard work and sacrifice, but because they are evil. Sadly, we do everything but empower those most in need to use or to develop their talents to not do for self. Don't take my word for it, read what Washington Post columnist Colby King said after Mayor Vincent Gray called D.C. a big-league city:

A big-league city even as many of our youth functions at a minor-league level? Even as residents endure some politicians whose moral principles are less than second-rate?

How can the mayor toss around such a term when only four in 10 D.C. third graders can read at grade level?

That is just one of several depressing statistics in a report released this week by Raise DC, a coalition of civic, philanthropic and community groups Gray created to evaluate city programs.

A "big-league city" when only six in 10 students graduate from high school in four years? When approximately 19 percent of District adults lack basic literacy skills?

We are a "big-league city" when 10,000 low-income persons 16 to 24years-old are out of work and out of school?

What's going to happen to those third graders who aren't passing reading tests? Will they miraculously reach proficiency by 10th grade? Or are they more likely, without a tremendous amount of remedial help, drop out of school?

What, pray tell, are those 10,000 adolescents in our "big-league city" doing when they are not in school or on a job?

Here are some of Raise DC's findings:

• About 11 percent of births in the District are to mothers under the age of 20
• More than 600 16 to 21year-olds spent their adolescence in foster care
• Each year, more than 1,000 youth are committed to the supervision of the juvenile justice system
• Nearly 30 percent of D.C. children live in poverty, and 1,800 are homeless

Sounds like a "big-league city," doesn't it?

When the report was released Monday, Gray suggested that the answer is better collaboration among programs that target social ills. Raise DC put it this way: "shape a civic infrastructure that moves away from the District's habit of isolated efforts toward a smarter and more integrated way of organizing existing funds, initiatives, and resources for children and youth."

Oh, please.

What it said here about D.C. is true of all of our major cities in America? What we need is a "civic infrastructure" focused on building stronger families: fathers living at home and married to the mothers of their children; parents who see that their kids get to school on time, ready to learn; children who are taught to respect others and themselves; no goals that are based on lifelong dependence on government; obedience to the law so that a broken justice and correctional system cannot destroy us. The men in our cities, or anywhere that are not taking responsibility for their children, need to be reminded in the strongest possible terms that Uncle Sam, the government, is not your baby's daddy, you are!

While the goal of every person and the objective of programs that help those in need should be self-reliance and financial independence. There will always be a need for programs that facilitate the transition from dependence to independence. What must change is the rules that create greater dependence and that destroy the dignity of the individual. Let me suggest some places to begin.

Right now if a woman wants to work she can't get assistance for childcare, but she can if she does not work. Neither can she get assistance if her child's father is in the child's life as though it is better for Uncle Sam to raise a man's child. Not only should people on assistance not be penalized for working and qualifying for child care, but there should be built in incentives for good parenting such as having both parents in the home, attendance at PTA meetings, and school attendance by their children. The last two should be mandatory. Sound cruel? If parents can line up for hours to buy the new Jordan's or Lebron James sneaker, they can be required to attend PTA meetings!

Many will say that these ideas are antiquated. I prefer to call them traditional values, American values, African-American values, whatever you like, but they work! What's needed could be gleaned from the mission of Raise DC:

"Together, raise DC by connecting resources to provide every young person the opportunity for success from cradle to career."

Resources = public dollars = bureaucracy = paperwork = reports on the shelf = more kids who can't read, babies having babies and young men off to jail until the next buzz word come to get the next hustle on with no intentions on really solving the problems before us. Then when a simple person comes with some common sense approaches that work, we let these greedy forces destroy the very people who had good intentions. One serious problem is that the welfare system has become a way to enrich the people who get funding for administrating the programs. This is a disincentive to truly help people move off the welfare and unemployment rolls.

The "War on Poverty" is nothing more than a fifty-year propaganda program that sends the message to the American people that the poor are helped by becoming dependent on government programs. The damage done in fifty years by President Lyndon Johnson's liberal Democrat "Great Society" dependency programs is immeasurable. That's not to say they did not have good intention, but what matters in the end are the results. Unfortunately, four generations later we have a higher percentage of blacks on welfare and unemployment than in any time in U.S. History.

A 1970's cartoon showed a wealthy couple looking out of their penthouse window at the "slums" burning in the distance. The pipe-smoking husband says to his wife, "No, my dear, the ghetto is not the problem, the ghetto is the solution." It shows how far we have gotten away from our core values when black politicians run on promises of entitlement programs that give people a fish rather than on training programs that will teach them to fish. Short-term financial assistance is compassionate, but in the long run it is gainful employment or owning a business that gives a man or woman dignity. The pursuit of happiness is an unalienable right, not the pursuit of a handout.

This is not a popular position among many of my people but it puts me in good company. Men like Abraham Lincoln, Mahatma Gandhi, Martin Luther King, Jr., Malcolm X, and of course, Jesus Christ literally lost their lives fighting for freedom, opportunity, and individual responsibility. Harriet Tubman did what was legally wrong but morally right when she led slaves to freedom on the "Underground Railroad." Others, like me, just have their character assassinated. I am proud to be drinking muddy water in such good company.

I am not comparing myself to those great heroes of the past, but I am comparing their enemies to those D.C. politicians now being investigated, indicted, and convicted for crimes against the people of Washington, D.C. Judases of the public trust that I call friendnemies who have once again come to destroy my name for speaking truth and fighting back. A friendnemy is a friend to your face and an enemy behind your back. A friend is honest to your face and always has your back. Remember, the same people who praised Jesus on Palm Sunday cried out, "Crucify him," on Good Friday. He warned us not to put too much stock in either praise or criticism from others.

Now I have a note to the party that I have embraced, but which needs to do a better job embracing my efforts to deliver a Civil Rights Republican message. There are millions of people who fit my profile who want what's best for America. The question remains, will we put aside perceptions and be more inclusive in solving our problems? Yes, I know I have a little mud on me from the political wars I've been through, but drinking so much muddy water will do that to you. Talking truth to power is a messy business. I have tried to learn how to use those experiences to improve myself. I have shared my experience in this book and my hope is to continue doing so as a Civil Rights Republican.

I am doing this because I know the political balance my people and country need at this moment in history. That is why I am a Civil Rights Republican. There have been so many black, white, and Latino Republicans that have shown me that there are as many, if not more, good folk over here than in the party I left. If it weren't for them, I would probably be an Independent. But I must warn my new home party that as long as blacks and minorities hear racist remarks out of a careless few Republican fools without the Party coming down hard on them, the battle to win black votes is going to be virtually hopeless.

Most minorities have not been exposed to the good things I now see in the Republican Party. Its message and policies are not just good for Republicans, but for all Americans of any color. My message to minorities and my black brothers and sisters especially is that we need to be represented in both parties. We need to regain the spirit of Black Rosewood and Black Wall Street for our communities. I was recently speaking at an event put on by former Representative J.C. Watts and Ohio Senator John Portman. They were addressing the Second Chance Act and mass incarceration. I received the following letter from Senator Portman after the event.

ROB PORTMAN
OHIO

UNITED STATES SENATE
WASHINGTON, D.C. 20510

March 20, 2013

Mr. Ronald Moten
4359 C St SE
Washington, D.C. 20019

Dear Ron,

Thank you offering your testimony during the INSIGHT policy briefing on reentry. Your personal commitment to this important work is inspiring, and I hope that you will consider supporting the Second Chance Act Reauthorization as part of your efforts.

I hope we can work together in the near future, and please keep in touch.

All best,

Rob Portman

This letter from Senator Rob Portman (R-Ohio) is evidence that the people I represent have a place "at the table" where decisions are made about Republican Party policy priorities. Republican principles are just one reason I am a Civil Rights Republican; the second reason is what I have repeated often in these pages, a more balanced representation for blacks in both parties. We need to be at the Republican as well as the Democrat table, not just one or the other.

In the spirit of being at both tables, I was also on a panel with Chicago Democratic Congressman Danny Davis dealing with some of the same issues. Participation in these events is a powerful way to get issues addressed that affect African Americans and other minorities. I also appreciate the fact that Rep. Eleanor Holmes Norton (D-D.C.) has continued to welcome me as a Republican to participate in the great work she is doing with the Commission on Black Men and Boys.

That's the balance I am advocating so that neither party can take us or our votes for granted. We have been drinking the one-party Kool-Aid for too long and it has produced very few lasting results other than to keep Democrats in power, breed corruption, and keep us on welfare.

I believe that having more blacks follow my lead and move to the Republican Party is important to the future of African Americans and, in fact, all Americans. I hope that the Republican Party is wise enough to know that I represent a lot of people who have been offended in the past by some of the ways in which a great message has been poorly delivered. These poor messengers just serve to confirm the stereotype that many blacks have about the Republican Party.

Minority ears will remain closed no matter how much sense the Party policies make until it finds the right ways and the right people to deliver its message in a way that recognizes the deep suspicion that has been planted by those who benefit from these misconceptions. It took me six years to open my ears, but even then I had been so conditioned by the other side that, as good as it all sounded, I resisted getting in bed with a political party that I was always told was racist. That's another reason why racially tone deaf comments by some Republican officials and office holders are so damaging and totally unacceptable.

The GOP needs to understand that there is a rich history of values in the black community that match up with much of what Republicans believe. There is also much in Democratic Party policies that is contrary to traditional black family values of self-reliance, faith in God, and the dignity of life. Wake up Republicans! Don't change the product; just expand the delivery system to include Civil Rights Republicans like me who know how to get the job done in the black community.

I often think about what my seventy-seven year-old grandmother told me. She said that when she was growing up they never even heard of welfare. They battled difficult situations as a family and community and didn't stop until they got the victory. Of course we had a village then that was healthy enough to help each other. I hope that rebuilding the village is the one thing everyone who reads this book can agree on so the American eagle can once again soar and every child will have the opportunity to live the American dream. In order for that eagle to soar again, its wings must be balanced, which in part means significant black and other minority representation in both political parties.

That balance will bring pressure to bear on both parties as they compete for our votes. Only when votes have to be earned is there any real pressure on politicians to do the right thing. One-sided black and minority representation distorts public policy because it allows our votes to be taken for granted. To this day my grandfather thinks this balance is impossible, but I am ready to help make it happen.

The Party of Lincoln must return to greatness and, once again, be the party "OF THE PEOPLE, BY THE PEOPLE AND FOR THE PEOPLE." The casualties and losses that come with division are too great. Abraham Lincoln was a statesman, but he was also a great political tactician. He never compromised on principle, but where he was in agreement with his political opponents, he was ready to work with them for the good of the country.

This country has seen division before. The divisions that caused the Civil War resulted in the loss of more American lives than all of the wars we have fought against foreign Armies. I am proud that I now belong to the Party of the man who had the wisdom to lead the country through those dark times. The words of Lincoln's Second Inaugural Address should guide us today as we seek to heal the deep divisions of our time. Let these words sink deep into your hearts and let's "pledge our lives, our fortunes, and our sacred honor" to once again becoming "one nation under God, INDIVISIBLE, with liberty and justice for ALL."

> With malice toward none, with charity for all, with firmness in the right as God gives us to see the right, let us strive on to finish the work we are in, to bind up the nation's wounds, to care for him who shall have borne the battle and for his widow and his orphan, to do all which may achieve and cherish a just and lasting peace among ourselves and with all nations.
>
> —Abraham Lincoln, Civil Rights Republican

It's time for REAL CHANGE, be a part of it. God bless you!

GLOSSARY

1-7 A neighborhood crew from 17th Street Northwest and Kalorama Road that often beefed (had feuds) with residents or crews from Gerald Street, NW.

Adrian Fenty Mayor of Washington, D.C. from 2007–2011. Fenty lost his bid for reelection because he angered some people who said he accomplished a lot but they didn't like his style. If he had the swagger of Corey Booker he would still be mayor because Booker had to deal with corrupt old school politicians also, but managed to do so and get re-elected.

ANC Advisory Neighborhood Commissioner is a unit of local government in D.C. ANC's have a say and obligation to weigh in on issues that affect their immediate community. Some ANC's are unorganized and self-serving, but when used for its intended purpose they are a great asset to the community.

Barry Farms A neighborhood and crew located in Southeast Washington, D.C. Members of the Barry Farms crew attended Ballou Senior High School and often had conflicts with members of Condon Terrace.

BHB Brothers Helping Brothers was a program created by Peaceoholics to address the social ills that affect the majority of African-American boys in the Nation's Capital.

Big-G Anwar Glover, former Hobart Star crew member who survived being shot thirteen times and became a D.C. Street Legend. He was a founding member of the famous D.C. Go-Go Band called The Back Yard Band and an actor who stared on HBO's hit series "The Wire"

Birds And Their Nest A term used to show that even birds with small brains understand that you must build institutions in order to have a stable family.

Black Neck Republican Black Republicans who pretend to be the voices of urban blacks in America but refuse to even engage with people who they consider below them in our poorest communities.

Bully A 2006 video game produced by Rock Star Games that encourages bullying. Peaceoholics fought its release and made national headlines by delaying its release. However, this and many other violent video games would be released and we warned people long ago that it would fuel the culture of violence in America forever, as it had.

Camp Oak Hill An historic African-American summer camp and retreat center in Lancaster County, Pennsylvania. It was founded in 1948 by two remarkable African American women from Philadelphia. It is just minutes from Lincoln University and historic Underground Railroad locations. The camp is still in operation and primarily serves children and families from Southeast, D.C. and other cities such as Philadelphia and Baltimore.

CSS Court Social Services is a federal agency that has control over youth on supervised probation under D.C. Superior Court. We had a partnership in which Peaceoholics provided Civil Rights Tours for youth under their supervision.

Change Agents A select few that have the courage, strength, spirituality, and motivation to start movements of change often defying the odds and naysayers.

Choppa City A D.C. crew located in the historic Anacostia corridor in Southeast Washington, D.C.

CHV A crew from Columbia Heights Village located in Northwest, D.C. that was involved in a lot of youth violence.

Check It The first ever documented gay gang in America.

Citizenship The obligation entitled to all people to protect, serve, and honor their community and country.

Civil Rights Republican A man or woman who adopts the principles of great Republican leaders of the past, such as Frederick Douglass, Abraham Lincoln, and Harriet Tubman, who all believe in freedom, family, and community as well as self-reliance. This political ideology is not based upon color. Instead, it is based on shared principles of life, liberty, and responsibility for all.

Condon Terrace A neighborhood and crew located in Southeast Washington, D.C. that attended Ballou Senior High School and often had conflicts with crews from Barry Farms.

Corrupt 7 Seven members of the D.C. Council who conspired to destroy former Mayor Adrian Fenty and his associates. Leading up to the election they metaphorically stabbed him in the back knowing he would bleed to death before he reached the finish line to victory. They destroyed plenty of positive black men in the process. These are the same people who often complain about what whites and Republicans do to blacks.

Crew It has similar behaviors and activities as a gang, but not an organized criminal enterprise deserving harsh punishment of the RICO laws. A crew is also a concentrated group that arises from a particular neighborhood in which members live and are often forced to represent or associate with the crew because they live in the community.

CTU Clifton Terrace University in Northwest Washington, D.C. which was a crew that operated out of Clifton Terrace apartments. This crew was often beefing with the Hobart Stars crew.

CYITC Children's Youth Investment Trust Corporation created by Mayor Anthony Williams, which several mayors later turned into a slush fund for corrupt politicians such as Harry Thomas, Jr..

DCPS D.C. Public Schools which spends more than $18,000 per child per year on education related expenditures. Despite these expenditures, DCPS ranks last in the nation education performance.

DOES District of Columbia Department of Employment Services.

Drinking Muddy Water This was a saying often used by many of my Civil Rights mentors reminding me that, "To be in the Civil Rights movement you had to be ready to 'Drink Muddy Water' and sleep in a hollow log."

Many of us find ourselves in the same position as we attempt to be Change Agents today, but far fewer of us are willing to "Drink Muddy Water."

DYRS Department of Youth Rehabilitation Services, which is a D.C. Government Agency responsible for rehabilitating youth in the District of Columbia. They have done a horrible job but it has been covered up by elected officials and people who benefit from the mismanagement.

East Of The River The side of the city that has some of the poorest and most forgotten residents. Often used by local politicians as a background for making promises they have no intention of keeping. This part of the city is the last section of the city to experience gentrification.

Emmanuel Bailey A businessman used by Mayor Gray and former Councilmember Michael Brown to replace W2tech in the lottery contract. Gray and the council did some gangster stuff taking a contract from a company who won it fair and square and when the heat came the contract went up in smoke.

Eric Payne An attorney and former director of contracts for the OCFO who was fired by the CFO after he resisted political pressure from Jack Evans, Jim Graham, and Vincent Gray to undo the properly awarded lottery contract earned by Intralot and W2Tech in 2008.

First Murder First murder known to mankind, the Cain and Able story, whose cause was never addressed therefore the dis-ease of homicide continues.

First Source A program that is supposed to ensure D.C. residents priority for new jobs created by municipal financing and development programs.

Friendnemies People who act like they are your friends, but really are around only for personal gain and/or to destroy you.

Go-Go Band A unique band that performs Go-Go music that has a leader talker who interacts with the crowd through call and response as he directs the band through a continuous beat.

Go-Go Music A subgenre associated with funk that originated in Washington D.C. In the mid-1960's to late 1970's (not to be associated with male and female dancers)

Grand Theft Auto Violent video game that trains our children to steal cars, rob, rape, use drugs, and commit other acts of violence.

Hobart Stars A D.C. crew located in Northwest Washington, D.C. which was known for violence

HOBO Helping Our Brother Out sportswear was an Urban Clothing Apparel business started by John & Angie Day

Irv Nathan District of Columbia Attorney General hired by Vincent Gray. Mr. Nathan is a premiere lawyer who worked for Arnold & Porter where he was a senior litigating partner and head of the firm's white collar defense practice. He is suing me but a recent Washington Business Journal article showed where he tried to steer a United Medical contract for Mayor Gray, which proves it's impossible for him to be unbiased.

Intralot A Greek company that sells integrated gaming, transaction processing systems, game content, sports betting management, and interactive gaming. They were awarded the lottery contract in 2008.

Jim Graham Ward 1 Councilmember who Peaceoholics assisted in addressing a rash of violence in his Ward. That did not keep him from turning on us for political reasons. He is currently under federal investigation for allegedly steering contracts. He is known as Grahamzilla the Black business Killa.

Kwame Brown Former D.C. City Council Chairman who cared about the children but was groomed by old school Politicians. They would not let him grow into leadership as Chairman and undermined him. He made a few transgressions that lead to a day of incarceration and resignation from office as part of his plea agreement.

Lynch Mob A D.C. crew located in Woodlawn Terrace in Southeast D.C.

Mary Cheh An aggressive councilmember who was corrupted by the corrupt six and made it the corrupt seven. She supported her friends with rewards just as she accused former Mayor Fenty of doing. When a reporter wrote a story to that effect, she had a fit as if she doesn't have to abide by the same standards. She was also a big Gray supporter who later asked him to resign.

MedStar Shock Trauma MedStar is a trauma/acute surgery team dedicated to provide comprehensive trauma care. U.S. News named it as one of best regional hospitals.

Michael Brown A Former City Councilmember and son of the late Ron Brown who recently pled guilty to Federal bribery charges. He is now cooperating with the feds against the Corrupt Seven.

MPD The Metropolitan Police Department of Washington, D.C.

Oak Hill A juvenile rehabilitation facility for delinquent youth whose name was changed to New beginnings after recent reform.

OCFO Office of Chief Financial Officer responsible for managing all public monies used to manage the District of Columbia. In Fiscal Year 2012, this budget was over $9 billion dollars. The Chief Financial Officer (CFO) is the head of this office and key player in municipal affairs.

Peaceoholics A popular grass roots organization that was started by two native Washingtonians. In six years Peaceoholics became one of the best and most effective nonprofits in the country. Peaceoholics trained and helped local governments in our hometown and throughout the country create strategies to end violence and empower the forgotten to uplift themselves and their communities. The group had an average of 60 staff and sent more than 160 children to college. We brokered more than 40 major truces among rival gangs and assisted more than 250 so-called unemployable people acquire employment. We help each of these people by assisting them to create value within themselves and advocate for opportunities for those ready to work or attend college. Peaceoholics challenged the government while at the same time depending on government funding for our operations. When those in power turned against us for political reasons, we realized that our funding was in danger. We learned the hard that in order to thrive and survive, nonprofits should have two arms. One that solicits funds from government and the other arm that builds revenue through businesses. Once caught up ugly and corrupt D.C. politics, Peaceoholics was virtually destroyed leaving a void that has yet to be filled.

Politricks The art often used by Politicians to deceive the people to get what they want, often manipulating people to fight each other so they can accomplish their mission of serving personal interest and not the people. Many Politicians forget everything they promised the people once they take their hands off the bible until they need votes again. This is the corruption of politics I see far too often.

Rebuild The Village Triangle In One Model A proven model developed by Peaceoholics co-founders, Ronald Moten and Jauhar Abraham, that helps reduce D.C. homicides and other violence crimes. The model empowered the very people who were part of the problem so that they could be a part of the solution with a holistic approach to solving community problems.

Returned Citizens A name that replaced ex-offender, ex-con, convict and many other unforgiving names that block citizens that have previously been incarcerated from receiving a second chance after their debt to society has been paid.

Rules To The Game The rules that a person should know to survive and be successful in America. These include the rules of the U.S. Constitution and other rules that govern society and the country.

SBC is a Street Background Check that we did on all employees and anyone whose background we needed to know. Our SBC's often told us more than a Homeland Security or FBI background check.

Shadow Campaign The illegal and hidden campaign that now Mayor Vince "I Know Nothing" Gray claim to know nothing about even though it raised over $650,000 off the books and enabled him to steal the 2010 D.C. Mayoral election.

Smoke Screens The illusion of smoke to hide wrongdoing often portraying innocent people as the problem or predator.

Snitching When a person commits a crime and then tells on someone else to either get a lighter sentence or get off the hook of receiving prison time.

SOS Saving our Sisters was a program created by Peaceoholics to address female gang violence when it was prevalent in the Nation's Capital.

Speaking Truth to Power Often the little people who speak to the people in power whether it be government or other leadership in the world. This practice often comes with negative personal hardships.

Street Commission Former rival gang and street leaders trained to be entrepreneurs and mediators in D.C. These young men were very instrumental in reducing homicides in the Nation's Capital but will never get credit.

Sulaimon Brown The guy Vince Gray threw under the bus after he paid him to taunt and distract Mayor Fenty during the 2010 mayoral debates. He was a candidate with no money, but a great hype man for Gray's planted clones who would boo Fenty at debates and straw polls. When Brown struck back to salvage his name and reputation, Vincent Gray and the Corrupt 7 lost control of D.C. Politics for good. As a hidden culture of corruption and Vincent Gray's shadow campaigns have been exposed to the nation.

Taking The Bait When a person takes the bait, which is normally an illusion of something good, but turns out to be something to benefit the provider of the treat.

Vincent Gray The former D.C. City Council Chairman who stole the election for mayor from Adrian Fenty in 2010. He is currently under investigation for running an illegal shadow campaign and ran on lies of wanting to help the poor and improve life for all citizens, especially African Americans. He has failed in all his promises and has become infamous for corruption and speed cameras. He helped destroy Peaceoholics and has a personal vendetta against me.

W2Tech A company that was wrongfully stripped of the lottery contract by a corrupt City Council who later installed the minority partner who they supported.

Washington City Paper A great investigative newspaper that can sometimes be a tabloid when it gets hooked on sensationalizing stories.

Weathering The Storm Understanding that in order to receive the fruits and flowers in life sometimes you have to go through a storm.

William C. Smith Developer and friend of corrupt Mayor Vincent Gray.

Woodlawn Cemetery An historic African American landmark located in Washington, D.C. It is the last resting place of numerous African American leaders. There is no other cemetery in United States with as many black leaders from post-Civil War era according to Congresswoman Eleanor Holmes Norton

Yvette Alexander Ward 7 Councilmember who is part of the corrupt 7. She was put into office with the help of Vince Gray when he gave up his seat to become council chairman. She was also used as the vehicle to call for the investigation of the Peaceoholics in order to influence the election. We were cleared by the audit of any wrongdoing, but because the audit findings were purposively not released for eighteen months, Peaceoholics was defunded and had to close. It would be revealed that only 5 percent of her constituents fund went to the needy constituents it was intended for. Instead, it was used to buy alcohol at a popular downtown tavern called Stan's.

BIBLIOGRAPHY

Red Ass Boy

D.C. Office of Cable Television. "DC People featuring Ronald Moten."
www.**youtube**.com/watch?v=N6GHegfb3OY

Dovey Roundtree News Clip- WJLA News 7, Feb. 2013
http://www.wjla.com/video/2013/02/roundtree-profile.html

Peaceoholics I

Howard Hilltop, "Peaceoholics Get People Hooked On Peace." November 2, 2006.

Mallory Kenneth, "Peaceoholics Positive Addiction Hooks Youth." African American Newspaper, August 12, 2005.

Lori Montgomery, "Mayor Pledges More Help After Ballou." Washington Post, Apr. 28, 2005.

Valencia Muhammad, "Teen Acquitted In Ballou Shooting." Afro American Newspaper, December 24th, 2004.

Jeffrey Anderson, "Ballou hoop dreams teen makes a slash in tournaments." Washington Times, Dec 31, 2010,

DMV Peace Authority "Moten Brings Stevie Wonder To Ballou."
http://www.youtube.com/watch?v=baDby1yoekc

Hamil R. Harris, "Bible, Breakfast Start the School Day at D.C.'s Ballou." Washington Post, May 15, 2008.

Theola Labbe-DeBose and Bill Turque, "5 Hurt in High School Melee." Washington Post, November 20, 2008.

Best of DC 2011, "Best Savior/Villain: Ron Moten." Washington City Paper.

Robert E. Pierre and Clarence Williams, "Trying to Hold On' Amid The Despair of D.C.'s Streets." Washington Post, August 9, 2008.

Robert E. Pierre, "Teens Who Left Trouble Behind Get Recognition and a Reminder." Washington Post, December 27, 2007.

"No more sugar and spice: Girl gangs on rise in D.C." Washington Times, March 30, 2006.

Darragh Johnson, "Beyonce's Opening Act; Before her concert, Music Star Drops To Talk With D.C. Girls As Part of Forum Against Violence." Washington Post, August 19 2007

Sylvia Mareno, "Spreading a Message of Peace in Troubled Barry Farm." Washington Post, January 27, 2008.

Hamil Harris, "In Spirit of '95 Million Man March, Rally Seeks End to Youth Violence." Washington Post, Oct 17, 2007.

Kimberly Kweder, "Marchers Want End To The Area Violence." Washington Times, May 4, 2008.

Choppa City

Courtland Milloy, "Young woman, saved from a violent life in D.C., seeks to empower others." Washington Post, May 17, 2011.

Robert Pierre and Clarence Williams, "Pulse of Go-Go, Promise of Peace Mingle at D.C. Dance Event for Youth." Washington Post, October 16 2006.

Robert E. Pierre, "2 Rival Groups Behind Fights On Metro buses Agree to Truce." Washington Post, December 19, 2006.

Robert Pierre, "Brokering Peace." Washington Post, January 14 2007.

Courtland Milloy, "Barry serving Free Turkeys With A Side Of Turkeys." Washington Post, Nov 23, 2012

Robert E. Pierre and Clarence Williams, "Trying to Hold On' Amid The Despair of D.C.'s Streets." Washington Post, August 9, 2008.

Robert E. Pierre, "Teens Who Left Trouble Behind Get Recognition and a Reminder." Washington Post, December 27, 2007.

Ann Scott Tyson, "Teen fatally shot in D.C. was in wrong place at the wrong time." Washington Post, Sunday February 20, 2011

Ruth Samuelson, "Truth And Consequences." Washington City Paper, May 30, 2008.

Alison Klein, "A Plea to the Code of the Streets." Washington Post, July 26, 2007.

Rachel Baye, "Crime Spike At DC Elementary Schools." Washington Examiner, June 7-8, 2013.

MPD website promotes and recognizes Peaceoholics as a model to teach children and parents how to avoid gangs. http://mpdc.dc.gov/page/understanding-and-avoiding-gangs

Colbert King, "Getting Fingers Off Triggers." Washington Post, Saturday, July 28, 2007.

Del Quentin and Allan Lengel, "Slain Youth Left Trail of Homicides, D.C. Police Believe." Washington Post, Sunday October 23, 2005.

Jeffrey Anderson, "Fenty targets crime areas." Washington Times, November 21, 2007.

Sylvia Mareno, "Spreading a Message of Peace in Troubled Barry Farm" January 27, 2008. Washington Post

Ann Scott Tyson, "Teen fatally shot in D.C. was in wrong place at the wrong time." Washington Post, Sunday, February 20, 2011.

Colbert I. King, "Big League City Would Not Fail It's Children." Washington Post, February 8, 2013.

Hamil R. Harris, "Bible, Breakfast Start the School Day at D.C.'s Ballou." Washington Post, May 15, 2008.

Alan Suderman, "Payback Is A Hitch." Washington City Paper, January 23, 2013.

The Gay Gang at Gallery Place – Check It

Courtland Milloy, "Gay black youths go from attacked to attackers." Washington Post, September 27, 2011.

Sam Ford, "Check It Performs for Chinatown Merchants." http://www.wjla.com/articles/2012/05/gang-check-it-performs-for-chinatown-merchants-75759.html, WJLA, May 8, 2012.

Lou, Chibbaaro, "Check It Clothing Line Gay Gang Gives Up Crime For Clothing Line." Washington Blade, July 13, 2012.

"Gay and Lesbian Gangs Add To Fights." Metro Weekly, August 2010

Clarence Williams, "D.C. crew uses fashion runway as first step toward redemption." January 15, 2010.

BIG G

Clarence Williams and Robert Pierre, "We're Tired of Seeing the Yellow Tape." Washington Post, Saturday, August 25, 2007.

Chuck Brown & Go-Go

Chris Richards, "Bounce beat' and go-go's generation gap." Washington Post, April 6, 2012.

Judson Berger , "Night Club Crackdown Could End Quietly." Gazette, April 5, 2007.

Thomas Lester, "Protestors Want To Be Part Of The Solution." Washington Post, April 4, 2007.

Power of the Womb

Adrian Washington, "Peaceoholics: Saving one young girl at a time." Washington Times, May 23, 2008.

Clarence Williams, "Trying to Build a Peaceful 'Village." Washington Post, May 11, 2006.

Peaceoholics II

"Peace At What Cost." Washington City Paper, October 9, 2009.

Keith Alexander, "Peaceoholics Mentor Found Guilty in Teen's Assault." Washington Post, September 05, 2009.

"Fenty Gets Peaceoholics to Assist in Snow Removal Project." http://www.washingtoncitypaper.com/blogs/citydesk/2010/02/15/fenty-gets-peaceoholics-to-assist-in-snow-removal-project/. Washington City Paper, January 15, 2010.

Audit

"Council Member Calls For Audit On Peaceoholics." http://www.tbd.com/articles/2010/08/d-c-council-member-calls-for-peaceoholics-audit-4581.htm. TBD.com, August 23, 2010.

Alan Suderman, "Peaceoholics Not Guilty Of Anything Too Serious." Washington City Paper, August 17, 2011.

Mike DeBonis, "Peaceoholics audit shows D.C. oversight lapses." Washington Post, August 17, 2011.

Patrick Madden, "Council Examines Peaceoholics' Grants."
http://wamu.org/news/morning_edition/11/10/03/council_examines_p
eaceoholics_grants. WMAU.org, October 3, 2011.

Tom Howell, "Graham requests new audit on Peaceoholics." Washington
Times, October 3, 2011.

Jeffery Anderson, "Feud fogs audit of nonprofit for youths." Washington
Times, May 4, 2011.

Daniel De Vise, "D.C. agency's handling of grant money labeled deficient in
audit." Washington Post, September 2, 2010.

Jeffrey Anderson, "Audit clears Peaceoholics cause for change in grant
program." Washington Times August 18, 2011.

Bruce Johnson, "Burglars Hitting Non-Profits And Small Businesses In SE."
http://www.wusa9.com/news/local/story.aspx?storyid=122907&catid=1
87. WUSA 9 News, November 29, 2010.

"Peaceoholics downsizing after cuts." http://voices.washingtonpost.com/local-
breaking-news/dc/peaceoholics-downsizing-after.html . Washington Post,
April 6, 2012.

"Peaceoholics Will Close Doors This Weekend Due To Budget Cuts."
http://www.wusa9.com/news/local/story.aspx?storyid=99588,
WUSA News 9. April 5, 2010.

P.J. Orvetti, "Peaceoholics VS ANC: Call In The FBI."
http://www.nbcwashington.com/news/politics/Peaceaholics-vs-ANC-
Call-in-the-FBI-97072279.html. NBC Washington, June 24 2010

DYRS

Colbert I. King, "Love Fest for a Troubled Agency." Washington Post,
December 8, 2007.

Deneen Brown, "Whatever Happened to ... the woman sued by Peaceoholics?"
Washington Post, November 3, 2011.

Politricks

Nikita Stewart and Mike DeBonis, "Mayor Grays 2010 Campaign had a
database of public housing residents." Washington Post, July 22, 2012.

Vincent Gray

"Homelessness Is A Gold Mine" Washington Times, February 8 1993.

"Efforts to Improve DC Procurement Seen as Fruitless," October 6 1993.

Tim Craig, "Gray, Supporters Accused of Luring Voters to Polls with Gift
Cards." Washington Post, Sunday, September 12, 2010.

Tim Craig, "Vincent Gray's first D.C. mayoral race TV ad attacks 'Adrian Fenty
for Cronyism.'" Washington Post, Wednesday August 25, 2010.

Liz Farmer and Alan Blinder, "Court papers offer inside look at shadow
campaign." Washington Examiner, July 12, 2012.

Mike DeBonis and Nikita Stewart, "Grays Ties To Scandal at Issue."
Washington Post, July 12th, 2012.

Jeffrey Anderson, "Gray May Owe Fines To City For property fence."
Washington Times, March 30, 2010.

Jeffery Anderson, "Statement, Faulty Timelines Cloud Gray's 'Exoneration.'"
Washington Times, April 20th 2010.

Tim Craig, Nikita Stewart and Paul Schwartzman, "Gray Says He'll Take On
Fenty For D.C. Mayor's Job." Washington Post, March 30, 2010.

Tim Craig and Peter Herman, "Mayor calls for more beat police after Capitol
Hill killing." Washington Post, December 27, 2012.

Bruce Depuyt , "New Allegations Against Gray Camp Featuring Moe Moten
and Mo Ellithee." http://www.tbd.com/blogs/news-talk/2012/07/new-
allegations-against-gray-camp-penn-state-sanctions-aids-report-card-
16225.html. News8 Video/TBD.Com, July 23, 2012.

Bruce Johnson, "DC Council Chairman Vincent Gray Fence Controversy."
http://www.wusa9.com/news/local/story.aspx?storyid=101689. WUSA
News 9, May 4, 2010.

Ann E. Marimow, "Gray's fence must be lowered or relocated." Washington
Post, May 27, 2010.

"Gray Clearing Up 2002 Traffic Ticket." Washington Post, July 8 2010.

Nikita Stewart, "Vincent Gray campaign under vigorous federal scrutiny."
Washington Post, October 16, 2011.

Mike DeBonis, Nikita Stewart, and Peyton M. Craighill, "Mayor Gray should
resign, most D.C. residents say." Washington Post, July 18 2012.

Alan Suderman, "Vince Gray From No Way To No Comment." Washington
City Paper, March 22, 2012.

Marc Fisher, "From Behind the Shades, Sulaimon Brown Talks to Council."
Washington Post, June 6, 2011.

Nikita Stewart, "Feds probe 'shadow campaign' for Gray." Washington Post,
March 21, 2012.

Nikita Stewart, "Council Approves Intralot Lottery Contract." Washington
Post, December 1, 2009.

Mike Debonis, "A Defiant Gray's Choice Words On Critics." Washington Post,
July 14, 2012.

Tim Craig, "Gray turning to China for DC projects." Washington Post, June 22,
2012.

Harry Jaffe, "Grays Security Detail Keeps him safe from DC Crime."
Washington Examiner, August 8, 2012.

Tim Craig, "Gray making mayoral race about ethics seen as risk." Washington
Post, May 6, 2010.

Lottery

Jeffery Anderson," "Gray Met with Lottery Executive Over Contract."
Washington Times, May 19, 2010.

Jeffery Anderson, "Council Passes Buck On Lottery, Members Defer to Chairman." Washington Times, July 8 2010.

Jeffery Anderson, "Shaky Bussiness, Suits Trail DC Lottery Partner." Washington Times, June 9, 2010.

Jeffery Anderson, "Court Filings Outline Steering of D.C. Lottery Deal." Washington Times, September 15, 2011.

Alan Blinder, "D.C. Lottery Suit Trial Likely in 2013." Washington Examiner, September 5, 2012.

Jeffery Anderson, "Emails show fight for D.C. Lottery contract." Washington Times, August 3, 2011.

Theo Emery, "Fired But Firing Back Over Dealings." N. Y Times, December 25, 2012.

Ben Nuckols,"DC Lottery Being Investigated By Federal Grand Jury." AP, December 10, 2012.

Kwame Brown

Del Quentin Wilber and Keith Alexander, "Ex-D.C. Council chairman Kwame R. Brown gets one day in custody, plus home detention." Washington Post, November 12, 2012.

Mike DeBonis, "If Earmarks were Prohibited, How Did The Harry Thomas Jr. Get Them." Washington City Paper, March 1h 2010.

James Wright, "D.C. Non-Profits Make Due Without Earmarks." Washington Informer, August 4, 2010.

Washington Post Editorial, "The tangled tales of Harry Thomas." Washington Post, December 12, 2010.

Allison Klein, "D.C. Police to Check Drivers in Violence-Plagued Trinidad." Washington Post, June 5, 2008.

Tim Craig and Mike DeBonis, "Ex-D.C. Councilmember Harry Thomas, Jr. gets 3-year sentence." Washington Post, May 03, 2012.

Mike DeBonis and Tim Craig, "Harry Thomas Home Searched by Law Enforcement." Washington Post, December 2, 2011.

Michael Brown

Mike DeBonis, "Mike Brown Charged With Bribery." Washington Post, June 7, 2013.

Jim Graham

Washington Post Editorial, "Jim Graham And Banneker, Metro moves Forward With Necessary Investigation."

Colbert King, "The Jim Graham scandal continues." Washington Post, May 8, 2013.

Fire Truck

Michael Neibauer, "Odd Deal Sends D.C. Fire Truck, Ambulance To Dominican Town." Washington Examiner, March 25, 2009.

Nikita Stewart, "Gift to Dominican Town Puts Spotlight on D.C. Nonprofit." Washington Post, April 06, 2009.

Alan Blinder, "D.C. lottery suit trial likely in 2013." Washington Examiner, September 5, 2012.

Mayor's Old School Ass Whippin'

Tim Craig, "Vincent Gray's Campaign Says Mayor Adrian Fenty Might Have Lead In Early Voting." Washington Post, September 8, 2010.

Washington Post Editorial, "Fenty's Terrible Week In Washington." Washington Post, August 17, 2009.

Tim Craig, "Gray's Record Assailed On Fenty Friend's Web Site." Washington Post, May 15, 2010.

Keith Alexander, "Peaceoholics Mentor Found Guilty in Teen's Assault." September 5, 2009. Washington Post

Jonetta Ross Barrass, "Pimps And Hustlers In DC." Washington Examiner, January, 2012

Tim Craig, "Peaceoholics' Moten, A Fenty Ally, Emerges As A Force In D.C. Mayoral Race." Washington Post, June 21, 2010.

Ann E. Marimow and Clarence Williams, "Mayor Fenty booed on delayed arrival at scene of fatal shootings." Washington Post, April 2, 2010.

Nikita Stewart, "Parks contract with D.C. defended." Washington Post, December 11, 2009.

Return Citizens

Joseph Young, "3,000 Ex-Offenders Meet Voter Registration Deadline in Nation's Capital." Washington Informer, Oct 16, 2008.

Tim Craig, "Ex-Offenders Go after Michael Brown." Washington Post, March 18, 2013.

Robert Pierre, "Ex-Offenders Protest Dearth of Jobs, Services." Washington Post, July 02, 2008.

Citizenships vs. Snitching

Ronald Moten, "Cracking the Snitching Code: NPR." http://www.npr.org/templates/story/story.php?storyId=13752977. NPR, 10:00 AM, August 20, 2007.

Ronald Moten, "The Real Meaning of 'Snitching." Washington Post, Sunday, August 19, 2007.

Housing

Lydia DePillis, "A Year After Peaceoholics Renovated Buildings, They're Mostly Still Empty." Washington City Paper, Jan. 19, 2012.

Hurt People Hurt People

Allison Klein, "Tears of Grief, Cries for Hope." Washington Post, September 3, 2006.

Robert Pierre, "Out of Grief, a New Search for Hope in D.C." Washington Post, November 3, 2006.

Bully/Gun Violence
Jose Antonio Vargas, "This Bully Isn't So Tough." Washington Post, Oct 17, 2006.
Robert Barnes, "Justices Reject D.C. Ban On Handgun Ownership." Washington Post, June 27 2008.
"Rockstar Controversial 'Bully' Game Not a Schoolyard GTA After All." http://www.mtv.com/games/video_games/news/story.jhtml?id=1538356 MTV.com, August 11, 2006.
"New Jersey Gun Laws Don't Curb Violence In Camden." USA Today, June 6, 2013.
Jose Antonio Vargas, "A Duo's Dynamic Attack on Video Game Violence Youth Activists Enlist Teens to Picket Stores." Washington Post, March 16, 2005.

Why I am Civil Rights Republican
Tim Craig, "Ron Moten Will Run For Council As A Republican." Washington Post, October 20, 2011.
Tim Craig, "Ron Moten, Don Folden, Clash at GOP Debate." Washington Post, March 6, 2012.
Michelle Alexander, *The New Jim Crow: Mass Incarceration in the Age of Colorblindness*. New York: The New Press (2012).
Courtland Milloy, "Peaceoholics Moten Is Fighting For a DC Council Seat." Washington Post, March 27, 2012.
Mike DeBonis, "Does Ron Moten Have A Chance For Ward 7." Washington Post, April 6, 2012.
Courtland Milloy, "Peaceoholics Moten Offers Tough Words for Tough Situation" Washington Post, May 11 2011.
Dian Alden, "Republicans and Civil Rights." http://www.errvideo.com/Articles/7/ Newsmax.com, December 14, 2002.

First Murder
Hamil R. Harris, "Story of Cain and Abel, Revisited." Washington Post, October 25, 2007.

INDEX OF NAMES
(Alphabetical by first names or title if first name is not known)

CPSIA information can be obtained at www.ICGtesting.com
Printed in the USA
LVOW10s2158140816

500381LV00028B/744/P

9 780615 702094